The Princess's Garden

Royal Intrigue and the Untold Story of Kew

Vanessa Berridge

AMBERLEY

To my mother, Patricia Berridge, who first inspired my love of history

This edition published 2017

Amberley Publishing
The Hill, Stroud
Gloucestershire, GL5 4EP

www.amberley-books.com

British Library Cataloguing in Publication Data.
A catalogue record for this book is available from the British Library.

ISBN 978 1 4456 6029 5 (paperback)
ISBN 978 1 4456 4336 6 (ebook)

Typesetting and Origination by Amberley Publishing.
Printed in the UK.

Contents

Foreword

Two garden visits were the genesis of this book. The first, over twenty years ago, was to Stowe in Buckinghamshire. At that time, I knew little about gardens and gardening, and even less about the history and iconography of this extraordinary site, but I remember well the Temple of Concord and Victory standing at the head of an overgrown valley. The image stayed in my mind and it was only fifteen years later that I began to make some connections.

By that time, I had launched and edited a magazine about gardens, become a freelance writer, and was increasingly interested in garden history. In the spring of 2004, I visited Mount Stuart, the Bute family's ancestral home on the Isle of Bute, and noticed the towering stone column that dominates one of the avenues. It was originally erected by John Stuart, 3rd Earl of Bute, in his garden at Luton Hoo in memory of Augusta, Dowager Princess of Wales and mother of George III. I learned of the part Bute played, in partnership with Augusta, in the early formation of Kew Gardens as a centre of botanical excellence. My imagination was snagged – I wanted to know more about Bute and Augusta and the relationship between them that had inspired such an extravagant gesture of affection. I also became intrigued by Augusta's husband, Frederick, eldest and hated son of George II, and one of only four Princes of Wales never to inherit the British throne.

These two visits set me on a path of ten years' study and exploration, of which this book is the result. It has been a fascinating journey, an intimate discovery of three lesser-known figures of the British Enlightenment.

The House of Hanover – Family Tree

George Louis, George I (great grandson of James I) 1660–1727 (1714) **m.** Sophia Dorothea 1666–1726

Sophia Dorothea 1686–1757 **m.** Frederick William of Prussia 1688–1740 (1713)

Frederick II (the great) 1712–1786 (1740)

Wilhelmina 1709–1758

George Augustus George II 1683–1760 (1727) **m.** Caroline of Ansbach 1683–1737

Frederick Louis, Prince of Wales 1707–51 **m.** Augusta of Saxe-Gotha 1719–1772

Anne 1709–59 **m.** William IV of Orange

Amelia 1711–86

Caroline 1713–57

George 1716–17

William Duke of Cumberland 1721–66

Mary 1723–72

Louisa 1724–51

Augusta 1737–1813

George III 1738–1820 (1760) **m.** Charlotte of Mecklenburg-Strelitz

Edward 1739–67

Elizabeth 1741–57

William 1743–1805

Henry 1745–90

Louisa 1749–68

Frederick 1750–65

Caroline Matilda 1715–75 **m.** Christian VII of Denmark 1749–1808 (1766)

(Those underlined are mentioned several times in the text; bracketed dates indicate accession)

Introduction

On a wet Saturday in February 1772, a solemn cortege made its way from Carlton House on Pall Mall to Westminster Abbey. At its heart was the lead-lined coffin of Augusta, Dowager Princess of Wales, mother of George III, and widow for over twenty years of Frederick, Prince of Wales, eldest son of George II. Aged fifty-three, she had lived long enough to see her children face tumult in both their public and private lives. Storm clouds were gathering across the Atlantic in America as she died, while two of her daughters, sent abroad to make dynastic and diplomatic alliances, struggled in loveless, turbulent marriages. Indeed, news that her youngest daughter, Caroline Matilda, Queen of Denmark, had been arrested for adultery may well have been the *coup de grace* that sent the ailing princess to her grave. Brave to the end, suffering from an incurable throat condition which was probably cancer, on the night before she died she had received her son, the king, and Queen Charlotte as usual.[1] Her passing is recorded with unusual sympathy by Horace Walpole, a man who seldom had a kind word to say for the princess, or for anyone else for that matter. He wrote that she 'kept them four hours in indifferent conversation, though almost inarticulate herself, said nothing on her situation, took no leave of them – and expired at six in the morning without a groan'.[2] It is a poignant scene.

Against royal practice, Augusta had asked not to be embalmed, so she was buried speedily, and with little ceremony, less than a week after her death. There were other reasons, too, for haste. The *Middlesex Journal* reported that 600 guards remained on duty in Palace Yard overnight, 'to prevent obstructions before and during the procession of the late Princess of Wales'.[3] Fears of trouble were not exaggerated. A large crowd gathered along Pall Mall, Horse Guards Parade and Whitehall to see the coffin on its way to its final resting-place in Henry VII's chapel in Westminster. She would lie beside her husband, Frederick, who was close in death to his little-loved parents as he had never been when alive. The Londoners lining the route on that dismal February morning had not come to cheer but to jeer, and Augusta was booed and hissed to her grave.[4]

The death of this unpopular princess is a fitting starting point for our story, partly because the virulence of the attack on Augusta reveals much about the political tensions during the first two decades of George III's reign. It is also because the princess, loathed in her lifetime and insulted in death, had left an extraordinary inheritance, valued to this day, though scarcely ever recognised as being her legacy. When Diana, Princess of Wales, opened the new Princess of Wales Conservatory at the Royal Botanic Gardens at Kew in 1987, all but the cognoscenti thought that the glasshouse had been named for her, being unaware of her rather less high-profile predecessor. For Augusta was de facto founder of those gardens, which evolved into a historical research institution of international significance and, since 2003, a UNESCO World Heritage Site. Her husband, Prince Frederick, had set the ball rolling at Kew in the 1740s, planting extensively, and also building temples and follies, which he invested with political meaning. After Frederick's death, Augusta transformed the 110-acre garden with the advice and support of her political advisor, and alleged lover, John Stuart, 3rd Earl of Bute. In the spirit of her age, she created a landscape of ideological importance – for in the eighteenth century, to adapt the feminist catchline of the 1960s and '70s, 'the horticultural was the political'.

In fact, eighteenth-century gardens played a significant role in the battle for the political soul and cultural identity of the British nation that raged throughout much of the century. After the bloody upheavals of the seventeenth century, the reigns of the first two Georges (1714–60) were a period of comparative calm, although the two Jacobite rebellions of 1715 and 1745 were serious threats to the new dynasty. Other fronts were also opened, on which aristocracy fought with royalty, Whig with Tory, English with Scots and the royal family with itself. These struggles concerned the type of constitution, monarchy and government that Britain would have, questions still not finally resolved after the civil wars of the seventeenth century.

The landscape movement was born at the same time, in part as a means of articulating, on the land, the political voice of the ascendant Whig aristocracy. As the nation also sought to create a new, distinctive culture for itself, the struggle was played out between such gardens as the magnificent landscape at Stowe, in Buckinghamshire, home of Lord Cobham, and the royal gardens at Kew. Gardens were turned into allegorical battlefields, with their layout and ornamentation used by both nobility and royalty to display political affiliation and to conduct political argument in front of their peers and the visiting public.

At Kew, Bute and Augusta intended to score points off the great Whig garden of Stowe in Buckinghamshire, but the princess's ambitions went beyond that; she also conceived of a physic garden which would, she said, 'contain all the plants known on Earth'.[5] Implicit in this was her awareness of Britain's developing role as a world trading power, forged through commercial muscle. There had been botanic gardens before, such as Oxford, founded in 1621, and the Chelsea Physic Garden, established in 1673, and there were the great landscape gardens such as Stowe, Stourhead and Studley Royal. Augusta's vision for her garden, however, was doubly innovative; she combined the landscape and the botanic in one garden for the first time, and she also collected plants for their intrinsic interest as well as their medicinal or economic value.[6]

In this endeavour, she was actively supported and advised by Bute, a botanist of distinction. As her eldest son's 'dearest friend' and head of his household from 1755, Bute educated the Prince of Wales on Tory lines, encouraging him to distrust morally corrupt Whigs, as he saw them, who had held his grandfather in their thrall. In so doing, he raised fears of a return to autocratic monarchy, untempered by Parliament.[7] When the inexperienced Groom of the Stole was promoted first to the Privy Council and then made Prime Minister in 1762, venomous attacks were launched on him, Augusta and the king by Whig leaders, supported by radicals such as John Wilkes and by the mob.[8] Augusta and Bute, described by Walpole as a 'passionate, domineering woman, and a favourite without talents', became the butt of scurrilous rumour.[9] Sexually explicit cartoons, which make Sarah Ferguson's toe-sucking exploits look tame, lampooned the couple and accused them of adultery. A Wilkesite paper, the *London Evening Post*, printed a list of anathema in 1770, which referred to Bute's work with Augusta at Kew. 'SECRET INFLUENCE, a *Scotch root*, as it now flourishes in the garden of Kew – Lord B-te.'[10] Bute, having masterminded the unpopular 1763 Treaty of Paris that ended the Seven Years War, was physically attacked, and windows were broken at his London home.

As a result, Augusta's and Bute's botanical achievements were obscured both at the time and subsequently, for the Whigs claimed that princess and adviser were dangerous amateurs – at both politics and gardening. Bute was underestimated as a botanist and reviled for his political failures and for his perceived malign influence on the young George III.

Augusta's passing brings together the themes of this book. Triggering Bute's resignation and replacement as director of Kew by Sir Joseph Banks, her death heralded the beginning of a new phase that looked forward to nineteenth-century imperial expansion. Banks saw the economic potential of plants and used the gardens at Kew as a home-based showcase of British power overseas.

When Bute died twenty years after Augusta in 1792, the waters seemed to close over the triumvirate which had been of such vital importance to one of the world's greatest gardens and to Britain's political life throughout the eighteenth century. The aim of this book is to show why these three people who contributed so much to British horticulture should not be forgotten and to restore them to their rightful place.

PART I

CHAPTER 1

A Chilly Summons

In the first week of December 1728, three riders battled their way towards Hanover in the teeth of fierce easterly gales. The unaccompanied men had ridden hard for several days across the Low Countries and the north German plain, snatching only a few hours' sleep at the roadside inns where they changed their horses. Weary and saddle-sore, they continued eastward with no time to waste, bound as they were on a secret and urgent mission for the newly crowned British monarch, George II.

The trio might have preferred to postpone their errand until spring, for as they would have known, winter comes early to Hanover, winds from Siberia driving relentlessly and unimpeded across Lower Saxony to the North Sea. The electorate was already manacled by cold, its roads pitted with snow-forced holes and frozen ridges. Icicle spears hung from the eaves of the half-timbered buildings that lined the route to the Herrenhausen Palace, the summer residence of the electoral family. The Grosser Garten of the Electress Sophia, grand-daughter of James I, was an icy baroque picture, with the formal lakes sheets of ice, the fountains stilled, the sculptures bound in hemp sacking and the long lines of hedges, concealing secret gardens, crisped by frost. The orange trees that decorated the terraces in summer were huddled together, craving warmth, in the elegant Orangerie, while botanic experiments in the hillside Berggarten had ceased for the duration of the cold. Small wonder that Sophia's ambition to grow rice in Lower Saxony had come to nothing; it was little short of a miracle that tobacco had flourished and that the leaves of Herrenhausen mulberries nourished the silkworms of nearby Hamelin's silk industry. But in December the silkworms were cocooned, awaiting the far-off arrival of spring. The cold was palpable, and even the River Leine, which lapped the walls of the Leineschloss in the city of Hanover itself, was frozen to a depth of several inches.

Within the ice-fortified palace, His Royal Highness the Duke of Cornwall and Edinburgh, eldest son of George II, and the effective if not titular head of the electorate, was hosting a Court Ball to launch the Christmas season, in an attempt to help his courtiers forget the winter chill for an evening. The diminutive, vivacious Prince Frederick Louis, popular with his attendants and with the people of Hanover, was the only member of their ruling dynasty to have lived there permanently since the elector, George Louis, had become King George I of England in 1714. When he departed to take up his throne, George Louis had been convinced that a senior member of the electoral family was needed to represent him during his extended absence in England. He was also implacably opposed to leaving his troublesome adult son and articulate daughter-in-law behind to undermine his interests in Hanover. So, with political expediency rather than common kindness uppermost in his mind, George decided that his grandson, Frederick, was the obvious choice; at seven years old, he was too young to be a political threat to his grandfather's interests, yet an ideal puppet focus of public loyalty and support.

There are no records of how the twenty-one-year-old prince would have been attired that December evening, the host of a courtly function as on countless times over the previous fourteen years. A fictional description based on Frederick in London, and written by Tobias Smollett, an advocate of the prince and a Scottish friend of John Stuart, 3rd Earl of Bute, gives an impression of how he might have appeared to his guests that fateful evening.

He was dressed in a coat of white cloth faced with blue satin, embroidered with silver of the same piece as his waistcoat. His hat was laced with silver and garnished with a white feather. But his person beggared all description. He was tall and graceful.' [princes, of course, are always tall, whatever their true height]. 'His limbs finely proportioned, his countenance open and majestic, his eyes full of sweetness and vivacity, his teeth regular and his pouting lips of the complexion of the damask rose. In short he was born for love and inspired it wherever he appeared. Nor was he a niggard of his wit, but liberally returned it, at least what passed for such. For he had a flow of gallantry for which many ladies of this land can vouch from their own experience.[1]

It is easy to imagine the now sexually experienced young man enjoying himself with gusto among the courtiers who had effectively been his family in the long years since his grandfather and parents had decamped to England almost a decade and a half earlier. Another account, reported in the popular English press, showed the prince taking part in winter sports; just a few days earlier, he had 'invited the principal Nobility of the Country and diverted himself with them in a Race of Sledges upon the Snow-Top by the Light of Flambeaux'.[2] But such gatherings were not laid on purely for courtly amusement; visiting princes from Germany and from elsewhere in Europe attended these functions to see and be seen. Sir Robert Walpole's brother-in-law, Lord Townshend, wrote back to the Prime Minister after a ball in Hanover in 1723, 'If there be a place in the world where faction and intrigue are natural and in fashion, it is here'.[3] As the prince entertained his guests 'with that pleasant facetious humour, which [was] easy and natural to him', he would have been mindful of the political importance of the occasion.[4] He would not, however, have been aware that forces beyond his control were closing in on him. What happened next was extraordinary even by the standards of Frederick's unusually troublesome family. With more than a hint of Gothic melodrama, a disguised, unnamed and unidentified man broke in upon the festive scene and called the unsuspecting prince from the ball. Startled, Frederick was taken to a house somewhere in the town, where he was confronted by the three riders. His initial consternation at the forced invitation might have been mitigated by his acquaintance with at least two of the three men. The Life Guards Officer, Lieutenant-Colonel de Launey, descended from French Huguenots, was probably a stranger to the prince, who had had only erratic contact with the English court and its attendants since 1714. But the other two men Frederick encountered that night in the dimly lit house had been members of his grandfather's court.

One was the Marquis de la Foret, another French Huguenot, and a major-general in the British Army, who had served in the Irish campaign of 1699. The leader of the party, Friedrich Ernst von Fabrice, had been familiar to Frederick since boyhood. The previous year in Osnabruck, George I had virtually died in the arms of the faithful Fabrice, who had then accompanied the king's body to his funeral and burial three months later in the family vault in the Leineschloss, at which Frederick had led the mourning. A diplomat of two decades' experience, Fabrice had been a Hanoverian-British delegate to the Congress of Brunswick in 1716, and two years later had brokered a political settlement between George I and Charles XII, King of Sweden. His diplomatic skills and personal relationship with the prince uniquely qualified him for a peculiarly sensitive undertaking. 'Under the exterior of a compleat courtier,' wrote one contemporary, Fabrice 'concealed as sincere a heart, and as benevolent a mind, as if he had never been connected with the great … This amiable person, who with the probity of a philosopher, was the finest gentleman of his time, and had as few faults, as is compatible with the infirmities of human nature.'[5]

Fabrice would have needed all his benevolence and amiability, for he and his companions had come to inform the prince that his father, King of England for a full eighteen months, now at last and immediately commanded the presence of his eldest son in London. Frederick had been closer to his grandfather than to his father, having seen the former on his regular visits to the electorate since his accession to the British throne. The presence, therefore, of one of George I's old and trusted friends offered some reassurance to the anxious young man as he stood before the shadowy group of figures in a darkened house, still dressed in his court finery. Kindly but firmly, Fabrice impressed on Frederick that it would be useless to resist his father's demands and that he needed to depart for England before the night was out. The prince was given no time to change or for farewells to the people among whom he had spent his entire life; the only delay permitted was a short courtesy visit to the President Bushe, the electorate chief minister, without which the king's command would have seemed even more politically inept and ill-mannered. Accompanied only by his favourite valet, Johann Holtzmann, and his de facto kidnappers, and, with no more than a warm cloak thrown over his flimsy costume against the gnawing cold, the prince left the electorate within hours, never to return.[6]

Why had George II finally chosen that moment to call Frederick to his side, and in such an eccentric and imperious manner? And why was the new heir to the British throne not summoned from Hanover as soon as George I died? The king himself had been crowned in Westminster Abbey amid much pomp in October 1727. For the ceremony, Handel had composed the spiralling anthem, Zadok the Priest, which helped to promote a new Biblically endorsed monarchy for Britain. Yet nowhere to be seen was the king's eldest son – to the curiosity of more than one observer. Frederick was feted, however, in Hanover on the occasion of the coronation. Verses from the Hanoverian people address him as 'Prince Friedrich, our King's son, he is our joy, he is Europe's star of hope and our country's son'. The verses conclude, 'We will do our best to keep you, Prince of Wales,' a title in which he would not be confirmed until January 1729.[7]

George II had begun his reign with a dishonest sleight of hand – the suppression of his father's will. The reasons for doing so provide insight into his foot-dragging about bringing Frederick to court, which had everything to do with his disinclination to have a potentially challenging Prince of Wales at his side. Like his father before him, the new king-elector was keenly sensitive to the tricky balance to be struck between the two very different countries over which he reigned. And, again like his father, he recognised the significance of having a senior member to fly the family flag in Hanover, one reason why Frederick's remaining there continued to be a good idea. Moreover, George II disliked the terms of his father's will, which had been lodged in 1716 with the emperor, Charles VI. In this document, the first George envisaged that he, his son and grandson would all reign as king-elector, but that thereafter, were Frederick to have at least two sons, the eldest would become king and his second son elector, to detach Hanover from the British sphere of influence. Despite the existence of this copy in the Imperial Treasury, George II had no compunction in immediately burying his father's will – an act in which he was supported by his advisors, both in England and Hanover, who were alert to the constitutional difficulties inherent in George I's plan.[8]

George II himself had been secretly making alternative plans for the succession, plans which would have had no fewer constitutional complexities had they been put into effect. The new British king had little problem with his father's idea for the eventual distancing of Hanover from Britain after their lifetime (certainly not within it). But he and Caroline proposed a different solution which would leave Frederick in Hanover and make their adored younger son, William, Duke of Cumberland, king instead.

Caroline may have described Frederick in a letter to the Duchess of Wolfenbuttel as '*le plus cher de mes enfants*', but there is little other evidence to suggest that this was the case. Violence done to her maternal feelings by her father-in-law's insistence on Frederick's staying in Hanover seem to have hardened into alienation while she fought to hold on to her remaining children. Prickly relations with her father-in-law had become thornier as the popularity of Caroline and the Prince of Wales with the English public infuriated the king as much as Frederick's subsequent crowd-pleasing ways would in turn anger them. Matters had come to a head in 1717 after the birth of a second son. Caroline wanted to call the boy William, but British ministers argued that the child should take the names of his father and grandfather and George William was agreed as a compromise.[9] Then George I required that the Duke of Newcastle, his Lord Chamberlain, should stand godfather to his new grandson. The Prince of Wales's dislike of Newcastle was well known, so the king's demand was deliberately inflammatory. In his exasperation, the Prince of Wales hissed at Newcastle, 'you rascal, I will find you'. Because of the prince's heavy German accent, the discomfited Newcastle misunderstood him as having said, 'you rascal, I will fight you'. Newcastle was a party-giver, legendarily so at his houses at Claremont in Surrey and in Lincoln's Inn Fields, but he was by no means a feisty duellist, and so hurried horrified from the scene to consult his friends.[10] News of the prince's alleged and outrageous challenge to his Lord Chamberlain and godparental appointee quickly came to the king's ears and gave him the opportunity he had been seeking; he first placed the prince under arrest and then banished him and the princess from St James's Palace. Without a qualm, having already deprived them of one son by leaving Frederick in Hanover, the king held on to the remaining children, including the tiny prince, George William, at the palace. 'The Princess,' wrote the king, 'is permitted to see them when she has a mind and ... the children are permitted from time to time to go and see her and my son.'

The infant George William, plagued from birth by a racking cough, sickened and died, provoking a legal inquiry into whether his death had been caused by separation from his mother. According to a note written by the chief physician, 'It appears ... that it was impossible that the young prince could have lived.'[11]

The finding of the inquiry can scarcely have comforted a mother whose baby had been snatched from her. Small wonder, then, that from his birth in April 1721, her next son, William Augustus, became the apple of Caroline's eye and the focus of her attention and hopes for the future. Things might possibly have been different had Frederick been allowed to accompany his parents and siblings to England in 1714, but Caroline, having lost two sons to separation and death, poured all her affection into this newest family member.

This occurred to the extent that, within four years of the boy's birth, she and George were contemplating switching heirs. They had become accustomed to the absence of Frederick, who seemed happy, settled and well-loved in Hanover. Why stir things up by bringing him to England? It is clear that the king and queen felt no desire to follow the obvious family precedent and send the seven-year-old William to be their regent in Hanover – he was the same age now as Frederick had been when he was left behind.

But they had reckoned without the power of British public opinion. Used to the more autocratic ways of the German states, they expected their subjects to be just that – subject to their will and pleasure. It took the influence of the wily Prime Minister, Sir Robert Walpole, to bring home to the royal couple the political importance of a visible heir (not just the spare) in Britain.

That was Walpole's priority in the closing weeks of 1728, although eighteen months earlier, it was his own position, rather than the prince's, that he had been intent on shoring up. At the beginning of the new reign, ever the chancer, Walpole rode pell-mell from London to Richmond to be first to inform the new king of his father's death in Osnabruck. As so often, the Hanoverians contrived to combine Grand Guignol with knockabout and farce with high drama. George was in bed with Caroline when Walpole was announced and was drawing on his trousers as Walpole informed him that he had become king. Instead of delighting in his accession, the tetchy, insecure new monarch focussed on his resentment of his hated father's first minister and sent Walpole packing with the peremptory command to 'go to Chiswick and take your directions from Sir Spencer Compton'.[12]

Although Compton held significant posts as Speaker of the House of Commons, Treasurer to the Prince of Wales and Paymaster to the Army, he lacked the fire and savvy of Walpole. In the slighting words of the diarist Lord Hervey, he was 'a plodding, heavy fellow, with great application, but no talents, and vast complaisance for a Court without any address ... as he was calculated to execute rather than to project, for a subaltern rather than a commander, so he was much fitter for a clerk to a minister than for a minister to a Prince.' As indeed was quickly proved. Realising he wasn't up to the task, Compton had to ask Walpole for help to draft George II's first speech to council, 'the last man in England he ought to have employed on this occasion'.

Lord Hervey disingenuously claims that 'Sir Robert Walpole had not the least hope of making his peace so far as to be employed in the new reign'.[13] It is unlikely that Walpole himself harboured such doubts about his political future. He had, after all, an important weapon in his armoury (apart from his own abilities, which were considerable) – the firm support of Caroline. Edward Pearce has written in his biography of the 'Great Man', 'Walpole took her seriously, talked policy, and, like all clever politicians, he listened. When Caroline talked to George she talked Walpole's views and Walpole's interest'.[14] The closeness and success of their political relationship is traced throughout the pages of Hervey, who wrote to Walpole as the queen lay dying, 'Your credit ... was through the medium of the Queen.'[15] He flattered her, encouraging her to manipulate the king on his behalf. Caroline, an able, intelligent woman, was alive to Walpole's stratagems, but she enjoyed his support not only politically but also for her costly horticultural endeavours at Richmond, which were contemptuously dismissed by the king. One source reports that 'he little suspected the aid Sir Robert Walpole ... furnished to her from the Treasury. When she died she was in debt to the King, to the amount of 20,000*l*.' At Richmond, she played her own political game, building in the 1730s the three-chambered, thatched Merlin's Cave, the message of which was overtly political. It was designed, by associating King Arthur's personal wizard with Walpole, as a defence of the Prime Minister in the face of concerted attacks by the Whig opposition and by Frederick.[16] The prince would choose, in contrast, to employ another legendary English monarch, Alfred (ascribing the Anglo-Saxon king's virtues to himself) in his iconography in his gardens at Carlton House.

These horticultural battles were for the future in 1727, when

Walpole's position was held by a thread – a silken thread drawn by Caroline. In his opening sally to gain the king's confidence, Walpole looked to Caroline and found her help forthcoming. The new queen was shrewd enough to realise that Walpole alone had the clout to pass measures to increase the Civil List, which was to be settled in Parliament within a fortnight of the king's succession. Walpole pulled off a tour de force, supported by the various Whig factions and opposed only by the veteran Jacobite leader, a Mr Shippen. The king was voted an income of some £900,000 a year (to include £100,000 for the Prince of Wales, the payment of which was left to the king's discretion, rather than going directly to the prince). Caroline herself was given Somerset House and Richmond Lodge, plus £100,000 a year, 'which was just double,' writes Hervey, 'what any Queen of England had ever had before.'

It worked, of course. Before Parliament was dissolved, the king wanted to confirm the appointment of his first minister. He 'ordered them both to make him a speech, and when he came to choose shook his head at poor Sir Spencer's and approved of Sir Robert's'.[17]

Once established as Prime Minister, Walpole remained in the king's confidence until 1742, when his eventual fall was engineered by the opposition Whigs and ironically orchestrated by the prince he had succeeded in bringing to England in 1728. Walpole, like George, would have been only too conscious that the presence of the heir would provide a rallying point for any discontented elements within the political classes – as the experience of the previous reign had shown. But he also knew the value of keeping the public on side, and informers from his spider's web of spies were telling him by early 1728 that the opposition was canvassing for support for a petition to embarrass the king into calling for Frederick. Throughout the year, he fought George's ingrained resistance and deep-seated belief that 'an adult heir would prove a nuisance, because his own experience had taught him how little scope the English constitution afforded to a Prince of Wales'.[18]

Gradually, Walpole and the other ministers began to work on the king, persuading him, according to Hervey, 'that if the Prince's coming was longer delayed an address from Parliament and the voice of a whole nation would certainly oblige His Majesty to send for him and consequently that he would be necessitated to do that with an ill grace which he might do with a good one'.[19] While the king continued to prevaricate, Frederick himself unwittingly – or perhaps even wittingly – played into Walpole's hands by meddling, unforgivably, with royal marital affairs. He was now twenty-one and of an age to be married, but he waited in vain for any movement on this front in the first year of his father's reign. So he decided to revive a plan first mooted while his grandfather was alive.

In the mid-1720s, a double marriage had been proposed. Frederick would marry his first cousin, Wilhelmina, daughter of King Frederick William I of Prussia and Sophia Dorothea, only daughter of George I. At the same time, Amelia, Frederick's second sister, would be married to Wilhelmina's brother, the future Frederick the Great. For George I, there would have been political advantages in the marriage, as it would have helped to free Prussia from Viennese hegemony. In furtherance of this aim, there had been return visits between Berlin and Hanover, which were not without incident. George I had subjected Wilhelmina to close scrutiny at a court party, alarming in itself for a girl still in her teens, but made all the more unnerving by the British king's collapse with an apoplectic fit while giving her the once-over.[20] This can hardly have made him a welcome guest with his hosts, although, for his part, George believed himself to be doing the Prussian royal family a favour by mastering his (not altogether unreasonable) dislike of his son-in-law, Frederick William. Although a fine military leader, the Prussian king was seriously unbalanced, executing his son's tutor in front of the boy, then court-martialing and imprisoning his son and even, if Voltaire is to be believed, threatening him with beheading.

The Treaty of Charlottenburgh was the result of this tepid accord between George I and his son-in-law, but it was never ratified by the British king, and Frederick William grew increasingly opposed to the marriage schemes. But Frederick of Hanover, young, romantic and loveless (apart from his brief affair with his father's and grandfather's mistress) developed an imaginary passion for Wilhelmina and determined to visit her in Berlin. He despatched Lamothe, a Hanoverian officer, with a message for his aunt, Sophia Dorothea, explaining that he meant 'to escape secretly from Hanover, brave his father's anger and marry the Princess'. Sophia Dorothea, who had always backed the marriages, was delighted, and in her delight, indiscreetly revealed Frederick's plans to the British envoy, who wasted no time in passing the news back to England.

This in itself would have been enough to incense George II. But, at the same time, it was discovered that Frederick had also been involved in negotiations to marry his mother's nephew, the seventeen-year-old Margrave of Ansbach, to Wilhelmina's fourteen-year-old sister, Frederica. This action, an attempt to establish himself in his parents' eyes as a political player, was nevertheless way beyond Frederick's remit and taken by his mother as a personal insult.

Frederick's meddling in pan-European marital affairs caused ripples of anger at the British court. Apart from the impropriety of a young, unmarried prince concerning himself with these alliances, his behaviour was likely to endanger current British-Hanoverian foreign policy, which did not then include any kind of alliance with expansionist Prussia. It was the final push that George needed to call his son to his side, for he understood, as his father had before him, that his heir was more dangerous out of sight than within his court. 'The King,' wrote Hervey, 'as children take physic, forced himself to swallow this bitter draught for fear of having it poured down his throat in case he did not take it quietly and voluntarily.'[21]

CHAPTER 2

A Boy in a Man's World

It was a bitter draught indeed, for it is difficult not to believe that the subsequent problems between Frederick and his parents, George II and Caroline of Ansbach, didn't date from that chilly December summons.

But then the Hanoverians had never been – and were never to be – the most skilful people at managing their personal relationships. Take the example of Frederick's grandparents, George Louis of Hanover (later George I) and Sophia Dorothea of Celle. Sophia was barely sixteen when she married the future elector, in 1682, but she did her duty by swiftly producing a son, George Augustus (the future George II), the following year, and a daughter, another Sophia Dorothea, in 1687. But the bubbly, youthful Sophia became fractious during her husband's long absences fighting against the Turks in 1684 and 1685 and was equally bored by his heavy, ponderous presence. She was chagrined, too, by his repeated and obvious infidelity, most particularly when he fell in love with Melusine von der Schulenburg (afterwards created Duchess of Kendal) in 1690. So when she was introduced that year to a charismatic young Swedish colonel, Count Philipp Christoph von Konigsmarck, she was ripe for romance. They became lovers in 1692, but, where extra-marital relations were concerned, it has never been a level playing-field between princes and princesses. George might be allowed to father and acknowledge two daughters by his mistress (in 1692 and 1694), but Sophia's unfaithfulness would not be tolerated by either her husband or his family. Matters came to a dramatic head when Konigsmarck was murdered in 1694, probably while attempting to visit Sophia at the Leineschloss.

George himself was in Berlin at the time, so took no direct part in the actual killing, but the fact that it was almost certainly carried out on his orders is suggested by the enormous and unexplained sum of 150,000 thalers (then about a hundred times the annual salary of the highest-paid minister) paid to an Italian member of the royal household, Nicolo Montalbano. Assisted by three German courtiers, the newly enriched Montalbano dumped Konigsmarck's body in the Leine River.

Sophia was divorced in December 1694, and incarcerated in the Castle of Alden, where she lived for over thirty years until her death in November 1726. Never again would she set eyes on either her husband or children.

George Augustus (the future George II) was only eleven when his mother was locked away. Denied access to Sophia, he never mentioned her name once he became an adult; there is no reference to her in any of his papers. On the day after his accession in 1727, however, George put up his mother's portrait in his dressing room, a rare recorded act of filial respect. But he jibbed at paying blackmailing prices for a cache of her love letters to Konigsmarck, which he was offered at the same time – no doubt in an opportunistic attempt to tap the new king's wealth.[1] Almost certainly as a consequence of his mother's treatment, George's relations with his father were chronically bad, resulting in a complete rift between them in 1717 during George I's reign – a rift which was to be re-enacted almost exactly two decades later when Frederick was Prince of Wales.

That said, the Hanoverians' dislike for their heirs was endemic, going back centuries to the middle ages.[2] 'It ran a little in the blood of the family to hate the eldest son,' wrote Horace Walpole when recounting Frederick's death in his *Memoirs of King George II.*[3]

And relations had not been straightforward since birth between Frederick and his parents. His Serene Highness Prince Frederick Louis was the first child of George Augustus and his remarkable wife, Caroline of Brandenburg-Ansbach. Orphaned at a young age, Caroline had received little formal education, so her handwriting and her spelling were always poor and idiosyncratic. But, from the age of thirteen, she had lived with her guardian, Sophia Charlotte, electress of Brandenburg and Queen of Prussia after 1701. The daughter of the electress Sophia of Hanover, Sophia Charlotte reigned over an enlightened and cultured court which actively encouraged and fostered intellectual debate. It was there that the young Caroline was introduced to the German philosopher and mathematician, Gottfried Wilhelm Leibniz, with whom she corresponded regularly until his death in 1716.

In 1703, a dazzling future was dangled before the twenty-year-old Caroline: marriage to the Archduke Charles, a possible future Holy Roman Emperor and King of Spain. Betrothal to a Hapsburg required the princess to become a Catholic, so a Jesuit priest, Father Orban, was commissioned to give the young woman instruction. Eventually, Caroline's dedication to Protestantism proved too strong; increasingly distressed by the tenor of their conversations and the priest's attacks on her Lutheran faith, she refused to convert, a stand of which she remained proud all her life. The steely courage it took to reject an emperor was recognised by Joseph Acres, who wrote in 1714, on her father-in-law's accession to the British throne, 'What a rare thing for a young Lady that has been bred up in the Softness of a Court, to decline the Pomp and Glory of the World.'[4]

So, instead, she was married in 1705 to the rather less glamorous George Augustus of Hanover, variously described as a 'philistine' and a 'tight-fisted bore'.[5] It seems, however, to have been a love match, on his side at least if not on hers. On his first visit to Caroline at Triesdorf, George was instantly impressed by her 'good character', according to Edmund Poley, the British envoy, who also added that 'he would not think of anybody else after her'.[6]

Despite his inharmonious family background, George II's own marriage was rather more successful, and even though he kept long-term mistresses, it often appeared he did so as much because he thought he ought to as because he wanted to, describing his conquests in lubricious detail to his wife. She in turn recognised the inverted compliment paid her, especially as the couple, by all accounts, enjoyed a successful sex life. Although perhaps temperamentally incompatible, George and Caroline, in the view of J. H. Plumb, were 'bound together in passion, knitted together by the lusts of their flesh'.[7] It is possible that had Frederick been able to grow up with his parents, rather than being left behind in Hanover on his own at the tender age of seven, he might have benefited from a more rumbustious childhood. With greater intellectual gifts than his younger and favoured brother, William (Duke of Cumberland from the age of five), he could have flourished within the court of his cerebral mother.

Controversy rather than delight surrounded the birth of Frederick a little under eighteen months after his parents' marriage on 20 January (old style) 1707 (1 February new style). The arrival of a son, after all, strengthened the House of Hanover's potential grip on the British throne, a third male heir-in-waiting in Germany to ensure the Protestant succession after the death of the now childless and ailing Queen Anne. Care, you might think, would be taken to ensure that the birth was officially overseen by an assembly of appropriate dignitaries, particularly in the light of the Old Pretender's notorious birth less than two decades earlier. This was surely not the time or place for a warming-pan moment, and yet proper forms were not observed; for some reason best known to himself, George Augustus organised that only the midwife and the court surgeon, Dr de la Rose, should be present during Caroline's labour. His decision irritated Emmanuel Scope Howe, English envoy to Hanover, who seemed almost to question the veracity of the pregnancy in a dispatch to his British masters in early February 1707.

> This Court having for some time past almost despaired of the Princess Electoral being brought to bed, and most people apprehensive that her bigness, which has continued for so long, was rather an effect of a distemper than that she was with child. Her Highness was taken ill last Friday at dinner, and last night about seven o'clock, the Countess d'Eke, her lady of the bedchamber, sent me word that the Princess was delivered of a son.

Testily, Howe writes in a later communication that he was not invited to the christening, nor allowed to see the baby for ten days, although he then does add, 'I found the women all admiring the largeness and strength of the child.'[8]

Courtly licence, perhaps, because Frederick was a small and delicate baby, whose sepia colouring gave rise to soon discredited rumours that far from being George Augustus's child, he was the illegitimate child of one of his grandfather's Turkish servants, Mehemet and Mustafa. George Augustus is subsequently reported as having called Frederick a *wechselbalg* or changeling, exclaiming in later years 'The beast is no son of mine'.[9] The family's nickname for Frederick helped give credence to the rumour – 'Griffin' or 'Griff', which in Louisiana French meant half-caste. Frederick's own subsequent sarcastic gloss on his father's decision to give him no more than a small private christening was that it was for reasons of parsimony. The prince wrote subsequently in his autobiographical fairy-tale, *Prince Titi*, that 'Prince Titi's parents regretted his prompt appearance on the ground of expense'.[10]

Even the choice of names for the young son caused eyebrow-lifting, suggesting as they did a distancing of George and Caroline from their heir. Frederick's godparents were his paternal grandfather, and his great-uncle, Frederick I of Prussia, after whom he was named. As the Hanoverian succession was virtually assured by 1707, Howe was surprised that no nod was made towards British royal customs in the naming of the new prince, and that his father's and grandfather's name was not used. It was almost as though Frederick was beyond the pale right from the start, given a moniker which would have no resonance at the English court, and which set him apart from his father.

Nevertheless, a glance at any portrait of Frederick quickly disproves Hanoverian court and diplomatic tittle-tattle which may have owed as much to popular dislike of Caroline's imperious manner as to genuine doubts about Frederick's birth. Portraits show that he had the characteristic short stature, bulbous eyes and thick lips of the Hanoverians and the soft, pale hair of his mother. But mother and son were never to be close, in part perhaps because Caroline was seriously ill with flu and smallpox within a few months of Frederick's birth. She was devotedly nursed by her husband, but her illness and the couple's mutual self-absorption left little space in their lives for a small sickly boy with rickets.

It was an inauspicious beginning and established the pattern for Frederick's future relationship with his parents. Often separated from his mother, he spent time instead with his great-grandmother, the electress Sophia, whose daily walks with him in the Baroque gardens of Herrenhausen were the perfect treatment for the prince's rickets, even though it was unlikely that anyone would have realised it at the time. The hours spent in those gardens of which the electress was so proud would have had their influence on Frederick in his lonely, early years. His horticultural tastes, however, were to develop in a less formal and more naturalistic direction, when as Prince of Wales he came under the spell of the mercurial William Kent and developed away from the rigid, absolutist style of Martin Charbonnier, the original Le Notre-trained gardener at Herrenhausen.

Gardening was a passion he was to share with his mother, too, although not his father; the survival of the Baroque garden at Herrenhausen is attributed to George II's lack of interest in gardens.[11] But it failed to bring them close, and indeed by the 1730s both prince and queen were using their gardens as symbolic weapons in their internecine warfare.

Caroline's ill-health, followed by the birth of three daughters in quick succession (Anne, 1709; Amelia, 1711; and Caroline, 1713), increased the distance between mother and son. His grandfather, the elector, took the lead in Frederick's upbringing, perhaps to atone for the failed relationship with his own son, George Augustus. The latter, in fact, was allowed little or no say in Frederick's education, the elector preferring to consult Count Bothmer, a Hanoverian servant familiar with England; Leibniz; and a Scot, George Murray, who had worked for the Duke of Celle in the early 1700s.[12]

In 1713, the elector chose Johann Friedrich Grote, a member of a high-ranking Hanoverian court family, to be Frederick's governor and senior tutor. A Latin scholar, Nikolaus Ernst von Neubour, became his sub-tutor, while, counter-intuitively, a Frenchman, Jean Hanet, was employed to teach the prince English.[13]

The prince was trained in the princely accomplishments of fencing, dancing and riding, while mathematics and science were taught through dialogue rather than on paper. There has been some dispute about how well Frederick was served by this regime. That relations between Neubour and Frederick were sometimes strained is suggested by the tutor's subsequent comments on his former pupil. 'He had the most vicious disposition, the most depraved nature, and the falsest heart that ever man had; and that his vices were so far from being the vices of a [Prince], that they were not the vices of a gentleman but the mean villainies and tricks of a footman.'[14] On the other hand, this condemnation was quoted in his memoirs by Hervey, never the most reliable of witnesses where Frederick was concerned.

Social pedigree rather than pedagogic abilities would have

been what counted in the choice of Grote as Frederick's tutor, as was almost always the case with royal education. The breadth and depth of Frederick's subsequent cultural interests, displayed during his years in England, suggest, however, that his artistic sensibilities must have been awakened at some point during his education. Significantly, both Grote and Neubour remained in senior positions in the prince's household when he came of age, raising doubts as to the credibility of the attack on Frederick quoted by Hervey.[15]

These men between them formed the framework of Frederick's life after 1714, when, at one stroke, he lost his great-grandmother to death and his grandfather and parents to England. The aged electress Sophia, grand-daughter of James I of England, died in June, missing by just six weeks the chance of inheriting the throne of her first cousin once removed, James's great-grand-daughter, Queen Anne. Sophia had been lobbying Anne for some time to give George Augustus, the future Prince of Wales, permission to visit England to take his seat in the Lords as Duke of Cambridge. Some knowledge of the country that they were expected to rule seems a not unreasonable aspiration, but Anne, a Tory by persuasion, and a Stuart, was only too happy to keep the Whig-supported Hanoverians on a string. She refused to allow a young prince to arrive in her country where he might sow seeds of disloyalty and unrest. Anne resisted Sophia's attempts, writing letters to the several members of the electoral family in case there should be any doubt about her position. To the elector, Anne wrote that she believed he, George Louis, was 'too just to allow that any infringement shall be made on my sovereignty which you would not choose should be made on your own ... I am determined to oppose a project so contrary to my royal authority however fatal the consequences may be.'[16] The elector's daughter-in-law Caroline was confirmed in her Whiggish sympathies by the queen's offensiveness, and was inclined to blame the manipulations of the maverick Tory leader, Lord Bolingbroke, who was subsequently to be a major influence on Frederick. She wrote to Leibniz,

We were in a state of uncertainty here until yesterday, when a courier arrived from the Queen with letters for the Electress, the Elector, and the Electoral Prince, of which I can only say that they are of violence worthy of my Lord Bolingbroke.[17]

Anne's comments were prophetic about the fatal consequences of her decision; on receipt of the queen's letter, the eighty-four-year old Sophia collapsed and died from a massive stroke while walking in the gardens of Herrenhausen with Caroline. Just six weeks later, on 1 August, Sophia's nemesis, Anne, was dead from erysipelas, and it was George Louis, Sophia's son, who became George I.

As the Jacobite threat was still a very real one, it is perhaps surprising that the first Hanoverian monarch was so tardy about claiming his throne; it was 18 September before George finally reached Britain. For George, Hanover was always *primus inter pares*, and his dilatory departure from the electorate gave him time to decide about its future governance.

Princelings have always spent more time with their nurses, tutors and governors than with their parents, so it is of course misleading to view what happened to Frederick in the early eighteenth century through the prism of modern child-rearing methods. But, however cool the relationship between parents and son, it must nevertheless have been a vertiginous moment for a young boy to stand watching on the steps of the palace as his father and grandfather, and then his siblings and mother, departed, leaving him with only courtiers and his great-uncle, George Louis's younger brother, Ernst Augustus, for occasional company. Frederick's correspondence with his parents was to be intermittent at best and to dry up entirely by 1725, when his eighteenth birthday, the age of majority for royal children, was ignored by George Augustus and Caroline. Caroline became increasingly engrossed with her younger children, mostly notably Prince William, born in 1721.[18] These years of emotional deprivation surely go some way to explaining Frederick's often adolescent behaviour when he was eventually reunited with his family at the end of 1728.

To maintain the public face of the ruling dynasty in Hanover, Frederick was called upon from the outset to represent his grandfather when foreign dignitaries and ambassadors presented their credentials at the court. George enhanced the boy's standing in the electorate and with visiting grandees by granting him further British honours and titles; on 30 April 1718, Frederick was installed, in his absence, as a Knight of the Garter in St George's Chapel, Windsor Castle, and eight years later, in July 1726, he was made up to Duke of Edinburgh from Duke of Gloucester (dating from 1717). The little prince was simultaneously aggrandised and cut down to size during these lengthy court ceremonials. George's portrait was propped up on the throne in the reception room, while the child stood nearby, greeting visitors, a boy swallowed up in a man's world.

Even allowing for a diplomat's syrupy gloss, a description by an English envoy, Anthony Hammond, written when the prince was nine, suggests that Frederick carried out his duties with some aplomb, uniting precocious poise with youthful high spirits, and perhaps relishing the freedom from parental restraint.

> Nothing can be more agreeable than the person of this young prince. His eyes are full of life, and vigour, his hair extremely fine, his complexion clear and fair, and his shape clean and exact: his constitution is very healthy, and the cheerful innocence and sweetness of youth, shine in his looks, and adds such an amiable grace to his whole deportment, as renders him the delight of all those, who have the honour and happiness to approach him.[19]

Hammond paints an appealing pen portrait of Frederick, who seems by this account to have adapted well to being his grandfather's surrogate. His views were echoed by other visitors to the electorate in the same year, 1716. The indefatigable traveller, diarist and letter-writer, Lady Mary Wortley Montagu, future mother-in-law of Frederick's friend Lord Bute, wrote in a letter to Lady Bristol, mother of Frederick's antagonist, John Hervey, that she was 'extremely pleased that I can tell you without either flattery or partiality that our Prince has all the accomplishments that it is possible to have at his age; with an air of sprightliness and understanding and something so very engaging and easy in his behaviour that he needs no advantage of his rank to appear charming. I had the honour of a long conversation with him last night before the King came in. His governor retired on purpose that I might make some judgement of his genius by hearing him speak without constraint; and I was surprised at the quietness and politeness that appeared in everything he said: joined to a person perfectly agreeable and the fine hair of the Princess [Caroline].'[20]

Further confirmation came from Charles Stanhope, cousin of James Stanhope, George I's Secretary of State, who described dining with Prince Frederick and finding him 'by much the finest youth I ever saw'.[21]

The Honourable John Hervey also took time out of his grand tour in 1716 to visit Herrenhausen and its young prince, who would then have been nine, eleven years Hervey's junior. Hervey knew how to make himself amiable, and, for Frederick, the witty young aristocrat must have blown into his stuffy court like a welcome blast of fresh air. A friendship was established, which was renewed when Frederick arrived in England as a man of twenty-one. It was a friendship, however, which was not to survive the irregularities of both men's sexual exploits, or the entrenched opposition of Hervey's patroness, Frederick's mother, Queen Caroline.

Rumours abounded in England that the neglected prince, lacking playmates of his own social standing, grew up heedless of birth or status, passing his time in the company of stable boys, grooms and footmen.[22] Dissipated nights in Hanover were reported, spent with his déclassé companions, breaking windows and mouthing insults as they racketed about the streets of the city on drunken sprees. But, for the most part, the people turned a blind eye to their prince's occasional excesses, taking a more indulgent attitude to his behaviour than his parents were to do fifteen or more years later. It seems that they understood that the solitary young man needed a chance to let off steam away from the stuffiness of court ceremonial.

Frederick is believed to have been deflowered by the time he was sixteen, at the tender hands of Madame d'Elitz, consecutively mistress to his grandfather, then father. The familial connection gave rise to ribald jokes, to the effect that Madame d'Elitz had lain above, between and below the electors. Sixteen, of course, was not an exceptionally young age at a time of tender diplomatic marriages to lose his virginity, but Frederick's public and solitary position meant that much was made of it. But if his sex life and his boon companions had a coarsening effect on the young prince, it was not observed by Sir John Evelyn, grandson of the diarist, who wrote on Frederick's arrival in England in December 1728,

> His face resembles the Princess Royal. His air is good and his motions graceful, he is shorter than the King, wears his own fair hair in a deep bag. Speaks English very well with a little foreign accent, and is extremely courteous.[23]

Frederick's isolation was not total; his grandfather spent a fifth of his British reign in Hanover, making extended visits in 1716, 1719, 1720, 1723 and 1725. And, in a rare example of maternal concern, Caroline, who had lost her own father to the disease, ordered that the prince should be inoculated against smallpox. The treatment was carried out in 1723 by Caroline's own doctor, Charles Maitland, at the eye-watering cost of £1,000.[24] But by the time Frederick was called to England, he had seen no member of his immediate family for three years, apart from his great-uncle, Ernst Augustus, by then Bishop of Osnabruck, who had died a year after his brother, George I, in August 1728.

Despite or perhaps because of his solitary childhood, Frederick seems to emerge from contemporary accounts as a courteous and good-humoured individual; even his subsequent antagonist Hervey admitted to 'the cheerfulness of his temper'.[25] Solitude taught the prince the value of getting on with his courtiers and subordinates and made him realise that he could not afford to be high-handed.

Frederick had a large staff to manage, which included gentlemen of the bedchamber and footmen, fencing and dancing masters, doctors, fiddlers and a resident organist, a dozen or more cooks, plus coachmen and postilions – although, interestingly, only one washerwoman, three more having been taken to England by the king.

Frederick's time cannot have been entirely misspent. He is quoted by one biographer as loving music, art and nature, interests which must have been fostered either by the prince himself or by his tutors as he was growing up in Hanover.[26] There is evidence aplenty that by the time he reached England at the end of 1728, Frederick's taste was already well-developed, for he certainly received no kind of cultural induction from his boorish father. He would have had shared interests with his mother, but she almost immediately washed her hands of him. Yet, within a few years, Frederick had made several outstanding gardens, introduced the rococo style into Britain through his furniture and silverware collections and clearly signalled his enjoyment of music by having himself painted playing in a trio with his sisters. This, too, was the man who commissioned William Kent to design him a gilt-encrusted state barge in 1731.

By the time he was called to England in 1728, Prince Frederick had become, on the surface, at least, a young man that any parent might have been proud of. He appeared genuinely distressed at his grandfather's death, writing to his sister Anne in England that 'I should be lacking in filial duty and the most ungrateful of men if it had not caused me great sorrow, for he treated me with especial affection and friendship. I was so overcome by sadness when they told me the news that I could not leave my bed for two days and fainted twice.' He adds, in an attempt to ingratiate himself with his parents, 'My only consolation in this sad affliction is the knowledge of my dear parents' goodness. I flatter myself that I shall always conduct myself in a manner deserving of their esteem and friendship for me. I pray you, dear sister, as you are by them, to remember me often to their Majesties.'[27]

One cannot help sensing a slight tongue in cheek when Frederick refers to his 'dear parents' goodness' – parents, that is, who had failed to correspond with him for over three years, and who were, at the time, attempting to lever Frederick from the succession to the English throne. In this instance, Frederick's letter to his sister is that of a diplomat, fully aware that he was writing not a private note *entre eux*, but a statement likely to be read out in public. Unsure what was going to happen to him on the death of his grandfather, Frederick was nevertheless preparing himself for a new role, even if his diplomatic touch was not always so sure – and even if he didn't know what that new role might entail.

This, then, was the state of affairs when the three horsemen rode into Herrenhausen to remove the prince to England. The journey to England was less pleasant and more perilous than the winter sports that the prince had recently enjoyed. Foret gave 'a long account' of the rigours of the trip to Lord Egmont, who recorded the party's 'likelihood of being lost on a marsh, which being covered with snow, was taken for plain ground, but proved to be water and ice, which broke with the first voiture that led the way'. Foret told moreover of 'their chance of falling from a dyke in Holland into one of the canals, their going from Helversluice in a small boat thro' the ice to reach the packet boat.'[28]

The prince was finally on his way to England to take his rightful place at his father's side as Prince of Wales and heir to the British throne. Rising excitement and anticipation, even eagerness to be reunited with his parents and siblings (three of whom he had never met), would surely have contended with alarm and trepidation in the prince's breast as his party struggled on over appalling roads. He would have been a strange youth indeed had he not resented the peremptory fashion in which his father had finally called him to England after a decade and a half of virtually ignoring him. The cool reception he was to receive on his arrival there would fuel bitterness between him and his parents, and lead indirectly to his creating an artistic and horticultural aesthetic of his own as he tried to find his own place in eighteenth-century Britain.

CHAPTER 3

'The Opulence of a Free Country'

Sometime in the 1690s, the traveller Celia Fiennes, daughter of a Cromwellian colonel, visited the home of Sir Richard Temple at Stowe in Buckinghamshire. She described the house as standing 'pretty high', with 'a vista through the whole house, so that on the one side you view the gardens which are one below another with low breast walls and taress [terrace] walkes, and are replenished with all the curiosityes or requisites for ornament pleasure and use'.[1] Fiennes was obviously impressed by Stowe's grounds, decked out with a rigid formality that owed much to the then-prevalent French style of landscape gardening. However, within a few decades, fashions – and the political picture – had changed, and the garden which Fiennes saw had been swept away. Temple's son, later Viscount Cobham, would transform the brick Caroline house into a Palladian mansion and remove the terracing and fancy topiary so that he could lay the bones of a garden which would be quite distinct from leading European gardens such as Louis XIV's Versailles and William of Orange's Het Loo. Stowe would break new frontiers in gardening and would remain the seat of Whig political power for more than six decades through a family network which included three Prime Ministers.[2]

Over that period, Cobham – and, after him, his nephew, Earl Temple – worked to lay out, improve and embellish their estate with the help of designers Sir John Vanbrugh, Charles Bridgeman, William Kent and 'Capability' Brown. The great garden, with its forty buildings or ornaments, became a large-scale, open-air statement of the Whig family's political beliefs and the cradle and embodiment of the English landscape movement. Stowe was pre-eminent among the gardens of the eighteenth century because it represented the three principal phases of the landscape movement, which are described today on the garden's information boards as 'Formality' (1713–30), 'Morality' (1730–40), and 'Naturalism' (1740–1813). These three phases map more or less on to different periods of political change or upheaval, and thus represent an ideological intervention within a real clash about the nature of power and Britishness.

As a political entity, Great Britain only came into existence in 1707 when the Act of Union united the legislature of England and Scotland in the year of Frederick's birth. After its creation, writers, commentators and artists (including garden designers as well as painters) together worked, in Jenny Uglow's words, 'to create a distinctive culture suitable to a new nation, celebrating the land, and the landscape itself'.[3] Forging this new cultural identity was a political act, and the evolution of this identity reflected the transitional state of Britain throughout the eighteenth century. Britain's future as a constitutional monarchy was by no means certain, especially as its new Hanoverian monarchs were accustomed to exercising a more highhanded form of government.[4] When Frederick arrived in Britain in 1728, the peoples of these islands were still coming to terms with the aftermath of the calamitous seventeenth century, which had seen civil war, regicide and eleven years of republican government after Charles I's execution in 1649. The monarchy was restored in 1660, but although Charles II was a cannier man than his father, the religious and constitutional issues which led the country to civil war in the 1640s remained unresolved. Charles's decision to rule without parliament for the last years of his reign, followed by the accession of his brother, the openly Catholic James II, led to the Glorious Revolution and the toppling of a second British monarch within forty years. In June 1688, five notable Whigs and two Tories, subsequently known as the Immortal Seven, invited William of Orange and his wife, Mary, the Protestant-raised daughter of James II, to usurp her father's throne. For the Tory believers in the divine right of kings, the fact that Mary was James's daughter smoothed through what might otherwise have been a contested succession.

During William's reign, in 1701, the Act of Settlement was

passed, which laid down in law that only a Protestant might accede to the British throne. This, together with the Act of Union, was part of what has been described by a twenty-first-century royal historian as 'an openly prepared and legally watertight process of succession-planning'.[5]

Which is why, in August 1714, on the death of Queen Anne – childless despite her seventeen pregnancies – the German George Louis, Duke of Brunswick-Luneburg, Elector of Hanover and a member of the ancient Guelf dynasty, became king of Great Britain and Ireland. Although he was a direct descendant of James I (grandson of James's daughter, Elizabeth, the Winter Queen of Bohemia), his claim was less strong than that of many other intervening members of European royal families. But he was a Protestant and that was crucial for the British ruling classes, most significantly for the Whigs. For them, Protestantism and liberty were synonymous; Catholicism equated to the kind of absolutist government imposed by Louis XIV, which they feared would be inflicted on this country by another French-educated, Catholic-professing Stuart monarch.

The Whig-driven Hanoverian succession after the death of Queen Anne in August 1714 was surprisingly smooth, leading to what Basil Williams has seen as 'an oasis of tranquillity' during the reigns of the first two Georges (1714–60).[6] Britain was, however, at war overseas for much of the period, with invasions in 1714 and 1745 adding to an underlying sense of unease beneath the apparently calm surface of the Whig supremacy. Meanwhile, the debate rumbled on well into the reign of George III about the type of constitution, monarch and government that the country would have, and whether it would be 'English' or 'British'.

George I's arrival was greeted with sporadic rioting as well as the raising of Tory voices in parliament against the new order. Their leaders were Henry St John, Viscount Bolingbroke; James, 2nd Duke of Ormonde; and Robert Harley, Earl of Oxford. Bolingbroke and Ormonde escaped impeachment for treason by decamping to France and joining cause with the Old Pretender, son of James II, while Oxford spent two years in the Tower of London before being acquitted by his peers in July 1717.[7] Only a year after George I's succession, the Earl of Mar, accompanied by 600 supporters, raised the would-be James III's standard at Braemar in August 1715. The death of Louis XIV, the Pretender's chief supporter in Europe, on

1 September, effectively sounded the knell for the insurrection, although James went ahead and landed at Peterhead in Scotland in December only to sail back to France from Montrose six weeks later, his forces harried and defeated.

The first, but not the last, test of the Hanoverian reigns had been passed. The new style of government in Britain impressed a visiting French noble, Monsieur Cesar de Saussure, who wrote home to his family in France in 1729,

> England undoubtedly is, in my opinion, the most happily governed country in the world. She is governed by a King whose power is limited by wise and prudent laws, and by Parliament ... The King cannot levy any new taxes, neither can he abolish privileges or make new laws without the consent of Parliament ... All civil and military posts are given away by the King. He also creates new peers, and has many privileges, in a word, the laws of Great Britain permit her kings to do all the good they may desire to do, preventing them at the same time from doing the bad.[8]

But despite this outsider's rosy assessment, the British identity remained in a delicate condition, in need of bolstering and development. In response, therefore, there were moves by Tories, Whigs and the royal family itself to define a new kind of Britishness through cultural artefacts. Frederick and his mother, Queen Caroline, were to join this artistic battle, at Kew and at Richmond, each to promote his or her own point of view.

There was nothing new in the idea of the landscape being used as a political canvas; gardens, although places of refreshment and leisure, had also always been invested with symbolism and were spaces where philosophical ideas could be aired and political points made. The garden is embedded in the classical and Christian heritage, both having resonance for educated, eighteenth-century gardeners. In ancient Rome, gardens were designed to astound visiting dignitaries with the power, brilliance and opulence of their creators. The Emperor Augustus branded his image on coins and on a thousand statues, which were erected in public places and in gardens across the Roman empire, making a god of a man who ruled territory from northern Europe to the Asian steppes. Medieval gardens, by contrast, were places for quiet contemplation, but not so the gardens of the Italian Renaissance, where upstart bankers like the Medici harked back to their Roman forebears and found a further arena, beyond painting and the decorative arts, in which to display and justify their wealth. The Boboli Gardens behind the Pitti Palace in Florence were central to Cosimo de Medici's botanical interests, and leading scientists from across Europe were welcomed there.

The garden could also be the setting for political courtship. In July 1575, Robert Dudley, Earl of Leicester, made a final, determined attempt to win the hand of Elizabeth I by creating a fragrant and colourful showpiece with which to press his suit at Kenilworth Castle. Inspired by the French and Italian Renaissance, two white marble Atlas figures at the centre of the garden supported a sphere down which the water cascaded. There were sandy paths, rose-covered pergolas and an aviary set with jewels and containing birds from all over the world. The plants themselves were rich in symbolism, chosen to emphasise the status of the garden's owner and the glory of his queen. The expense was all for nothing; the queen resisted Leicester's blandishments and remained unmarried.

It was always unwise for courtiers to try to impress their monarchs with their estates; one of the many luckless dukes of Buckingham lost both his castle at Penshurst in Kent and his head after inviting Henry VIII to admire what he had done there. In the first decade of the seventeenth century, James I was so captivated by the work of the legendary gardener and plantsman John Tradescant for Robert Cecil at Theobalds in Hertfordshire that Cecil was forced to offer up his grand new home to the king and take in exchange the more ramshackle royal residence of Hatfield House.

The garden is also a potent Christian symbol, with the Garden of Eden being the scene of man's lost innocence. It is the central image in Milton's *Paradise Lost* (1667), which set up the restored Stuart monarchy as the fallen angels and sees the failure of the republic as a 'loss of Eden'. Milton, a Whig hero, is included in the Temple of British Worthies at Stowe, and his portrait of Eden in *Paradise Lost* influenced eighteenth-century thinking about gardening. Sir Robert Walpole's son, Horace, for instance, suggested in *The History of the Modern Taste in Gardening* that Milton 'seems with the prophetic eye of taste … to have conceived, to have foreseen modern gardening'.[9]

Walpole's use of the word 'taste' to describe Milton's political and religious epic may strike a jarring note to a modern ear, but questions of taste were fundamental to the aesthetic and political discussions of the eighteenth century. For 'taste' had a wider meaning then; it was not merely about personal preferences or style, but about moral interpretation. 'What is called Taste,' wrote Edmund Burke, '... is not a simple idea, but is partly made up of a perception of the primary pleasures of sense, of the secondary pleasures of the imagination, and of the conclusions of the reasoning faculty ... concerning the human passions, manners and actions'.[10]

The connection between beauty and morality was a crucial component in all the arts, not least in gardens, as was outlined in *Characteristicks of Men, Manners and Opinions, Times,* by Anthony Ashley Cooper, 3rd Earl of Shaftesbury. He was the grandson of another Whig hero, the first earl, who played a major role in the Exclusion Crisis of 1678 to 1681. The crisis brought the Whig and Tory parties into being, as the former attempted to exclude the Catholic James from the succession, in the teeth of resistance from the Tories, a political faction loyal to the divine right of kings. *Characteristicks* detailed his views on the harmonisation of ethical and aesthetic experience, and his emphasis on liberty and toleration. He wrote that 'the horrid graces of the wilderness represent nature better and are more engaging than the formal mockery of princely gardens'.[11] Gardens, he suggested, could be used to express 'moral objects', to help form 'taste' as a manifestation of a certain kind of elitist patriotism. Shaftesbury's book was an artistic credo for Whig gardeners; he proposed that features in a garden should be 'disposed at proper distances and points of sight, with all those symmetrys which silently express a reigning order, peace, harmony and beauty'.[12]

The difficulty, as the political writer Joseph Addison identified in *The Spectator* in 1712, was to reconcile nature and art. 'There is something more bold and masterly in the rough careless strokes of Nature, than in the nice touches and embellishments of art,' he wrote, 'yet we find the works of Nature still more pleasant, the more they resemble those of art.'[13] Despite these contradictions, the idea of a cultivated, yet unconfined, naturalistic garden was an Enlightenment trope, with its humanist suggestion of man's infinite capacity for reason, expansion, exploration and invention.

But the Tories and Whigs interpreted taste, or political morality, according to their own lights. Walpole applauded Bridgeman's 'capital stroke' in introducing the ha-ha at Stowe and its imitation at his father's estate at Houghton in Norfolk in a 'simple though still formal style'.[14] But Houghton, on which Sir Robert Walpole allegedly spent over £200,000, struck the Tories as anything but 'simple'.[15] Walpole's political enemies hit out at him by criticising his taste, and therefore, by implication, his moral and political values. Visiting Houghton in 1722, the Tory Earl of Oxford described the house as 'neither magnificent nor beautiful. There is a very great expense without either judgement or *taste* [my italics].'[16]

It was in this context that Cobham and other Whig grandees developed their gardens, using them as flamboyant means of displaying their fitness for political power, and reinforcing in their smooth, undulating contours the success of their Glorious Revolution. As garden designer Humphry Repton wrote later in the century, 'the neatness, simplicity, and elegance of English gardening' was a visual symbol of the English constitution, itself 'the happy medium betwixt the liberty of savages, and the restraint of despotic government'.[17] Bridgeman's vistas at Stowe ran apparently seamlessly out into the surrounding countryside across an unseen ha-ha. These views represented the new, more open political order which sought to uphold parliament, curtail the power of the crown, and maintain the Protestant succession. Cobham, also the descendant of a Cromwellian colonel, would have believed that this was the 'happy medium' for which his ancestors had fought in the civil wars of the seventeenth century.[18] As one of Marlborough's generals, and ennobled by George I in 1718, Cobham was a significant beneficiary of the Hanoverian succession. But he, along with other Whig grandees, was also a midwife to that succession and to constitutional government which was still in its infancy when Frederick stepped ashore at Harwich in December 1728. It remained, however, an aristocratic settlement, for few Whig leaders espoused political values that would be seen today as genuinely democratic.[19] An 'enlightened' oligarchy, they believed, was the best system for running a country; writing later in the century, Horace Walpole quoted Lord Augustus Cavendish as saying that he 'liked an aristocracy and thought it right that great families with great connections should govern'.[20] The monarch, in their view, was merely first among equals, and effectively chosen by them; he was little more than a titular head and with none of the power of an absolutist such as Louis XIV.

So the garden at Stowe was created initially as a counterblast to the overweening ambitions of Louis XIV's gardens at Versailles, although it would later come to challenge the policies of other, British leaders. Previously the definitive political garden, Versailles had been designed by Le Notre and had sparked copies across Europe. William of Orange's elegant canal garden at Het Loo owed its symmetry and firm lines to Versailles, and indeed inspired a brief fashion in the 1690s England during his reign; the water garden at Westbury Court, by the Severn in Gloucestershire, is a rare survivor of the style.

Le Notre had come to attention of Louis XIV when in 1661 the king visited Vaux-le-Vicomte, the estate of his finance minister, Nicolas Fouquet. Like Buckingham before him, Fouquet made the mistake of showing off the magnificence of his taste and his ambition. No subject, in Louis's view, should be allowed to get so above himself, and, almost within hours, Fouquet was arrested for corruption and imprisoned for life. Le Notre went to work instead for Louis, and together monarch and designer turned a small castle outside Paris into a formidable expression of absolute monarchy. As Louis's power spread across Europe, and as he triggered the War of the Spanish Succession in 1701 by attempting to put a Bourbon king on the Spanish throne, Versailles became the emblem of his dominance and influence, *le jardin sans pareil*. From the giant equestrian statue of Louis in front of the palace to the strict geometry of Le Notre's layout of canals, fountains and sandy walks radiating out from the palace, the gardens demonstrated that all power was centralised in the hands of the monarch. Versailles was a very public affirmation of the absolute authority of the Sun King, designed not only to hold his courtiers in his power, but also to trumpet to France and to other nations Louis's Apollo-like status. The gardens, the king's Great Apartment and the Hall of Mirrors were open to all and could be visited like a museum, while the king himself would be seen in the morning by the visiting public as he made his way to chapel.

Louis's statue, centred on the front of the palace, is also aligned with the main vista behind. This vista represented the Catholic vision of the way through earthly life, leading to heavenly glory – above all, Louis was suggesting, for the king.

It was away from this image of absolute monarchy, and indeed from everything that the Catholic king represented, that first England, then Great Britain, attempted to steer in the late seventeenth and early eighteenth century. At the same time, the new cultural identity that British politicians were fashioning for Britain did not include bestowing on their monarch semi-divine status.

The extreme formality of Le Notre-style French parterres, with their savour of regal control and absolutist government, were rejected by Cobham at Stowe and Lord Burlington at Chiswick. Instead, their new gardens, although equally artificial, appeared at least to mimic nature, equating 'naturalism' with hard-won British freedoms. These two gardens were the cradle of the English landscape movement, brought into being by and representing the new political order.

Lord Burlington created his Palladian villa and garden at Chiswick with the help of painter and designer William Kent. Kent, along with Charles Bridgeman, also worked variously for the Earl of Carlisle at Castle Howard, for the Duke of Newcastle at Claremont and for his brother, Henry Pelham, at Esher Place, and for Queen Caroline at Richmond Gardens. Kent would also come to work for Frederick at Kew, and, more influentially, at Carlton House in London.

Burlington's miniature Italian idyll on the outskirts of London owed many of its features, such as its exedra, to classical, Roman inspiration, although given an English twist; a curved hedge of dark yew, rather than a stone screen, was erected as a backdrop to Burlington's collection of ancient and eighteenth-century sculpture.[21]

The appointment of Bridgeman at Stowe coincided with the accession of George I in 1714. Appropriately, the Temple family motto was *Templa quam dilecta* ('How beautiful are thy temples'), so Cobham and his successors filled Bridgeman's formal landscapes with temples, monuments and other ornamentation, which had a clear meaning not only to fellow aristocrats but also to the visiting – mostly educated – public.[22] Although much work was still follow, Cobham's achievements at Stowe were soon acknowledged; by 1724, Sir John Perceval, later Lord Egmont, was writing that Stowe 'has gained the reputation of being the finest seat in England'.[23]

Cobham's appointment of Bridgeman, Vanbrugh and Kent was the opening sally in a political and aesthetic battle about the nature of Britishness – and its monarchy – which was to be played out well into the reign of George III. As concepts of nationhood subtly changed and shifted, so too were these shifts reflected on the cultivated landscape.[24] As Tories, different Whig factions, and members of the royal family attempted to define their individual notions of Britishness, they helped to engineer the birth of British gardening. The English landscape garden, known as *le jardin anglais*, became a key British export. It influenced other rulers, including Catherine the Great of Russia, whose estate at Tsarskoe Selo featured buildings reminiscent of those at Stowe, most notably the Palladian bridge.

Cobham wanted to display his wealth, but more importantly to develop a style of gardening with a distinctly British aesthetic. The Whig cultural hegemony he fashioned, however, was concerned with a very limited notion of Britishness – leisured, knowledgeable and wealthy. As aristocratic wealth and self-confidence grew, which they continued to do throughout the course of the eighteenth century, the gardens became increasingly informal. First Kent, then Brown softened the strong lines of Bridgeman's original design at Stowe, for instance, although they left his encircling ha-ha in place. As Horace Walpole was later to write about gardens, 'The expence is only suited to the opulence of a free country.'[25]

A free country, with a fast-growing empire abroad and burgeoning tourism at home, without which Cobham might not have gone to such lengths at Stowe (nor Caroline at Richmond, or later Augusta at Kew). The benefits of freedom, commercial success and imperial expansion were recognised as early as the 1720s by the novelist, journalist and pamphleteer, Daniel Defoe. Defoe, who had actively promoted the Union with Scotland, saw Britain as 'the most flourishing and opulent country in the world'. He applauded 'this great British Empire', which, with mercantile expansion abroad, brought 'improvement, as well in culture, as in commerce'. He notes in his *Tour through the Whole Island of Great Britain* 'the new seats and dwellings of the nobility and the gentry; also the encrease [sic] of wealth, in many eminent particulars'.[26]

The homes 'of the nobility and gentry' that attracted Defoe's attention were also central to a road atlas published as early as

1675 by mapmaker John Ogilby. On detachable sheets, *Britannia* contained a series of structured journeys across the country to landed estates, which reflected political authority and social status.[27] That these estates needed an audience, or consuming public, was recognised in the seventeenth century by Celia Fiennes. Defoe also understood that the estates themselves had become commodities, to be 'bought' by the visiting public. The popularity of tourism in the eighteenth century was a feature of a consumer revolution, creating a market for guidebooks, accommodation, personal guides and transport, and involving several social classes. George Bickham describes this in one of his guidebooks to Stowe.

> Besides, there is another advantage in wealth laid out in this elegant manner ... the money spent in the neighbourhood, by the company daily crouding hither, to satisfy their curiosity. There is a kind of continual fair ... several of the inhabitants of *Buckingham* [Bickham's italics] say, that is one of the best trades they have: their inns, their shops, their farms, and shambles, all find their account in it.[28]

The act of visiting established a relationship, albeit at arm's length, between different levels of society, and reinforced the elite's picture of itself, in which visitors from lower social classes were allowed briefly to share. Tourism also promoted Britain's position in the world, especially through the landscapes of its leaders.[29] This is also summed up in the same edition of Bickham's guidebook. 'Another advantage of a public nature, derived from these elegant productions of art and Nature ... is, their tendency to raise us in the opinion of foreigners.'[30]

The rhetoric of Stowe guidebooks suggests that a well-ordered estate offered public instruction and a chance for this 'great concourse of people' to share briefly in a privileged world.[31] 'A Sunday evening spent here adds a new relish to the day of rest, and makes the sabbath appear more chearful [sic] to the labourer, after a toilsome week.'[32] That is how Lord Cobham saw his work at Stowe. To that end, he opened what must surely have been the first ever visitor centre in 1717. The New Inn was leased out by Cobham to a series of innkeepers, responsible for feeding, watering and offering overnight accommodation to visitors to the estate, admitted only when the Temple family were not at home. It was even used by members of the aristocracy who weren't Cobham's personal friends, although one of them was Sir John Perceval, who complained in 1724 that the accommodation provided was 'scurvy'.

Jacques Rigaud's 1730s engravings, which still adorn the mansion at Stowe (now a school), are imaginary projections; both general public and house guests are shown viewing the landscape simultaneously. The public, however, were never admitted while the family was in residence, and tourists were only quasi-members of an elite club. Posture and clothing identify each group. House guests drift around, the women elegantly clad, the men bewigged, all deep in conversation and apparently unconscious of their surroundings; the political meanings of the landscape are taken by them as read. By contrast, the paying visitors, clearly of the 'middling sort', wear outdoor clothes, the men hats and serviceable coats, the women wide-brimmed bonnets, and all gesture eagerly around.

Even another fellow aristocrat, Viscount Torrington, could not gain admission to the grounds when Cobham's great-nephew was in residence later in the century. 'Unluckily for our intention,' he wrote, 'the Mss of Buckingham is return'd to Stowe, else we had thoughts of surveying it.'[33]

The inn was just up the lane from the Bellgate, to which visitors would stroll and pull the bell to gain admittance to Cobham's didactic landscape. A clear path was laid out for them once through the gate, with the political message reinforced at every turn.

Although the private Cobham might well have preferred to retreat into the fortified island encircled by Bridgeman's ha-ha, the public man wanted to show off his taste and worldly success to the voting public. Adam Smith neatly summed up this desire for display in *The Wealth of Nations* (1776).

> With the greater part of rich people, the chief enjoyment of riches consists in the parade of riches, which in their eyes is never so compleat as when they appear to possess those decisive marks of opulence which nobody can possess but themselves.[34]

Cobham recognised that the estate was his power base to be used to advertise his party's and his family's fitness to govern. Although the passing of the Septennial Act in 1716 meant that MPs only had to face re-election every seven years, the voting public still needed wooing; as a young man, Cobham had won his parliamentary seat (for Buckinghamshire) in 1704 by just two votes.[35] Stowe was always intended to be seen by outsiders, not just by Cobham's social equals.[36]

What Cobham did at Stowe was, effectively, to reinvent Versailles. The main axis of the garden, as at Versailles, was also intended to represent the path through earthly life, with paths of virtue and of vice on either side offered as choices of thoroughfare to garden visitors. Embodied within these landscapes were Anglo-Saxon legends, with Kent's landscaping of the groves of vice conjuring up a particularly raunchy story from Edmund Spenser's *The Faerie Queene*. Reference to Anglo-Saxon history was quite deliberate; the Temple family saw themselves as the contemporary descendants of the Saxons who appointed their kings through early forms of parliament. King Alfred – a hero of the Whigs, who mistakenly believed him to be the architect of British justice – was commemorated in Kent's Temple of British Worthies, set in the Elysian Fields on the side of virtue.

Monuments were erected by Cobham to 'Britannify' the new German dynasty, but also to make a further point about how that dynasty came to enjoy its position. An equestrian statue of George I still dominates the approach to the north front of Stowe, standing in the same position as the similar statue of Louis XIV at Versailles. Again, this is no accident. Louis sits astride his horse, his right hand held out triumphantly, pointing out that he is master of all he surveys. George I, however, has his right hand hanging down decorously to his side. The statue was erected by Cobham in tribute to the king who had raised him to the nobility, but there is a further message to be decoded. Louis's statue stands in front of his greatest palace, while George's statue is before the palace of one of his subjects. The inference is clear; George is king because Cobham and his ilk have deemed that he should be. This is no absolute monarch, but a king with his power circumscribed by the Whig oligarchy.

In a further twist, the statue of Queen Caroline, George I's daughter-in-law, gracing a tall Ionic plinth, is set in the Garden of Vice, an indication that by the mid-1730s, the Cobhamite Whigs would be at odds with George II and his wife.

❉

Small wonder, then, that Caroline, first as Princess of Wales and then as queen, in the face of such competition from an over-mighty subject, would wish to put forward her own, and personally self-aggrandising, interpretation of British history on another, previously Jacobite, landscape.

On the western, riverside half of what is now Kew Gardens stood a lodge built by James, 2nd Duke of Ormonde, in 1704, on property leased from the Crown.[37] Just over a decade later, in 1715, the Tory duke, described by Basil Williams as 'a futile grandee', was impeached for treason, along with Bolingbroke, for their pro-Jacobite manoeuvrings, and, like Bolingbroke, escaped to France to offer his services to the Pretender.[38] In 1721, George, Prince of Wales, took on the property from Ormonde's brother, the Earl of Arran, and it was there that his wife, Caroline of Ansbach, began to enjoy the fashionable pursuit of landscape gardening. Caroline employed Charles Bridgeman at Richmond throughout the 1720s, appointing him Royal Gardener in 1728 after her husband's accession to the throne. She also worked closely with William Kent, who was responsible in the 1730s for the design of two idiosyncratic buildings, the Hermitage and Merlin's Cave.

Like Cobham at Stowe, Caroline devised her own iconography at Richmond to claim the moral high ground for herself and her husband and to demonstrate her aesthetic taste and judgement. She employed the British nation's legends, manipulating them for vindication and authentication. Bridgeman's landscape and Kent's buildings can still be seen at Stowe, but we have to rely on contemporary engravings of Caroline's contributions to the debate, for her buildings were razed later in the century by 'Capability' Brown, working for her grandson, George III.

The Hermitage was described in a 1761 guidebook, *London and Its Environs*, as 'a grotesque building, which seems as if it had stood many hundred years'.[39] It appears to have been a hut-like construction with rusticated walls and an incongruous classical pediment. This ancient-style shrine was peopled by contemporary figures, in contrast, for example, with Cobham's Temple of British Worthies at Stowe, which featured heroes from several centuries. Inside were marble busts, still in the Royal Collection, commissioned by Caroline in 1731 from Giovanni Battista Guelfi, who had worked with Kent and Burlington at Chiswick. At the centre, raised higher than the others and with a sunburst behind him, was the chemist, physicist, philosopher and founder member of the Royal Society, Robert Boyle. He was flanked by mathematician Isaac Newton and the Whig philosopher John Locke, and by two contemporary divines, Samuel Clarke and William Wollaston. The choices of these heroes displayed Caroline's interest in Enlightenment ideas, as well as her devotion to the Church of England; the shrine was a tribute to the divine gift of human reason.[40]

Even odder in appearance was the three-chambered Merlin's Cave, which looked like Big Ears' toadstool. If the message of the Hermitage was scientific and religious, that of Merlin's Cave was overtly political and intended to defend her ally, Britain's first Prime Minister, Robert Walpole.[41] The thatched building had small Gothic windows in a reference to British vernacular architecture and was lined with bookcases. Wax figures inside of Elizabeth of York, wife of King Henry VII, and of Elizabeth I associated Caroline with Tudor queens who had brought peace and unity. Elizabeth I also figures in the Temple of British Worthies at Stowe. Merlin, according to an article in *The Gentleman's Magazine* in December 1735, was 'born a Welchman', to enforce Caroline's pan-British credentials.

Merlin was associated with Walpole, which was, perhaps, unwise. The same magazine article refers to the mythological character as 'that great Man', an allusion to the contemporary and derisive description of Walpole. The building was savaged in the Tories' political magazine, *The Craftsman*; the article linked magic and cunning, wizardry and political corruption.[42]

Caroline, like Cobham, opened her garden to the public so that they should link the new Hanoverian dynasty with ideas of Britishness. To help make the point, she employed a hermit, pastoral poet Stephen Duck, to live in the Hermitage, while his wife, Sarah, explained the elaborate conceits of Merlin's cave to visitors. The pro-Walpole and anti-*Craftsman* journal, *The Gentleman's Magazine*, pointed out the significant role of the royal family as social and cultural leaders.

Most nations form themselves upon the model of their princes. Vice and virtue, as well as arts and sciences, flourish in proportion as the court either practises or encourages them. For the taste of the court is always the standard of every thing, but liberty, to the rest of the nation.

The great concourse of people, that have lately flock'd to view
that celebrated edifice call'd *Merlin's* Cave, the universal applause
it has met with … prove the truth of this maxim.[43]

Both Cobham and Caroline were hard at work on their new
gardens when Frederick, Prince of Wales, was called to London
by his parents in December 1728. It was an interesting time, both
personally and politically, for the prince to arrive.

CHAPTER 4

'This Is Not a Son I Need Be Much Afraid Of'

The scene was set for the arrival of Frederick in the country where he expected to reign. Britain had achieved some kind of uneasy peace, the king had been crowned in Westminster Abbey with his younger son, the six-year-old Prince William, rather than his heir at his side, and the Whigs had put down their marker firmly on the land and in Parliament, eclipsing the Tories for a generation. The government was headed by Sir Robert Walpole, the owner himself of a splendid estate, where he had erected his own bust in a Roman toga alongside those of would-be emperor Julius Caesar and the emperor Marcus Aurelius. In so doing, he evoked imperial rather than republican Rome, the latter being the political model favoured by Cobhamite Whigs. In their view, Walpole had corrupted the republican ideal and so they made party with Frederick against the king and Prime Minister. Walpole came to regret accommodating his restive backbenchers by bringing the prince to London.

On 7 December, Frederick landed at Harwich. He would never become king, but nor would he again leave British shores in the remaining twenty-three years of his life. He had crossed the Channel anonymously on an ordinary packet boat, and, after a night in Colchester, he made his way to London, where he was greeted without ceremony or special notice. This was recorded the following day in the *Daily Post*.

Yesterday His Royal Highness, Prince Frederick came to Whitechapel about seven in the evening, and proceeded thence privately in a hackney coach to St. James's. His Royal Highness alighted at the Friary and walked down to the Queen's backstairs, and was there conducted to Their Majesty's apartment.[1]

There is pathos in this description of Frederick's first appearance in London after almost a decade and a half without seeing his parents. The key lies in the only descriptive word in what is otherwise a baldly factual account; the adverb 'privately' points up the oddness of the long-awaited Prince of Wales's arrival in London being so furtive, as hugger-mugger, indeed, as had been his departure from Hanover. The writer would have been aware that it was strange that the prince had to hire a hackney coach and then be shown up the backstairs to his mother's apartments, rather than being greeted publicly in the state apartments.

There have been suggestions that Fredrick deliberately came post-haste and without fanfare in the hope of surprising his parents after their protracted separation. If so, the element of surprise was lost, as Egmont records. Foret complained to the king about Alderman John Philipson, commissary of the packets boats at Harwich, 'who having discovered the Prince was landed sent immediately an express of it to his friends in London, which defeated a pleasure the Prince had conceived to surprise the King with his sight even before he could know he was landed'.[2] The young man, having departed precipitously from Hanover, was impatient to be at court, to see his parents, and to establish himself in his new role as Prince of Wales. As for the family reunion, he was to be bitterly disappointed.

If there were surprise, it must surely have been more on Frederick's side than his parents' – surprise that after the abrupt order for his appearance no plans had been made for his arrival in London. What the frosty reception would have underlined was the unwillingness of George and Caroline to instate their eldest son in the British court. Frederick's portrait had been included in Sir James Thornhill's royal family portrait in the Painted Hall at Greenwich, Thornhill having visited Hanover in 1719 to make sketches of the prince. Fine to have the prince's image at Greenwich, indicating the Hanoverian succession's strength in depth, but George and Caroline were less willing to actually have him in London with them. Their own experience as Prince and Princess of Wales had forcefully taught the couple the ambiguous nature of the heir's role, and in part explains their joint reluctance to have their elder son join them in London.

George II was a short-tempered, peremptory man, with a childhood overshadowed by his mother's disgrace, and always at loggerheads with his father; it was not the upbringing to make him emollient or considerate towards the feelings of his own son. Caroline's behaviour is harder to understand. Caroline of Ansbach is arguably the most thoughtful and cultured consort that any British monarch has had, thanks to her privileged adolescence, the guidance of two highly intelligent women and her regular correspondence with Leibniz, Newton and with leading divines. She showed imaginative kindness in paying a pension to the poverty-stricken grand-daughter of John Milton.[3] She was influenced by the latest medical developments and, to the horror of the court, had all her children inoculated against smallpox.

The arrival of her eldest son, from whom she had been separated for more than fourteen years, might, one would have imagined, have been a moment to gladden a mother's heart, especially as that son already showed signs of cultural refinement himself. And yet she followed her husband's lead in cold-shouldering the young prince on his arrival, and indeed her hostility to Frederick became deeper and more engrained as the years passed. It is possible that this antagonism grew out of a mother's feelings of guilt at having abandoned her son, however unwillingly, when he was a mere child. The death of her baby son, and her separation from her older daughters after her husband's vicious row with his father, perhaps forced her to cover up feelings for her children that were very real – and which were indeed revealed in the affection correspondence she shared with her elder daughter, Anne, after her marriage to William IV of Orange in 1734. Nevertheless, whatever caused Caroline's antagonism to her eldest son, hostility between the two grew.

The king and queen were determined that their acquiescence to public opinion in bringing the prince to England should be sufficient. They did not wish to fete him before their subjects and so risk him becoming a focus of opposition. Like other European monarchs, including the Sun King himself, they dined in public once a week, on display within a barricaded enclosure at St James's Palace. On the first Sunday after Frederick's arrival, it was anticipated that the heir to the throne would join his parents to be shown to the people.

He did not appear, although he was seen to guide his mother into her pew at the Chapel Royal that day.[4]

Nevertheless, the public were eager to see the new prince and he was soon the talk of the town. A large crowd turned up at the palace on the morning after Frederick's backstairs arrival, as reported in *Brice's Weekly Journal*. 'Infinite numbers of people assembled before the apartment of His Royal Highness Prince Frederick. His Royal Highness looked from the window with great affability, upon which the crowd expressed their satisfaction with loud acclamations.'[5] This was just the kind of demonstration that the king and queen had hoped to avoid, especially as the prince's first faltering words in English were accompanied by a carillon of bells from St Michael's, Cornhill, in the City of London.

Frederick became quickly visible to more than just the court, attending plays, balls, masks and concerts. The week of his arrival, he was seen at a play, *The Constant Couple*, along with three of his sisters, Anne, Amelia and Caroline. He seemed, the newspaper remarked, 'to express a particular liking to our English comedies, and the English actors'.[6] On New Year's Day, he attended a performance of John Gay's *The Beggar's Opera*, which Robert Walpole had sought to have supressed, as two of the crooked characters, Peachum and Macheath, were not very well disguised attacks on the Prime Minister; the whole play was a biting satire on the concentration of political power in Walpole's hands. Frederick may well not yet have been aware of the implications of the play, but it is intriguing that he was watching anti-Walpolian drama within a fortnight of coming to London. It was a presage of things to come.

Frederick also started to move into society and behaved, like all the Hanoverian princes of Wales, as a fashionable member of the aristocracy rather than as royalty. He began to acquaint himself with some of England's great houses and gardens. In July 1729, for example, he accompanied the queen, Princess Anne and his younger brother to dine with the Earl of Orkney at Cliveden in Buckinghamshire, a house he later leased and where he entertained extensively. In August, he dined with the Duke of Newcastle at Claremont in Surrey, where he saw the work of Sir John Vanbrugh, Charles Bridgeman and William Kent.[7]

The formalities were also observed; in January 1729, Frederick was invested as a Knight of the Garter (the ancient order of chivalry instituted by Edward III in the fourteenth century) and introduced to the House of Lords formally as Prince of Wales. He also attended the House of Commons in February, where he was congratulated by the members of Parliament on his safe arrival in England. The prince replied, in a statement no doubt pre-prepared for him by court officials,

> I return my thanks to the House of Commons for this very obliging message. I esteem their kind notice of me, as a fresh mark of that zeal and affection which they have, upon all occasions, shown for his Majesty and his family.[8]

Frederick received foreign deputations, was welcomed to London by the Lord Mayor and Court of Alderman, formally greeted at the Royal Society by Sir Hans Sloane, who had succeeded Isaac Newton as president two years earlier, and made Chancellor of Dublin University in 1729, although he never visited Ireland. He was taking his place in the family firm, and an attempt was made to present unity at the heart of the royal family.[9] He also played a leading role in marking his mother's birthday. 'His Royal Highness the Prince, who was dress'd vastly fine, led the Queen to the Room of State.'[10]

There are accounts of Frederick attending functions, appearing on occasion with his family and filling certain ceremonial roles. But there are no records of guidance or training offered to Frederick either by the king or by his leading ministers such as Walpole – nothing indeed along the lines of the letter that Frederick was to leave for his son, the future George III, on his early death in 1751. Yet, despite his lack of preparation for the role of Prince of Wales, he generally made a good impression, as Lady Bristol wrote.

> He is the most agreeable young man it is possible to imagine without being the least handsome. His person is little, but well made and genteel, a liveliness in his eyes that is undescribable, and the most obliging address that can be conceived.[11]

According to Lady Bristol's son, Lord Hervey, Frederick was also 'in great favour' with the king when he first arrived in London, although 'it lasted not long'. 'The King was pleased with him as a new thing,' wrote Hervey, felt him quite in his power, contemned him as rival, made him no great expense and looked upon his being here with so little court paid to him as an escape from a danger which he had dreaded, and yet was obliged to expose himself to. Sir Robert Walpole told me one day that the King, speaking to him of his son, soon after his arrival, said with an air of contempt and satisfaction: "I think this is not a son I need be much afraid of."[12]

It is hard to imagine just how strange it must have been for Frederick, dragged away from Hanover without warning and confronted with six siblings, all of whom were virtual strangers to him. His three elder sisters, Anne, Amelia and Caroline, now nineteen, seventeen and fifteen, were small girls when they left for England with their parents in 1714. Since then, George and Caroline had had four more children: George William, who died in infancy; then William Augustus, Duke of Cumberland, born in 1721; Mary, born in 1723; and Louisa, born in 1724. With Anne, Frederick had had a desultory correspondence over the years; it was to her that he wrote of his emotions on the death of their grandfather, George I, although the tone of the letter (quoted in Chapter 2) suggests that he was writing for court consumption rather than sending a personal note to a beloved sister. His next sister, Amelia, made friendly overtures to the prince, but he quickly discovered that she was spying on him for his mother, to whom she confided the fact that Frederick had left behind a pile of debts in Hanover.

This was hardly an auspicious start. Having been at the centre of his own court for the past fourteen years, Frederick might reasonably have expected to have been given a separate establishment and paid the same allowance as his father had received when Prince of Wales. The king, who had no intention of making his son independent and therefore a focus for opposition, sent him instead back to the nursery to live with his siblings, the youngest barely five years old, a dramatic contrast with the position which he had held in Hanover. The king paid him just £2,000 a month, which, together with his revenues from the Duchy of Cornwall, gave him an income of about £34,000 a year; not much for a prince who had already shown himself inclined to run up gaming debts. Far from keeping the prince away from the opposition, the king by his parsimony pushed his son straight into their hands, as Hervey recalled. 'The opponents, who had a mind to get him, began their attack by telling him how ill his father used him in giving him this short allowance.' He unflatteringly describes Frederick's reactions. 'The Prince, on this occasion, as on all like occasions afterwards, between anger and timidity went just such lengths with those who were against the Court as served to irritate his father and not far enough to attach them to his service.'[13]

Hervey had perhaps underrated his man, for the prince was within a few years to have become more than a figurehead of the Cobham-led opposition to Walpole, an almost inevitable result of his parents' conduct. Brought over to London, apparently on a whim, given no political or ceremonial role and consigned to the royal nursery, it is scarcely surprising that a young man should seek out an occupation for himself, nor that he should sow a few wild oats, as is suggested in this description of Frederick from Lord Egmont's diaries.

> He has no reigning passion: or if it be, it is to passing the evening with six or seven others over a glass of wine and hear them talk of a variety of things; but he does not drink. He loves play, and plays to win, that he may supply his pleasures and his generosity, which last are great, but so ill placed, that he often wants wherewith to do a well-placed kindness, by giving to unworthy objects. He has had several mistresses, and now keeps one, an apothecary's daughter of Kingston; but is not nice in his choice, and talks more of feats this way than he acts. He can talk gravely according to his company, but is sometimes more childish than becomes his age. He thinks he knows business, but attends to none; likes to be flattered. He is good-natured, and if he meets with a good Ministry, may satisfy his people; he is extremely dutiful to his parents, who do not return it in love, and seem to neglect him by letting him do as he will.[14]

Egmont's astute and subtle description of Frederick conveys both the strengths and the weaknesses of the prince's character, and hints at teenage rebellion staged a decade late – and to a large extent triggered by his parents. He had a succession of mistresses, partly, Egmont believed, because no marriage was arranged for him; he seemed to believe as late as April 1730 that Wilhelmina of Prussia might still be in contention. He wrote that the Prince had lately engaged a mistress in his neighbourhood, a Papist, and taken a house and furnished it just over against her father's; that her father's name is La Tour, the man in the playhouse plays the hautboy. That the discourse is the Prince has bought her for fifteen hundred pounds. I was very sorry to hear it, and do heartily wish the project of his marriage with the Princess Royal of Prussia may come to effect, upon which I am persuaded his Royal Highness will forsake this kind of life.[15]

The prince sounds no worse than many Princes of Wales before and after him; the behaviour of Frederick's grandson, the future George IV, and, like Frederick, an avid collector, was to be much more reprehensible. Frederick was indeed keen on gambling, and would lose £1,000 a night. He seems often to have been on the edge of trouble, happy to mix with the general public in the streets, despite the disapproval of his parents, allegedly boxing the ears of an abusive man at a masquerade and being robbed at night in St James's Park. On another occasion, he 'resorted to a prostitute', and had his watch and money stolen.[16] Hervey compares the prince's behaviour to that of the Roman emperor Nero.

I have often thought there was a great similitude in many particulars (cruelty excepted) between the characters of Nero and the Prince of Wales. Nero at the beginning of his reign was as much admired and loved as the Prince of Wales at his first arrival in England, and both of them soon after were as much hated and despised ... Both of them were extremely lewd and both extremely inconstant. Both of them as false to their mistresses as their friends, and no more capable of attachment by constitution to the one than they were of fidelity by principle to the other. They both loved feasts, fine clothes, expense, shows, masques, revelling and drinking, and loved too in drunken company to scour the streets, beat the watch and molest everybody they met ... the Prince in an exploit of this kind as narrowly escaped being shot from the Duchess of Buckingham's house in the park whilst he and his company were taking the diversion of breaking her windows.[17]

Given Hervey's habitual malicious exaggeration, it seems fair to assume that Frederick was, in effect, a classic man about town.

He made valiant efforts to speak the language, thereby winning the hearts of Londoners. They were particularly impressed when he was involved in handing buckets of water alongside firefighters to put out a fire in the Inns of Court in January 1737. Lady Irwin reported the event and reactions in a letter to her father, saying that 'there was a dreadful fire last week at the Temple ... The Prince stayed from 12 at night till 6 in the morning, directing the soldiers and encouraging the firemen to work both by his presence and money, and 'tis said he did a great service. He need not this to make him popular.'[18]

Frederick also came to love the British sport of cricket, sponsoring the London and Middlesex team in 1735 to play a Kent team raised by Charles Sackville at Knole for a stake of £1,000. In 1737, John Sackville, again with the prince's help, arranged a game on Kennington Common, described by the *London Evening Post* as 'the greatest match of cricket that has ever been contested'. It attracted a crowd of about 10,000, and 'the crush outside the Prince of Wales's pavilion was such that a poor woman by the crowd bearing upon her unfortunately had her leg broke, which being related to his Royal Highness, he was pleased to order her ten guineas'.[19]

Such acts of bravery and of generosity meant that 'the town' and 'all ranks' were on the prince's side when it came to money matters, too, as Egmont also recorded.

> It is inconceivable how much the town resents the King's usage of the Prince with respect to money matters; the enemies of the Government are loud against it, because they are glad of any handle to make a noise, and the friends are deeply concerned for the reflection it draws on the King, and the injury it does to the Prince, both in health, credit and temper, for his necessity may turn him from being the most generous and best admired man in the world to be of a sordid temper and to abandon himself to pleasure to stifle concern. The fault is laid at Sir Robert Walpole's door, who is said to encourage the King in his parsimonious temper, by which he preserves His Majesty's favour, and gains the disposal of all places, which he only bestows on his creatures.[20]

Walpole was no more anxious than the king to see the prince playing anything other than a strictly ceremonial role, and also wanted to limit his activities by keeping him short of money. The plan backfired, as Walpole would discover to his cost over the next thirteen years. Frederick's relationship with Walpole was never good, and his reputation was permanently tarnished by Hervey's spiteful machinations. Alienating the British Saint-Simon of the time was possibly Frederick's worst mistake, resulting as it did in his name being blackened by the elegantly barbed pen of Hervey. The diarist was ruthless, unforgiving and fearless in his attacks, as he himself admitted. 'Those who expect that I should be very choice in my language or methodical in my arrangement will be extremely mistaken, for I seek rather to please people's curiosity than to promote my own reputation.'[21] Pouring scorn on the heir to the throne and revealing disharmony at the heart of the royal family was more likely to attract the attention of potential readers than being a smooth-tongued flatterer.

Writing always in the third person, Hervey made himself unpopular with many people, not the least the Dowager Duchess of Marlborough, widow of the victor of Blenheim, who described him as 'the most wretched profligate man that ever was born, besides ridiculous'.[22] He also offended the greatest poet of the age, Alexander Pope, who launched an excoriating attack, matching Hervey in its venom, in his early 1730s Epistle to Dr. Arbuthnot.

> Let Sporus tremble – 'What? that Thing of silk,
> Sporus, that mere white Curd of Ass's milk?
> Satire or Sense alas! can Sporus feel?
> Who breaks a Butterfly upon a Wheel?'
> Yet let me flap this Bug with gilded wings,
> The painted Child of Dirt that stinks and stings.[23]

As already mentioned, Frederick and Hervey had first met in Hanover in 1716, when the former was nine, the latter twenty. Hervey, in Europe on his Grand Tour, had been encouraged by his father, the 1st Earl of Bristol, to detour to Herrenhausen to nurture a potentially useful relationship with the young prince. A handsome man, a fact admitted even by Pope, Hervey attracted the attention of the beautiful Molly Lepell, a maid-of-honour to the then Princess of Wales. By the time Frederick arrived in London, Hervey and Molly were married and had four children, although Hervey himself was abroad travelling in Italy with Stephen Fox, a young Tory landowner with whom he was in love. Hervey returned from continental Europe in October 1729 and was appointed Vice-Chamberlain at the court in May 1730, giving him frequent entrée to members of the royal family. Frederick would have done well to keep Hervey at a distance, but he may have been pleased in a still unfamiliar situation to come across a man he remembered from boyhood. Initially, the two men struck up a friendship, corresponding when apart, and Frederick stood godfather to Hervey's third son in August 1730.[24] They even wrote a play together. *The Modish Couple* opened in January 1732 at the Theatre Royal, Drury Lane, and, on the third night, Frederick appeared 'to one of the finest Assemblies of Persons of Quality that has been seen'. The following night, however, the play was booed off the stage, thus ending Frederick's aspirations to be a playwright.[25]

The friendship is believed to have ripened into a sexual one. It is hard to chart its development and then its falling off, as the relevant pages of Hervey's *Memoirs*, from May 1730 to late summer 1732, were destroyed in the nineteenth century by descendants of Hervey, wishing to protect the reputation both of their family and of the ruling Hanoverian dynasty.[26] Certain causes of dissatisfaction on Hervey's part with Frederick, however, are clear. The first was Frederick's appointment of the corpulent wit, George Bubb Dodington, as his political advisor, thereby implicitly replacing Hervey as his favourite.

The other bone of contention was Frederick's affair with Hervey's mistress, the Honourable Anne Vane, a maid-of-honour to the queen and daughter of the second Lord Barnard. It was all very public, so much so that when Anne gave birth to a son on 4 June 1733, she did so in her apartments at the palace and the boy was openly acknowledged by the prince and christened in the Chapel Royal, as reported in *The Gentleman's Magazine*. 'On the 17th June, 1733, the son of a Lady much talk'd at St. James's was Christened by the Name of Fitz Frederick of Cornwall.'[27] When Anne was dismissed by the queen and turned out of her apartments, Frederick found her a house in Grosvenor Square and gave her an allowance of £1,600 a year.[28]

The affair made both Frederick and Hervey the butt of a number of literary squibs, including *The Humours of the Court, OR Modern Gallantry* and *The Fair Concubine: Or the Secret History of the Beautiful Vanella*, both published in London in

1732. In the preface to *The Humours of the Court*, the anonymous author writes that 'it is not designed as a satyr upon any one person particular', but adds that if the cap fits, wear it. The story involves three people: Adonis (Frederick), Aldemar (Hervey) and Vanessa (Miss Vane). The two men appear as rivals, with Adonis saying to Aldemar, 'Have her I must and will.' Vanessa initially modestly rejects Adonis's advances, admitting to her potential lover's confidant Modish, 'That princely youth and I can never meet as lovers, Fate has put such bars between us as are not to be moved; nor can I e'er be his, but upon terms so shameful, as I much blush to think on.' Modish replies insinuatingly, 'Can any thing be shameful with a Prince? Don't you consider that a Prince's name gives sanction to every thing?' The rejected Aldemar's response to his almost inevitable usurpation by Adonis is the ungallant urging of Vanessa 'to go thy ways, next to enjoying a new mistress, the greatest pleasure is to get rid of an old one'.[29]

The Fair Concubine tells much the same tale about 'the beautiful Vanella', like 'Vanessa', a clear pseudonym for Miss Vane. In this account, Vanella becomes pregnant by both a young nobleman, Albimarides, and by Prince Alexis. For Albimarides, 'honourable Love was a Stranger to his Heart; for he used it like a Cloak to cover his libidinous Designs.' When Vanella finds herself pregnant by the prince, she writes to him, saying, 'Methinks I am the Laughing-Stock of the Court'.[30]

Neither Frederick nor the prince come well out of this sorry story – or indeed Miss Vane herself. Hervey, despite being aggrieved at losing his mistress to the prince, was quite happy to use her to spy on her new lover. He found out that Dodington was no longer in Frederick's favour through 'Miss Vane, with whom he was now privately reconciled, and who ventured to meet him in secret once or twice a week, and at these meetings entertained him with the account of everything she learned from the Prince or observed either in him or the people about him'.[31]

Frederick remained faithful to Anne for about three years, but eventually broke off the affair when he was attracted by Lady Archibald Hamilton, a woman ten years his senior and the mother of ten (a mother figure for the prince, perhaps?). Anne was sent off to Bath, where she died, only a week after her son had died from 'convulsion fits. The Queen and the Princess Caroline told Lord Hervey that they thought the Prince more afflicted for the loss of this child than they had ever seen him or on any occasion, or thought him capable of being.'[32]

The effect of Hervey's attacks on him, his conniving with Walpole and the queen against Frederick, and Frederick's own sometimes unwise behaviour, made the prince conscious that he had what we would now call an image problem. If he were going to be seen as a creditable figure and a worthy heir to the throne, he needed to reinvent himself in the public eye. This he did through his connoisseurship of painting and the fine arts, and through the gardens he created at Carlton House and at Kew.

CHAPTER 5

'Fretz's Popularity Makes Me Vomit'

Personalities help shape events, and the story of Frederick is a very personal tale of political infighting, of high policy and historical drama. There are distinct echoes for today; a Prince of Wales, thwarted by a long period in waiting (twenty-four years in Frederick's case), trying to find his role in the court and the wider world, often out of sorts with his parents, and with his considerable achievements undervalued – certainly in his own opinion. 300 years after the Hanoverian succession, the cultural and political legacy of the dynasty's founding members and their supporters is still not fully understood or appreciated. Each generation left a considerable legacy, despite their being described by one commentator as 'one damp squib monarch after another'. Frederick, and after him his wife, Augusta, contributed in large measure to that legacy. Their achievement, which can be seen today in the Royal Collection and on the ground at Kew Gardens, is often ignored.

This is in part because Frederick's behaviour was at times callow and foolish, the result of both his upbringing and his unsatisfactory relationship with his parents. He was not helped, either, by alienating Lord Hervey, the most outspoken voice of his father's reign and one which has been heard down the centuries. As intimate friendship turned to rancour, Hervey poured vitriol on the Prince of Wales. With a venom-tipped pen, he wrote of him as 'the prince who never forgot an injury or remembered an obligation'.[1]

Unkind words, but Frederick could be a foolish hedonist, happy to lose large sums of money at cards, sexually reckless – at least until his marriage in 1736 – and subject, like many other royals, to damaging flattery. But he was also the first major Hanoverian patron of the arts, in an age of conspicuous consumption. As Britain's trading empire expanded, the numbers of the super-rich grew rapidly, creating a market for paintings and precious objects. Frederick, a man of his age, quickly appreciated that in order to be a major player on the London political scene, he needed to demonstrate that he had fashionable taste.[2]

Questions of taste were fundamental to the aesthetic and political discussions of the eighteenth century. 'Taste', as we have seen, was not merely about personal preferences or style, but about morality. In all his cultural endeavours, therefore, Frederick had to tread a fine line, to show that he had taste and an awareness of contemporary fashions, but also that he possessed discernment for what was best and morally valuable. Several pieces still retained in the Royal Collection amply reveal that Frederick liked eye-catching objets d'art, allegedly spending £700 in a single visit to a shop selling trinkets such as golden snuff boxes and other curios. To mark the christening of his eldest son, George, in June 1738, Frederick presented an elegant and graceful ewer and basin to his wife, Augusta. In 1745, he paid £695 14s 4d for an elaborately wrought, silver-gilt epergne by George Wickes, after a design by William Kent.

These magnificent pieces are indicative of Frederick's taste for the rococo, inspired in part by the opulence of the gilded Baroque interiors of his childhood homes at Herrenhausen. One of his early commissions from William Kent, in 1731, was a fabulous gilded barge, costing over £1,000 at the time, and still on view today in the National Maritime Museum in Greenwich. It was built in 1732 by John Hall in a boatyard across the Thames from Whitehall, and has a wherry-style hull in a nod to the day-to-day traffic then thronging the river. The ostentatious carving is by James Richardson, successor in 1721 to Grinling Gibbons as Master Carver to the Crown, and the gilding is 24-carat gold leaf. It is emblazoned with symbols. The shell motif edging the canopy of the cabin and Vitruvian scrolls along the sides of the barge, echoing the waves of the river, have classical precedents, while British military and naval power are evoked by swags of oak, the British national symbol, and by mythical sea creatures. His initials, FP, are carved above the cabin, while the Garter Star is on the stern beneath the Prince of Wales feathers. This sixty-three-foot barge, which needed twenty-one oarsmen, proclaimed the prince's desire to be seen and to be taken seriously as someone who understood classical symbolism, and who placed himself at the heart of the new British polity.

On the barge's first outing, Frederick took his mother and his four sisters from Chelsea Hospital to Somerset House to inspect the restoration of royal paintings being carried out there. It would have been a grand procession on the river; the royal barge was accompanied by two other, less ornate, barges, one transporting officers and ladies, and the other musicians.

The barge was often used for musical parties, of which Frederick was fond, being a competent musician himself. Among his possessions was a harpsichord, with plectra made from the quills of Tower of London ravens. His purchase of this fine piece in 1740 set a fashion; harpsichords were later commissioned from the Swiss-born maker, Burkat Shudi, by Frederick the Great of Prussia, Catherine the Great of Russia and the composer Handel.

Frederick was a competent cellist, managing thereby once again to incur Hervey's contempt. In a further unfavourable comparison between Frederick and the Roman fiddler, Nero, Hervey wrote, 'Nor was Nero fonder of his harp than the Prince of his violoncello.' In 1734, Hervey had 'seen this Prince once or twice a week during this whole summer at Kensington seated at an open window of his apartment with his violoncello between his legs, singing French and Italian songs to his own playing for an hour or two together'. Again, Hervey accused Frederick of toadying to the general public. 'His Royal Highness never began this performance till nine or ten o'clock at night, which, by the multitude of lights he had in the room where he played, made this royal object of theatrical attention still more conspicuous than he could have been at noon-day.' To Hervey's disgust, the prince's audience was composed of 'footmen, scullions, postilions, and lower order of domestics ... chamber-maids and *valets de chambres* ... laundry-maids and their gallants.'[3]

In 1733, Frederick, with a group of opposition Whig nobles, set up and funded the Opera of the Nobility in Lincoln's Inn Fields as a rival company to Handel's Haymarket Opera, to which George II subscribed £1,000 a year. The king and queen, according to Hervey, 'sat freezing constantly' in Handel's theatre, 'whilst the Prince with all the chief of the nobility went as constantly to that of Lincoln's Inn Fields. An anti-Handelist was looked upon as an anti-courtier, and voting against the Court in Parliament was hardly a less remissible or more venial sin than speaking against Handel or going to the Lincoln's Inn Fields Opera.'[4] Frederick's opera company, however, struggled in its first season, despite recruiting the services of the fashionable castrato, Farinelli. Its musical directors, first Giovanni Bononcini and then Giovanni Battista Pescetti, are also barely footnotes in musical history compared with the more illustrious Handel. The opera eventually went bankrupt and was dissolved in 1737, one of the less fruitful of Frederick's artistic initiatives.

Frederick came more into his own in the fields of painting and portraiture. He had a great deal in common with his Stuart great-great-great uncle, Charles I, much of whose art collection had been dispersed or sold off during the Commonwealth. 'No prince since King Charles I took so much pleasure nor observations on works of art or artists,' wrote the antiquary George Vertue.[5] He was a discriminating collector, who bought contemporary and seventeenth-century Italian and Flemish masters, including Guido Reni, Claude Lorrain, Gaspard Dughet, Carlo Maratti and David Teniers. He also reacquired works by Sir Anthony Van Dyck, Charles I's court painter. A portrait of a man painted in about 1630, and a double portrait of Thomas Killigrew with an unidentified man, possibly his secretary, from 1638, were both acquisitions by Frederick. *The First Georgians: Art & Monarchy 1714–1760*, an exhibition at the Queen's Gallery in 2014, revealed the extent of Frederick's contribution to the Royal Collection. Through his commissioned portraits, it is abundantly clear that Frederick wanted to establish himself as the Renaissance prince that his resolutely reclusive and often philistine father failed to be. Carved rococo frames were specially designed for his purchases of works by Lorrain, Poussin and Teniers, indicative of the care with which the prince displayed his collection.

It is surprising that Frederick is not a more familiar figure today, as his only royal rivals in image production before the advent of photography were Elizabeth I and Victoria; his father and son were far more 'camera shy'. He understood the importance of branding as well as any celebrity or media manipulator today. Portrait painters Jacopo Amigoni and Philippe Mercier were on his payroll. They, and many others, painted dozens of portraits of Frederick over the twenty-two years he lived in England, and had any of the painters been as distinguished as Van Dyck, then maybe Frederick's face would be almost as well-known today as is Charles I's.

Frederick was portrayed in many different and carefully calculated guises. In one portrait, by Charles Philips, he is seen presiding over the Knights of the Round Table. He is drinking with boon companions, a Prince Hal for the 1730s, a clubbable men among men – unlike his father, who isolated himself with his wife and a succession of plain mistresses.

Philippe Mercier, a Berlin-born French Protestant and Frederick's painter and librarian from 1728 to 1738, painted *The Music Party* in about 1733. This was at the height of the Excise Crisis, a political debacle that irrevocably split the Whigs and pitted Frederick and Cobham against Walpole. In this conversation piece, Frederick projects an image of family harmony that did not, in fact, exist, as he tended to quarrel as much with his sisters as he did with his parents. The prince is shown playing his cello, peering rather myopically and slightly anxiously at his music (he had only begun learning the instrument the previous year). He accompanies his sisters Anne on the harpsichord, Caroline on the mandora (a type of lute), while a third sister, Amelia, listens reflectively, a volume of Milton open on her knee. There are two versions of the painting. In one, the setting is almost certainly Frederick's much-admired garden at Carlton House in London, for visible through a window are a line of loosely clipped trees, a bank of bushes and gravel paths against the backdrop of a grand terrace of houses. In the other version, the musicians are playing outside the little palace in the gardens at Kew, another place dear to Frederick's heart. The message is clear. Frederick is a cultured man, a proficient enough musician to play with the Handel-trained Princess Anne, and at ease with his sisters, although, as we have seen, music was the cause of dispute rather than rapprochement in the royal family. But Frederick is making a good fist of it, and the choice of the republican poet Milton for Amelia's reading matter is not accidental, either; this would have told the Cobhamite Whigs that the prince stood firmly with them.

John Wootton, the first English landscape painter of any significance, also worked for Frederick. His brushwork was more rustic than the smoother contemporary Continental style, anticipating by half a century the work of Constable and Turner. In one of Wootton's paintings, Frederick is out and about hunting with John Spencer, grandson of Sarah, Duchess of Marlborough, and Charles Douglas, 3rd Duke of Queensberry. The prince didn't, in fact, share the enthusiasm of the rest of his family for country sports; nor, to his father's horror, was he the least interested in genealogy or military history.[6] But Frederick knew the value of at least being seen to care about these subjects, and, in virtually every portrait, Frederick is on the move, a man of action, parading his credentials. There is one notable exception; in a portrait by Thomas Hudson, at Trinity College, Dublin, of which the prince was chancellor, Frederick sits on a raised throne-like chair, its back surmounted by the feathers of the Prince of Wales crest (as on his barge). Frederick looks not at the viewer, but away to the left, reaching out stealthily to the crown on the table at his side. This is a man eager for the throne.

The unattributed picture which perhaps gives the sharpest impression of how Frederick intended to project himself was painted sometime after 1745. *St James's Park and The Mall* bustles with life, as different social classes apparently rub shoulders as they stroll about public streets and park. To the left, a woman sells tin cups of milk from a pail at a bar, with the provider, a large tawny cow, looking sleepily at the observer. Nearby a woman has lifted her skirt to pull up a stocking, a dog in the middle foreground defecates, while across to the right, a woman suckling her child is salaciously pointed out by a couple of swarthy ne'er-do-wells. Soldiers from several regiments strut about, an allusion to military strength. Two in tartan dress are reminders of the recent defeat at Culloden of the Jacobites, led by Bonnie Prince Charlie, Frederick's younger contemporary and a romantic figure even at the time. It is Frederick, however, who is now the undisputed heir to the British throne.

The Prince of Wales himself is at the heart of the picture, wearing his Garter Knight sash and badge, and surrounded by ordinary people. This is, of course, just an illusion; it is noticeable that the courtiers and people of fashion are corralled within a low walled platform, and therefore set apart from the middle and working classes who mill around the sanded walks of the park. Nevertheless, this faintly pompous figure, hand on hip, wearing bright red trousers, is showing himself to be a man of the people, a champion of British liberties. Although his parents dined in public, they would never have appeared in the streets among their subjects, as Frederick does here. To the royal family, however, such accessibility seemed nothing more than vulgar playing to the gallery, akin to Prince Edward and the Duchess of York appearing on *It's a Knock-out*. That was the expressed view of Queen Caroline, reported by Hervey. '"My God," says the Queen, "popularity always makes me sick: but Fretz's popularity makes me vomit."'[7]

Hervey, as ever, went further. In a masterpiece of reiteration and qualification, he casts aspersions on the prince's pursuit of popularity and wish to ingratiate himself. His words could almost act as a caption for *St James's Park and The Mall*.

> The Prince's character at his first coming over, though little more respectable, seemed much more amiable than it was upon his opening himself and being better known. For though there appeared nothing in him to be admired, yet there seemed nothing in him to be hated – neither nothing great nor nothing vicious. His behaviour was something that gained one's good wishes, though it gave one no esteem for him. For his best qualities, whilst they prepossessed one the most in his favour, always gave one a degree of contempt for him at the same time, his carriage, whilst it seemed engaging to those who did not examine it, appearing mean to those who did; for though his manners had the show of benevolence from a good deal of natural or habitual civility, yet his cajoling everybody, and almost in an equal degree, made those things which might have been thought favours, if more judiciously or sparingly bestowed, lose all their weight. He carried this affection of benevolence so far that he often condescended below the character of a Prince, and as people attributed this familiarity to popular and not particular motives, so it only lessened their respect without increasing their good will, and instead of giving them good impressions of his humanity, only gave them ill ones of his sincerity.[8]

The more charitable interpretation is that the painting demonstrates Frederick's determination to become an English (or British) prince, rather than a German one, here on sufferance *faute de mieux*. The painting neatly encapsulates the prince's view of himself as a man who has been integrated into British society. Equally, it reveals that, even eight years after his antagonistic mother's death, Frederick continued embattled, eager to set his own interpretation of British royalty against that of his father. It is noteworthy, too, that Frederick chooses to be seen in St James's Park, which was on the doorstep of his home at Carlton House. He had other town residences, in Leicester Square and St James's Square, but his political headquarters was Carlton House, perhaps not coincidentally the focus of his gardening activities throughout the 1730s.[9] Although his garden was tucked away behind the high walls visible in the Mercier conversation piece mentioned earlier, this painting suggests that the prince can, at will, cross the boundaries between his cultivated life and the activities of his future subjects. And Westminster Abbey, glimpsed through the trees in the background, is a reminder that Frederick hopes to be crowned king there one day. Foolish he could be at times, but these paintings, along with his horticultural interests and his extensive purchases for the royal collections, hint that he was a prince very conscious of the role that he expected to play, and that he attempted to prepare himself thoroughly for it. The fair-haired figure, with the characteristic ex-opthalmic eyes of the Hanoverians, is a beguiling figure – a fond brother, a man of the people, a clubbable chap and someone prepared to join in with sports he found less than appealing.

Far from Frederick's artistic patronage making a bond between himself and his mother, it drove them further apart. Both parents looked at his expenditure as gross extravagance, and deplored the fact that even with an income of £34,000 a year the prince was unable to break even. They failed to appreciate his attempts to anglicise, as it were, the new Hanoverian dynasty. He distanced himself from his childhood and youth in Hanover, to which he never returned, unlike his father. George II's frequent visits caused anger and consternation among his British subjects, who feared that the king was likely to put Hanoverian interests above those of Britain. Each visit served commensurately to increase Frederick's general popularity, as Lady Irwin wrote. ''Tis not to be imagined the outrageous things that is [sic] every day spoke against the King, and on the other hand how exceedingly the Prince is caressed by all ranks.'[10]

In 1729, the year after Frederick's arrival in London, George II himself returned to Hanover for the first time since his own father's accession in 1714. Perhaps unreasonably, given that he had only been in Britain for a few months, Frederick expected to be made regent in his father's absence, or at the very least to be included in a regency council. Instead, Caroline was placed in sole command, and Frederick was passed over, as he was to be on three subsequent occasions when he might have been thought better equipped to play his part. The effect of these slights was to make him easy prey for the opposition, who in Hervey's words 'would enrich themselves with any bit of him they could catch, and not care a farthing what they tore or spoiled'.[11]

Frederick tried, through his artistic patronage and through his image-creation in portraiture, to show himself to be a man of taste, fit to rule. He no doubt attracted his fair share of unhelpful sycophants, among whom George Bubb Dodington can probably be numbered, to say nothing of Hervey before they were alienated. But he also drew supporters such as Lord Cobham and Alexander Pope to his side. Their friendship may not have been entirely disinterested, but they were no men of straw.

While the bad relations between the prince, his parents and Walpole rumbled on, described in painstaking and graphic detail by Hervey, political events began to shape Frederick's future. Feted by both the Tories and by opposition Whigs, such as Cobham, he was to find himself in an anomalous position, destined to create a permanent wedge within the royal family.

The Whig government was not without its internal divisions, nor were the Tories completely silenced by Whig victory in 1714 or by the defeat of the 1715 Jacobite rebellion. Financial scandals such as the South Sea Bubble in 1720 exposed Whig political and social leaders, such as Sarah, Duchess of Marlborough, as avaricious capitalists, even though the South Sea Company was, in fact, founded by the Tory Robert Harley, Earl of Oxford. Walpole had swept to power in the early 1720s, managing to distance himself successfully from the wave of revulsion against the perpetrators of the financial collapse, despite having himself profited substantially from it. Tory thinkers such as Henry St John, Lord Bolingbroke, took issue with the Whig hegemony and with the concomitant glorification of the Hanoverians. An implacable enemy of Walpole's, and a Jacobite sympathiser, Bolingbroke was a spokesman for gentry resentment and nostalgia against the new mercantile wealth of the Whigs. He spent most of George I's reign in exile, returning home in 1725, before fleeing back to France a decade later. Far from seeing the Whig ascendancy as asserting British liberties, he believed Walpole's government endangered traditional, community values through its rampant materialism.

The Tories rejected the exclusive and artificial enclosures of the first phase of the landscape movement, as represented by Charles Bridgeman's ha-ha, which turned Cobham's garden at Stowe into a military redoubt. *The Nobleman, Gentleman and Gardener's Recreation* (1715) by Stephen Switzer provided a blueprint for a 'farm-like way of gardening', which should be about husbandry and good estate management rather than ornamentation.[12] Bolingbroke adopted the style at his manor house, which he styled 'Dawley Farm', from where he wrote attacking editorials for the anti-Walpole paper, *The Craftsman*, which he himself co-directed. He created a *ferme ornée*, a Tory interpretation of the Whig landscape garden, describing it to Pope, 'I am in my farm, and here I shoot strong and tenacious roots: I have caught hold of the earth.' It had grass plats and orchards near the house, and woodland and fields anchored the ornamental garden firmly in an agricultural landscape. Thus it emphasised the values of good farming practice, and the connection of the landowner with the people and the land, rather than their remote exploitation from within what looked like a military fortification such as Stowe. But although Bolingbroke may have fancied himself as a horny-handed son of toil, Dawley Farm was as artificial a construct as Stowe.[13]

For the Tory political view was not entirely consistent, and Tory paternalism was often more rhetorical than real. Land was equally important to the Tory leaders, especially as they often represented smaller landowners without the financial muscle of the London-based aristocracy. They feared that the commercial interests of the wealthiest landowners were themselves undermining an aristocratic ideal of enlightened ownership and contented peasantry.[14] Cobham, for example, owed his ability to put his grandiose garden plans into practice to his wife's fortune, which was derived from brewing. The Tories, recognising that they faced a long period in opposition, chose, therefore, to characterise themselves as the representatives of traditional, virtuous husbandry, as opposed to the corrupt Whig commercial exploitation and enclosure of land; whole villages were moved at Stowe and Chatsworth to ensure that the views of the aristocrats were unencumbered. In his political works, and in his gardening, Bolingbroke represented opposition to the Whig oligarchy's centralisation of power and to the unaffordable magnificence of their gardens.

The Whigs were fissiparous, too, however, and the fluidity of the Tory and Whig positions was revealed through the financial battles between George II and the Prince of Wales and in the aftermath of the Excise Crisis of 1733. The crisis was sparked by the proposal of Walpole to introduce duties on tobacco and wine, and to extend the search-powers of revenue officers, thereby endangering the Englishman's much-vaunted right to privacy. So, instead of finding the country leaders on his side, Walpole succeeded in uniting peasant and peer. Riots broke out, and images of both Walpole and of the queen were burned in the streets. Walpole was defeated in the House of Commons, but not before he had irrevocably divided the Whigs. Round one to Frederick, who had backed the opposition Whigs on this issue, sensing an opportunity to get one over his mother.

Cobham, dismissed from his regiment by George II for his opposition to Walpole, retired to Stowe to lick his wounds. He gathered around him the 'faction of cousins', which would include over the years three future Prime Ministers, George Grenville and the Elder and Younger Pitts, forming what became known as a 'Patriotic Opposition'.[15] The views of 'Cobham's Cubs' or 'Boy Patriots', such as Pitt and Lyttelton, another Cobham nephew, were influenced in the 1730s and 1740s by that of Bolingbroke, whose book *The Idea of the Patriot King* was written and circulated during this period. When it was finally published in 1749, it was dedicated to Frederick, Prince of Wales, who took ideas from it in instructions left to his young son, George, on his death in 1751. Bolingbroke advocated a monarch who would end the dominance of a central ministerial government, such as Walpole's, which had come to seem odious to the Cobhamite Whigs as well. He took as his model Elizabeth I, a heroine adopted by both Whigs and Tories, who was enshrined in the Temple of the British Worthies at Stowe and used to help wage the moral battle of Cobham's 'Patriotic Opposition'.

Cobham and his associates focussed their efforts in the late 1730s and beyond on Frederick, as he fought acrimoniously with his parents and with Walpole. In one stand-off over Frederick's allowance, Walpole attempted concessions to the prince, but when push came to shove, the prime minister plumped for the king's cause. He called the Tories' bluff by defending the king's prerogative to decide on his son's finances – causing forty of their MPs to leave the Commons rather than vote against the monarch's rights for which they had so long fought.[16]

These political developments coincided with the second, William Kent-led, 'Morality' phase of the landscape movement. This was marked by Kent's softening of the landscape, his experimental use of woods and water and the construction of buildings and ornamentation full of social and political allusion. During this period, Frederick visited Cobham at Stowe; indeed, the prince had his own Morocco-leather-bound copy of *A general plan of the wood, park & garden of Stowe*, dedicated to Cobham by Charles Bridgeman's widow, Sarah, and illustrated with sixteen engravings by Jacques Rigaud. One of Frederick's biographers, more interested in his connoisseurship than in his politics, has argued that the prince's passion for gardening preceded his interest in politics. She has suggested that it was visiting Stowe and the friendship of Kent and Pope that encouraged him to espouse the political standpoint of Cobham and his cronies, rather than the other way round.[17] This underestimates Frederick's active, if not always successful, involvement in politics, although it also highlights the synergy between politics and gardening at that period. Frederick was politically aware, and because he was initially an outsider, was more able to identify the grounds on which to attack his father. On his father's long absences in Hanover, Frederick set himself up in opposition to George, in Hervey's words, as 'an idol of the people'.[18]

Whichever was chicken and which egg, the prince's politics and his gardening interests became indissoluble, as they did for his contemporaries. Through the 1730s, Cobham, Queen Caroline and the Prince of Wales vied vigorously to provide their own interpretation of Britishness at Stowe, Richmond and Carlton House respectively, displayed in the ornamentation of their gardens.

CHAPTER 6

'There Is a New Taste in Gardening'

'Gardening, in the perfection to which it has been lately brought in England, is entitled to a place of considerable rank among the liberal arts,' wrote Thomas Whately in his 1770 *Observations on Modern Gardening*. 'It is as superior to landscape painting, as a reality to a representation: it is an exertion of fancy, a subject for taste; and being released now from the restraints of regularity, and enlarged beyond the purposes of domestic convenience, the most beautiful, the most simple, the most noble scenes of nature are all within its province.'[1] Back we come again to the subject of taste as a key means of expressing both artistic discernment and moral value. At Stowe, you can still see these values embodied in the work of Lord Cobham and his nephew, Earl Temple, but there are few physical traces of Frederick's endeavours at either Kew or Cliveden, and his house and garden at Carlton House were razed by his grandson, the prince regent. Nevertheless, the work that he carried out at Carlton House and began at Kew made a permanent mark on the future of British horticulture. In the case of Kew, Frederick's foundations, built on by his widow, Augusta, and Lord Bute, led to the establishment of the world-famous Royal Botanic Gardens.

Hervey's pen, the source of so much information about the royal family in the 1720 and 1730s, is unusually quiet about Frederick's gardens, and indeed Caroline's, too, perhaps in part because he appreciated that horticulture was not an interest of the king's. There is just one reference to Caroline's Merlin's Cave, when Hervey reports a conversation between the king and queen. Caroline mentions that the building has been sharply criticised in Bolingbroke's opposition paper, *The Craftsman*. '"I am very glad of it," interrupted the King: "you deserve to be abused for such childish silly stuff, and it is the first time I ever knew the scoundrel in the right.'"[2]

Until the early nineteenth century, the two royal gardens, Richmond and Kew, were separated by an ancient bridle-way, Love Lane. The riverside half, Richmond Gardens, formed the grounds of Richmond Lodge and belonged to the king and queen. A lease on the eastern gardens, around Kew House, later the White House (demolished in 1802), was bought by Frederick in 1730.

When Frederick arrived in England in 1728, Caroline had been at work for some years at Richmond, laying out grass plats, kitchen gardens, tree-lined walks, and several wildernesses, one with a large oval glade. That year, she appointed Charles Bridgeman Royal Gardener and bought the early-seventeenth-century Kew Palace, on the cusp between the two gardens, for her oldest daughter, Anne, the princess royal. The palace and its gardens are featured in one of the two versions of Philip Mercier's painting of Frederick's *Music Party*, and it is not a coincidence that Frederick should have chosen this backdrop, which related to both royal estates.

The prince bought a home at Kew, possibly in order to irritate his parents but conceivably as a conciliatory act, as Egmont believed. He wrote that the prince 'put himself to an inconvenient expense to purchase his house at Kew, that he might be near his Majesty when at Richmond'.[3] The house was less than two miles from Richmond Lodge, the king's summer retreat, next door to his sister's home, and adjacent to Caroline's wilderness garden, where William Kent was just beginning to work his magic. Frederick bought the lease on the house and eleven acres of grounds from the Capel family, adding to his estate over the years, so that by her death Augusta would be presiding over 110 acres. The gardens had been originally laid out by Lord Capel in the seventeenth century and, in an earnest of things to come, had become celebrated for their collections of rare plants. The diarist, John Evelyn, described a visit to Kew in August 1678. 'I went to my worthy friends Sir Hen: Capels (bro: to the Earle of Essex) it is an old timber house, but his garden has certainly the choicest fruite of any plantation in England, as he is the most industrious, & understanding it'. Returning in March 1688, Evelyn noted that Henry Capel's 'Orangerie & Myrtetum, are most beautifull, & perfectly well kept: He was contriving very high palisades of reedes, to shade his oranges in during the Summer'.[4] Leasing a garden that was near his parents and already had a planterly reputation provided Frederick with the canvas he needed to make his mark – and, of course, he called in Kent.

William Kent, architect, painter, furniture and landscape designer and unpredictable genius, was approaching the height of his fame when he began working for the warring members of the royal family. Born about 1685 in Bridlington in Yorkshire, the son of a successful joiner, he spent a decade training as a painter in Italy and sketching Palladio's work in the Veneto. By the time he met Richard Boyle, 3rd Earl of Burlington, he had already been in the service of Thomas Coke, the future Earl of Leicester, for whom he would build the Palladian palace of Holkham Hall on the north coast of Norfolk. He returned to Britain to work for Burlington at Chiswick House, an early testing-ground for the landscape movement. There, Kent painted the interiors of the neo-Palladian villa and designed the landscape garden, making an exedra opening out from the house, with an arrangement of radiating avenues in the shape of a *patte d'oie* or goose's foot. He dammed a stream, turning it into a naturalistic lake, built a cascade at one end, and added a Doric column and Ionic temple, a miniature version of the Pantheon in Rome, to be glimpsed through trees about the landscape. Copies of Kent's sketches for the various scenes he created can be seen in position around the gardens today. A Jacques Rigaud etching of 1733 shows the proximity of the villa to Burlington's older, Jacobean house, and sphinxes atop the gate piers on the public road. A square in front of the villa is lined on two sides with tall Cedars of Lebanon which have had their lower branches removed to give a smooth, elegant line. When Burlington, with debts of over £200,000, stopped work on Chiswick in 1738, Kent moved on to work for General Dormer at Rousham in Oxfordshire and created the garden which is his masterpiece.[5]

In the meantime, Kent had been employed by George I to paint the main staircase at Kensington Palace, a tumultous parade of people that included a democratic mix of royalty, aristocracy, entertainers and servants, and was probably inspired by the Sala de Corazzieri at the Quirinal Palace in Rome.[6] Kent was ecumenical in his customers, happy to work for the Tories (Burlington was

82   *The Princess's Garden*

always thought to be a covet Tory), the different Whig factions, and for the belligerent members of the royal family. The joiner's son became one of the main players of the day, a friend of the nobility, whose taste and abilities were generally applauded by most people, apart from Hervey. As was so often the case, he put in his vindictive three ha'porth when he described Kent as 'a man much in fashion as a gardener, an architect, a painter, and about fifty other things, with a very bad taste and little understanding, but had the good luck to make several people who had no taste or understanding of their own believe that they could borrow both of him, and had paid for their error by ruining their fortunes in making gardens and building houses that nobody could live in and everybody laughed at'.[7]

A visit to Holkham or to Stowe today will give the lie to Hervey's description, for few could fail to be impressed by the scale of Kent's ambition, while an afternoon in the serenely beautiful and perfectly composed garden at Rousham is proof enough that Kent had 'taste' in the eighteenth-century understanding of the word, as Horace Walpole appreciated. He entered the lists on Kent's side in his 1771 book, *The History of the Modern Taste in Gardening*, understanding how Kent's training as a painter developed his eye for landscape. He wrote,

At that moment appeared Kent, painter enough to taste the charms of the landscape, bold and opinionative enough to dare and to dictate, and born with a genius to strike out a great system from the twilight of imperfect essays. He leaped the fence, and saw that all nature was a garden. He felt the delicious contrast of hill and valley changing imperceptibly into each other ... and remarked how loose groves crowned an easy eminence with happy ornament ... We owe the restoration of Greece and the diffusion of architecture to his skill in landscape.[8]

Walpole was well qualified to understand the links between politics and gardening; he was the son of a Prime Minister, Sir Robert Walpole, was an MP himself for twenty-seven years and had a keen understanding of gardening from creating his own mini-paradise at Strawberry Hill.

❋

Kent was pitched into the royal battleground when he was appointed architect to the Prince of Wales in 1732. He worked simultaneously for Caroline and Frederick, more as an architect than as a landscape designer initially. It was Kent who designed the Hermitage in 1732 in Caroline's Richmond Gardens, followed by Merlin's Cave three years later. Alongside the busts of Elizabeth of York and of Elizabeth I, Caroline also invoked Prince Arthur. It has been argued that Caroline did so in order to seduce Frederick away from Cobham and his supporters who were gaining influence over the prince at the time.[9] This seems an unconvincing argument, judging by other evidence from the queen herself. Caroline may have regretted the trouble caused to her and the king by Frederick's alliance with dissident Whigs, but it is more likely she was advertising what she saw as her son's signal failure to live up to the princely ideals of Arthur and to be the heir that Britain needed. 'My dear first-born is the greatest ass,' she declared to Hervey, 'and the greatest liar, and the greatest *canaille*, and the greatest beast in the whole world, and I most heartily wish he was out of it.'[10] Hardly the stuff of Arthurian legend.

It must, then, have been a red rag to a bull to have her son living across Love Lane and employing Kent there to rebuild a timber-framed Tudor house virtually in front of the windows of the princess royal's Kew Palace. The exterior of the White House was designed in the solid Palladian style which was almost a badge of Whig ideology.[11] Kent appears to have made little contribution to the garden during Frederick's first phase at Kew; the only concrete evidence of garden work carried out there by Kent is an illustration in Sir William Chambers' 1763 book, *Plans, Elevations, Sections, and Perspective Views of the Gardens and Buildings at Kew in Surry, the seat of Her Royal Highness the Princess Dowager of Wales*. This shows a garden shelter with a classical pediment with sinuous arcading around the front.

The White House and its interiors were an important architectural commission for Kent, who turned the manor house into something more akin to a palace. He devised an integrated design for the decorations and furnishings in the rococo style which Frederick favoured, as is described by Chambers, later architect to Frederick's wife, Augusta, and to his son, George III. In the same book, Chambers lists Kent-designed ceilings and chimney pieces in the drawing room, Augusta's bedroom, the Gallery and on the great staircase. He also mentions 'a very good hunting piece by Mr Wootton, wherein are represented his Royal Highness Frederic Prince of Wales, lord Baltimore, lord Cholmondely, lord Boston, colonel Pelham, and several of his Royal Highness's attendants'. In two other 'very fine' pictures by Wootton, the prince is seen returning 'from the chace'.[12]

Frederick, already a student of botany, drew up lists of flowers, herbs, bushes and trees which he wanted to plant at Kew and decided also to grow rare plants from abroad. In the early 1730s, however, he did not give free rein to his imagination at Kew; by all accounts, in contrast with the artificial wilderness of his mother's garden across Love Lane, Frederick chose to stay with the formality of the earliest phase of the landscape movement. The garden façade resembled the front of Chiswick House, with square lawns framed by trees and hedging.

Whether or not Frederick initially planned to have the White House at Kew as his family home, that is what, in time, it became. It was furnished, decorated and ready for his future wife, Augusta, to move to after her arrival in England in the spring of 1736. Frederick would also eventually take on Leicester House, his parents' home while themselves Prince and Princess of Wales, and, after a fatal dispute with his mother in 1737 (of which more later), he would establish his family at Norfolk House in St James's Square, where the future George III was born in 1738. What he did need in the early 1730s was a political headquarters in London, and so in 1733 he bought Carlton House in Pall Mall from the dowager Lady Burlington, mother of Kent's patron at Chiswick.

Frederick was still kept on a short financial rein by the king, being given an allowance of £25,000 per annum, paid out in instalments to the prince's treasurer, as opposed to the £100,000 George II had enjoyed while Prince of Wales. Although this was supplemented by £14,000 per annum from the Duchy of Cornwall, Frederick was spending large sums of money on the house and gardens at Kew, so 'borrowed' £5,000 of the £6,000 he needed to pay for the house from George Bubb Dodington. According to Horace Walpole, who matched Hervey in spite when it came to the prince, Frederick boasted that he had no intention of paying Dodington back. Seeing Dodington walk past his window, the prince said to his treasurer,

John Hedges, 'That man is reckoned one of the most sensible men in England, yet with all his parts, I have just nicked him out of five thousand pounds.'[13] Dodington may have been more clear-sighted than either Frederick or Walpole gave him credit for. His house was adjacent to Carlton House beside St James's Park, with a connecting door between the two gardens, so the shrewd and wealthy Dodington may have calculated that easy access to the heir to the throne was worth £5,000. Other, kinder commentators argued that the prince was never motivated by money or a lust for power. The Earl of Stair, for example, claimed, 'I love the Prince well for many valuable qualities, especially for his good head; which I think does not dispose him to be overfond of money or power.'[14]

Frederick wanted a canvas for his ideas. The tide of events seemed to be flowing in his direction, with the Excise Bill the first open trial of strength between him and George II. Frederick regarded himself as a champion of the people, a breath of fresh air against the rampant commercialism and cynicism of Sir Robert Walpole. In this, he was aided by Cobham, who believed Walpole's form of Whiggery was destroying all that had been achieved in the Glorious Revolution of 1688 and by the Hanoverian succession. Frederick was increasingly being encouraged by his supporters, such as Dodington, Bolingbroke and Cobham, to believe that he could in future become, in the words of E. P. Thomson, 'an enlightened monarch' with the 'means to elevate himself, as the personification of an "impartial", rationalizing bureaucratic state power, above and outside the predatory game' being played by Whigs such as Walpole.[15]

It was precisely this image of himself as the 'patriotic prince' that Frederick was eager to embody in the garden at Carlton House. Whether or not he was 'overfond of money or power', he meant Carlton House to be his flagship, where he would display his taste and the depth of his moral and cultural understanding, with its references in style to the paintings of Claude Lorrain and its invocations of classical Rome and of high points of English history.

There were two main influences on Frederick as he began gardening at Carlton House: Alexander Pope and Lord Cobham, their views and their very public gardens. It is hard to overestimate just how important these two people would be to the prince's emerging political plans over the next few years, and how he would emulate what they had done in order to put himself into a position of recognised political and social influence.

Pope's friendship with Kent didn't preclude the poet attacking Robert Walpole, Kent's *quondam* employer, as Pope aligned himself with the Cobhamite Whigs. Two of his *Moral Essays* were dedicated to anti-Walpole dissidents; the first, to 'brave COBHAM' (1734), was about the corruption of political power.[16] His *Epistle to Burlington* (1731) was both a dissection of the moral responsibility of riches and a manifesto for garden design, for this, Pope suggested, is a proper use of wealth. 'Consult the Genius of the Place in all,' he advised, and, to create an artistic whole, the garden should be related to the surrounding countryside.

> Still follow Sense, of ev'ry Art the Soul ...
> Nature shall join you, Time shall make it grow
> A work to wonder at – perhaps a STOW.

The Catholic Tory Pope had no quarrel with the Whig Cobham's judicious employment of his riches at Stowe, and indeed was also a close friend of Bolingbroke, whose ideas were holding sway there at the time. But he was critical of what he saw as the crude opulence of Walpole's Houghton, where money had been squandered. Walpole is equated by Pope with Timon, the epitome of Athenian corruption.

> At Timon's Villa let us pass a day,
> Where all cry out, 'What sums are thrown away!'
> So proud, so grand, of that stupendous air,
> Soft and Agreeable come never there ...
> The suff'ring eye inverted Nature sees,
> Trees cut to Statues, Statues thick as trees.[17]

A friend of both Bridgeman and Kent, Pope was at the heart of the gardening world at that time, and poems such as these were by way of being an artistic manifesto. Pope's poetry and his gardening style took their inspiration from classical Rome, where gardens were the setting for discussions of philosophy and politics. Ornaments, statuary and seats were carefully placed about his garden at

Twickenham, as at Stowe, to trigger debate.[18] The ornamentation included a shell temple, an obelisk and elaborate grotto, in the style of ancient Italy, decorated with coloured mirror glass. There was a main axis, off which paths meandered to small clearings and framed different vistas. One of the most charming legacies of Pope's garden – apart from the grotto, which can still be visited by special appointment – is a pencil sketch made by Kent. In it, Kent stands with his arm on Pope's shoulder, the two men looking up at a large, and fantastic, domed temple, while Pope's dog, Bounce, jumps around them. It is a snapshot of friendship and of shared cultural views.

Pope also became a friend of the prince's, who visited the poet at his own home in Twickenham more than once before he bought Carlton House. Allegedly, on one occasion, Frederick's verbosity on the subject of poetry caused the ailing poet to fall asleep. The prince commissioned two sets of small marble busts of Dryden, Milton, Shakespeare and Spenser, all patriotic poets of the last two centuries, from a leading contemporary sculptor, Peter Scheemakers, one for Carlton House and the other for Pope's Twickenham villa.[19] In 1738 Pope gave Frederick a small dog, with the following couplet inscribed on his collar, 'I am His Highness' dog at Kew. Pray tell me, sir, whose dog are you?'[20]

Shakespeare and Milton are also commemorated by Scheemaker busts in Kent's Temple of British Worthies at Stowe. Pope was an admirer of Cobham, and although it is scarcely possible to compare the poet's five-acre estate with the massive acreage of Stowe, the two men were influenced by the ideals of Augustan Rome. Both gardens had a moral purpose, and, as Cobham fell out irrevocably with Walpole over the Excise Bill, so he retired to Stowe to launch his own rear-guard action there against the Prime Minister.

Writing later in the century, the farmer/observer, Arthur Young, describes what Frederick would have seen at Stowe on his first visits in the early 1730s. The gardens, says Young, 'were for many years the admiration of all that viewed them, not only for their real beauty, but the scarcity of other improvements of the same kind'. Like Pope, Cobham also had a grotto from which visitors were led

to that part of the garden, called the Elysian-fields, which are beautiful waves of close shaven grass; breaking among woods, and scattered with single trees; bounded on one side by thick groves, and shelving on the other down to the water, which winds in a very happy manner; and commanding from several spots, various landscapes of the distant parts of the garden. From the temple of Antient [sic] Virtue, you look down on a very beautiful winding hollow lawn, scattered with single trees in the happiest manner, through the stems of which, the water breaks to the eye in a stile admirably picturesque. Near to this temple in a thicket is the well known satire, the temple of Modern Virtue in ruin.[21]

This is a remarkable evocation of Kent's genius at work at Stowe. Bridgeman had set the ball rolling, but the garden, with its straight avenues and encircling ha-ha, still had something of the feel of a military emplacement. Kent, however, began to flatten out the hilly slopes and to plant trees and channel water naturalistically through the landscape. All of this served to reflect well on Cobham's credentials as a British peer, in touch with the countryside of his homeland. But the message still needed to be underlined, which is why the buildings were raised on either side of the Elysian Fields.

On a slope overlooking the dammed lake still stands the Temple of Ancient Virtue. In the Ionic Rotunda, designed by Kent, were placed the statues of four great ancients: Lycurgus, the lawgiver; Socrates, the philosopher; Homer, the poet; and Epaminondas, the military leader. These four men, according to George Bickham's 1753 guide to Stowe, 'made virtue their only pursuit, and the welfare of mankind their only study; in whose breasts, mean self-interest had no possession. To establish a well-regulated constitution, to dictate the soundest morality, to place virtue in the most amiable light, and bravery to defend a people's liberty; were [their] ends.' Over one of the doors to the temple read the inscription, 'To be dear to our Country, to deserve well of the State, to be honoured, reverenced, and loved, is truly glorious; but, to be dreaded and hated of Mankind, is not only base and detestable, but highly impolitic likewise, and hazardous.'

And, as an indication of the hazards of falling below the level of these high classical – and Whig – ideals, nearby stood the ruinous Temple of Modern Virtue (no longer extant, unlike the Ancient Virtue rotunda). Built deliberately as a ruin, it was surmounted by a headless statue, variously believed to be Louis XIV and Robert Walpole, the two bogey-men of the Whig opposition. Bickham notes about the ruin that 'this fine moral may be drawn, that glory, founded on true merit, is solid and lasting; while a reputation, built on the empty applauses of the multitude, soon fades away'.[22] Kent, in juxtaposing these two buildings, was re-enacting what he would have seen in the Tivoli Gardens in Rome, thereby giving a classical imprimatur to Cobham's contemporary political point-scoring. This apposition was intended to be one in the eye for Walpole.

Further reinforcement comes from a building already alluded to several times – the semi-circular Temple of British Worthies, also designed by Kent – on the other side of the Elysian Fields. This Temple, with its line of Whig heroes, was central to Cobham's iconographical programme in this part of the garden, landscaped in the years after the Excise Crisis of 1733. Alexander Pope represented poetry, along with Shakespeare and Milton. The Black Prince and King Alfred, putative founder of the British constitution, were commemorated, too. Roger Bacon, scientist and empiricist philosopher, together with Locke and Newton, hint at Cobham's interest in Enlightenment ideas (and a counter-blast to Caroline's busts of Newton and Boyle at Richmond). Sir Thomas Gresham, founder of the Royal Exchange, and Sir John Barnard, Lord Mayor of London in 1737, flag up the mercantile interests of this Whig family – an acknowledgement of Britain's standing as a trading power. It was nothing less than a political credo in stone.

Alexander Pope, by then something of a national treasure, opened his garden to the public, who continued to throng there even after his death in 1744. Given the didactic purpose in opening, many stately homes had visitor guidebooks by the mid-eighteenth century. Stowe led the way, with guides, some in the form of Socratic dialogues, produced from 1744 by Benton Seeley, a Buckingham bookseller, and by a plagiarist, George Bickham.[23] The guides were sold in London, Buckingham and at the New Inn near the gate into the garden. Some were illustrated, with antiquary George Vertue among the engravers, and had pull-out maps. The prices varied greatly, from sixpence for a simple description of house and gardens without plan or illustration, to two guineas for a deluxe version with thirty coloured plates, two views of the house and a plan of the garden.[24] A guide, published in 1748, is believed to have been by William Gilpin, later a respected traveller and commentator on the Picturesque.[25]

The guides imply that visitors would easily understand the

classical illusions embodied in its buildings and ornamentation. The 1748 and 1751 dialogues take place between two gentlemen: Polypthon and his friend, Callophilus, both clearly regular travellers. Polypthon 'was a gentleman engaged in a way of life, that excused him two months in the year from business; which time he used generally to spend in visiting what was curious in the several counties around him'.[26] The 1751 version refers to the men having 'made a tour into the North of England', and in both accounts, Polypthon recognises the resemblance between the Palladian Bridge at Stowe and Lord Pembroke's at Wilton.[27]

Callophilus displays his understanding of Stowe iconography as he guides Polypthon. 'You have just seen the flourishing condition of antient [*sic*] virtue; see here the ruinous state of modern ... Polypthon said, he was glad to find his walk grew a little more moral.'

The two men discuss the lie of the land, the success or otherwise of the vistas and their ornamentation, and comment on fashions in gardening. Polypthon criticises 'our clipped yews, box-wood borders, and flourished Parturers [parterres] ... as opposite to that notable simplicity, which is the foundation of true taste in every thing.'[28]

Although these guides were not published until after Frederick had carried out his major work at Carlton House, he would nevertheless have been conscious of the political and moral philosophy behind what he saw both at Twickenham and at Stowe. As he grappled with his own personal and political problems, he would have been happy to have been lionised by Cobham, and encouraged by Pope and Kent to create his own horticultural idyll along contemporary lines.

There are marked similarities between the layout of Pope's garden and that which Kent would design for Frederick at Carlton House, partly because the poet's five-acre estate was a better template for the prince's twelve acres at Carlton House than the massive acreage of Stowe. Both Carlton House and Pope's Twickenham were enclosed gardens, with the eye drawn inwards, as at Burlington's Chiswick House. This is not to say that Frederick was less ambitious than Cobham in what he was trying to express, more that he cut his coat according to his cloth. Fifteen years later at Kew, he would conceive of landscape gardening on a grander scale, although even there he was more constrained by space than the Temples were at Stowe.

Frederick, conscious of his mother's work at Richmond, and of Cobham's at Stowe, reinforced cautious co-operation with the Whig opposition by constructing his own value system at Carlton House. William Woollett's 1760 engraving shows a lawn framed by plantations of trees and two mirrored exedra with niches for statues, similar to that created by Kent for Burlington at Chiswick. There is a hint of paths snaking off the main vista on either side, similar to Pope's garden. At the far end can be seen an octagonal *bagnio* or pavilion, a miniature version of Burlington's Palladian villa. Standing in niches along the wall of the octagon are busts by Michael Rysbrack of King Alfred and the Black Prince. Frederick was clearly identifying himself with England and claiming as his own the virtues of the medieval vanquisher of the French – in contrast to his mother's less favourable interpretation at Richmond (that Frederick represented a falling off rather than a fulfilment of earlier Arthurian ideals). The inclusion of the Black Prince at both Carlton House and in Cobham's Temple of British Worthies now seems ironic. Frederick would not have realised that he was tempting fate by invoking a Prince of Wales who predeceased his father, as Frederick was himself to do.

The pavilion stood on the western side of a wilderness, with an unbroken view of some 800 feet across the landscape and down an avenue flanked by terms or half-figures. These included Pope's four Scheemakers' statues, plus four others by Joseph Pickford and Peter Rubens. The garden was costly, as is shown by invoices from various nurserymen in the prince's household accounts. Richard Butt, Robert Furber and John Swinhoe of Brompton Park were respectively paid £938 6s 1d, £273 4s 10d and £81 12s 9d in August 1736 for trees, shrubs, climbers, bulbs and herbaceous plants. Robert Singer, 'Church Warden of Barns' [*sic*], invoiced for £77 10s for '31,000 of Turf deliver'd from Septb 28 to December 3d 1734 at 5d pr thousand'. In June 1735, Robert Furber delivered more herbaceous plants, bulbs, shrubs and trees 'to make good the defficiences'.

It is estimated that there were probably over 15,200 trees at Carlton House, of which some 2,000 were what we would now describe as border and climbing shrubs. These included 1,500 elms, 400 cherries, 1,400 hornbeams, 500 yews, 150 oaks, several tulip trees, mulberries, laurels, roses, honeysuckles and jasmines. The garden was characterised by its flowering trees and shrubs, a distinctive difference from the largely evergreen Stowe, and a decade ahead of later developments at Kew. Frederick's household accounts indicate expenditure on plants including 'Sweet Bryers', 'Sirringo Roses', 'Gilded Roses', 'Honeysuckles', 'persian Jasmins', 'Jacobea or Sea Ragwort', 'Stars of Bethlehem', 'Turkey Renuncalas' and 'Dutch Tulips'.[29]

The style and ornamentation of Carlton House, and its semi-informality, demonstrate the influence of the landscape movement on Frederick. The lists of plants in Frederick's household accounts are long and lavish, however, revealing that the prince was more of a plantsman than many of his friends and political cronies, whose concentration was rather on landscaping and statuary. These lists are half prophetic, for, as the words 'Persian', 'Bethlehem' and 'Turkey' suggest, Frederick gathered plants from across the Middle East, indicative of the incipient internationalism which would inform Kew. His subsequent meeting with a dedicated botanist, John Stuart, 3rd Earl of Bute, would further develop the prince's interest in plants.

For the meantime, though, Frederick's garden at Carlton House quickly made waves and had its own reciprocal effect on the gardens which had influenced him. A letter written in 1734, only a year after the prince started work, pays tribute to Kent's contribution and stresses the political importance of a princely commission. The much-quoted letter was from Sir Thomas Robinson to his father-in-law, the Earl of Carlisle, creator with Sir John Vanbrugh of the baroque palace and garden at Castle Howard.

> There is a new taste in gardening just arisen, which has been practised with so great success at the Prince's garden in Town that a general alteration of some of the most considerable gardens in the kingdom is begun, after Mr. Kent's notion of gardening, viz. to lay the mont, and work without level or line. By this means I really think the 12 acres the Prince's garden consists of, is more diversified and of greater variety than anything of the compass I ever saw; and this method of gardening is more agreeable, as when finished, it has the appearance of beautiful nature, and without being told, one would imagine art had no part in its finishing, and is, according to what one hears of the Chinese, entirely after their models for works of this nature, where they never plant straight lines or make regular designs. The celebrated

gardens of Claremont, Chiswick and Stowe are now full of labourers, to modernise the expensive works finished in them, even since everyone's memory. If this grows a fashion, 'twill be happy for that class of the people as they will run no risk of having time lay on their hands.[30]

Gardens are dynamic places, and the Temple family was not yet finished with the landscape at Stowe. Future building projects there would flag up differences between younger members of the family and Frederick's future wife, by then working closely with Lord Bute. And the reference in Robinson's letter to Chinese style was also prophetic; Frederick and then Sir William Chambers were to invoke China at Kew.

PART II

CHAPTER 7

'As Anxious as a Good Child to Please'

When Frederick, Prince of Wales, bought Carlton House from the dowager Lady Burlington in 1733, he was twenty-six and still a bachelor. It was an advanced age in the eighteenth century for a prince to remain single; his father and grandfather had been twenty-one and twenty-two respectively when they were married. Frederick's excursions into the marriage market had been markedly unsuccessful; his grandfather's vetting of Wilhelmina, daughter of King Frederick William I of Prussia, had, as mentioned, alarmed the girl when he collapsed while examining her. Frederick's subsequent meddling attempts to engineer a marriage between himself and Wilhelmina, while also negotiating a union between his mother's nephew, the Margrave of Ansbach, and Wilhelmina's younger sister, Frederica, had precipitated his parents' decision to call him to London.

No further plans were made for the marriage of the heir to the British throne after his arrival in England. The subject was shelved, while Caroline took over the reins of government during her husband's increasingly frequent absences in Hanover, and the prince was sidelined.

Frederick eventually began to look about for himself, and, like another Prince of Wales two and a half centuries later, he found himself manipulated by an ambitious grandmother. The formidable Sarah, Dowager Duchess of Marlborough, was the widow of the victor of Blenheim and the grandmother of an earlier Lady Diana Spencer. She had lived most of her life at the heart of court circles, having been a friend of Queen Anne's from girlhood until their spectacular falling-out in the middle years of the queen's reign

– largely as a result of the duchess's bullying ways. She remained a fearless and outspoken critic of those with whom she disagreed. Her diary entries show her firmly on Frederick's side and against the king when the subject of the prince's allowance came up for yet another airing in Parliament in 1736. 'The Court carried it by a majority of thirty, not without the expense of a great deal of money and a most shameful proceeding to threaten and fetch sick men out of their beds to vote … But not withstanding this the minority for the Prince was two hundred and four … who were certainly on the right side of the question. And I am apt to think that men who have been so base with estates and so mean as to act against the interest of their country, will grow very weary of voting to starve the next heir to the Crown.' Frederick, she adds, 'in all this affair has shown a great deal of spirit and sense; and the intolerable treatment which he has had for so many years will no doubt continue him to be very firm and act right'.[1]

Given her predisposition towards Frederick, small wonder then that the ambitious duchess sought to snare him for her own grand-daughter. The story of the clandestine plan was later put about by Horace Walpole, whose father had reasons a-plenty for stopping the match and curbing the ambitions of the dowager duchess. According to Walpole *fils*, a visit of the Prince of Wales to Windsor Castle in September 1730 coincided with Sarah and her grand-daughter, Diana, spending time at the duchess's lodge in the Great Park.[2] Sarah was allegedly prepared to buy her way into the royal family, and the £100,000 dowry suggested was a considerable inducement to the perpetually impecunious prince. The king and queen were not consulted; instead, a scheme was hatched that the couple should be married secretly at one of the duchess's Windsor homes. Walpole's vigilant spies, however, discovered the plot and the Prime Minister stepped in to stop it. The union would have been perfectly legal, for this was before George III introduced the Royal Marriages Act, which laid down that members of the royal family had to have the monarch's permission to marry. One historian believes that the marriage would have been generally popular, apart from with the king and queen. 'The English people would have found themselves with a genuinely English Princess of Wales, grand-daughter of a national hero,' he has written, adding unkindly, 'and far superior in birth, beauty and wit to the German bride whom Frederick eventually married.'[3]

Frederick's marriage prospects were kicked into touch yet again, and insult added to injury when the marriage was arranged in 1733 of his sister, Anne, the princess royal, almost three years his junior. Her bridegroom was to be William, Prince of Orange, of whom 'she was resolved, if it was a monkey, she would marry him', according to Hervey.[4] The marriage was intended to bring about a welcome alliance with the United Provinces, thus forming a Protestant bulwark against the continued might of France. It also served the domestic purposes of George II, who was becoming increasingly unpopular as a result of his prolonged absences in Hanover. On one of his Hanoverian trips, an angry placard was nailed to the gate of St James's Palace, saying,

> Lost or strayed out of this house, a man who has left a wife and six children on the parish, whoever will give tidings of him to the Churchwardens of St James's so he may be got again shall receive four shillings and sixpence reward. N.B. this reward will not be increased, nobody judging him to be worth a crown.[5]

News of his daughter's betrothal to the Dutch prince was greeted enthusiastically by Parliament and did something to restore the regard in which the king was held by the general public. Not by Frederick, however. Already poor relations between brother and sister were further strained by Anne's getting ahead of him in the marriage stakes, especially when Anne was granted £80,000 on her marriage. Double the size of any prior royal dowry, it was funded by the sale of colonial lands in the West Indies and was bitterly resented by the bachelor prince.[6]

The nuptials seem to have been handled with a certain cack-handedness by the king, who, running true to form, awarded the bridegroom no public honours when he arrived in England in November for his marriage, just as he had previously ignored his son. 'The opinion [the king] seemed to desire tacitly to inculcate, was that the Prince of Orange was a nothing till he had married his daughter.' Lord Hervey was sent instead to Somerset House, where the prince was staying, with a goodwill message from the king and queen. Caroline had no high hopes of the Dutch prince, asking Hervey 'to let her know without disguise what sort of hideous animal she was to prepare herself to see'. Hervey was able to reassure her that 'he had not found him near so bad as he had imagined; that she must not expect to see an Adonis; that his body was as bad as possible; but that his countenance was far from disagreeable, and his address sensible, engaging, and noble'.[7]

The nuptials ran into problems. William collapsed with a fever on the eve of the wedding, and was thought for three weeks to be dying. Fearing that his illness might be infectious, the king ordered the royal family not to visit the ailing prince. Frederick, however, took a different tack; according to Hervey, he 'forced himself to be tolerably civil to the Prince of Orange, though he was hurt at the distinctions paid him by the nation. Yet the Prince of Wales had at least this satisfaction in obliging himself to do what he thought right on this occasion, that he was sure that what he was doing was disagreeable to his father.'[8]

On his recovery, William went off to Bath for several months for a cure, returning to London via Oxford, where he was given an honorary doctorate. Anne and he were finally married in the Chapel Royal at St James's in March 1734, four months after the bridegroom had first arrived in England. On her entry into the chapel, the Princess Royal was supported by her brothers, the twelve-year-old Duke of Cumberland and the Prince of Wales, the latter no doubt with clenched teeth. The wedding was followed by six weeks of celebrations, during which Frederick invited the newly-weds to a command performance at Drury Lane of the ironically entitled *The Careless Husband*. The prince didn't attend the emotional farewells when the couple finally departed, claiming that he and his 'beloved' sister might be too afflicted by their separation.[9] The queen's distress at her eldest daughter's departure was, however, genuine, and in marked contrast to her feelings about Frederick. She wrote, 'Dear Hart, My sadness is indescribable, I never had any sorrows over you Anne, this is the first cruel one'.[10]

Over a year later, Frederick was still pressurising his father to let him marry. Egmont records that at an audience with the king in August 1734, 'the Prince desired his Majesty would consider his age, and think of marrying him. The King replied that he was impertinent; that he would do it when he saw proper; that he should expect no regard from him while he was uncivil to those who were in possession of his favour, and received all those who were under his displeasure.' In October 1735, Egmont reports, 'It is yet doubtful what Princess is designed for the Prince of Wales, the King having sent for the picture of the daughter of the Duke of Wurtemburg Stutgard, who is reported a fine young lady, but seems a little too young, being as I think but 13 years old.'[11]

Finally, in April 1736, Frederick's own marriage took place. 'It had been so long talked of without anything being done to forward it,' wrote Hervey, 'that everybody began to think it was not designed, when a step was taken that showed at last the King was in earnest.'[12] On his 1735 trip to Hanover, George II took the opportunity of interviewing a potential bride for his son. Born in November 1719, the then fifteen-year-old Augusta was the daughter of Frederick II, Duke of Saxe-Gotha-Altenburg, a minor German prince. As the eighteenth of his nineteen children, Augusta would not necessarily have been expected to make as glittering a match as the heir to the British throne, and her Lutheran family were pleased at her marrying into one of Europe's foremost Protestant houses. On her betrothal, it was suggested to her mother that it might be a good idea for Augusta to learn English. The duchess thought this quite unnecessary, assuming that as the Hanoverians had reigned in Britain for over twenty years, everyone there must now speak German. 'A conjecture so well founded,' said Hervey sarcastically, 'that I believe there were not three natives in England that understood one word of it better than in the reign of Queen Anne'.[13] The duchess's instructional programme for Augusta was also scorned by the intellectually able Queen Caroline, who wrote to her daughter, Anne, in Holland, 'I could scold the old duchess for not having given the poor child a better education'.[14]

Augusta pleased her future father-in-law with her humility and unaffected friendliness, and George may have hoped that she would have a calming effect on his errant son. He took a favourable report back to Frederick, arranging through five members of his Cabinet Council that 'if His Royal Highness liked it, [he] would demand the Princess of Saxe-Gotha for him in marriage. The Prince made answer with great decency, duty, and propriety, that whoever His Majesty though a proper match for his son would be agreeable to him.'[15] Despite his dutiful answer, Frederick wasn't taking such an important point on trust; he sent his confidential valet to inspect Augusta before assenting to the match in February 1736.

Augusta, by then aged sixteen, duly landed at Greenwich in late

April, escorted by Lady Irwin, daughter of the Earl of Carlisle, who had been appointed as one of her three ladies-in-waiting by Queen Caroline. Like many royal brides, the ingénue was barely out of the nursery and there are touching accounts of her first, nervous days after she arrived in England, when she was observed by servants still playing with a doll. Augusta made a good impression on Lady Irwin, who described her in a letter to her father.

> I think the Prince has great reason to be satisfied, to speak without the flattery of a courtier; she's a very agreeable woman, very affable in her behaviour, a good deal of address, and her person what may be called a pretty woman.[16]

Other observers, including Egmont and Sir Edward Southwell, remarked that Augusta's face was marked by smallpox scars, an issue about which Hervey was unusually reticent, due perhaps to the fact that his own complexion was covered with paint to hide a multitude of scars and blemishes.

Frederick made his way to Greenwich to greet his bride, arriving at the Queen's House with grand eclat in his William Kent barge, his white silk standard flapping in the spring air.[17] According to Lady Irwin, the meeting was successful.

> The Prince and Princess supped together in public ... in the evening I made tea for the Prince and Princess in private: the Prince seemed vastly pleased and embraced the Princess I believe ten times while I was in the room; and afterwards with great civility kissed me, and thanked me for the care I had taken of the Princess.[18]

After his experiences over the past eight years with his own family, Frederick was delighted that his father had found for him a bride who was cheerful, good-natured and willing to take his part. The fact that she was less sophisticated, and less likely to orchestrate political power than his mother, would also have been attractive to the young prince. He won his bride's trust by arranging, at her request, that her childhood governess, Madame Rixleiven, should be brought over to England, against the king's command. A kind gesture, but Frederick made sure that this rare victory over his father's wishes was widely known.[19]

Frederick took Augusta for a trip on his barge from Greenwich to the Tower of London, and must have been gratified by crowds gathering on the bank to cheer them. 'The ships saluted their Highnesses all the way they pass'd, and hung out their streamers and colours, and the river was cover'd with boats.'[20] The following day, Frederick returned to central London, while the king sent a coach to take Augusta to Lambeth, refusing the prince's request that she should be allowed to drive with an official guard through the City of London.[21] She crossed the river to Whitehall by barge, and was then carried by sedan chair through St James's Park to the palace, to be met again by Frederick at the steps to the king's apartments. In front of the assembled Court, she was reintroduced to her father-in-law and met Caroline for the first time, prostrating herself on the floor in front of first one, then the other. 'This prostration was known to be so acceptable an accosting to His Majesty's pride that, joined to the propriety of her whole behaviour on this occasion, it gave the spectators great prejudices in favour of her understanding, which on better acquaintance afterwards soon mouldered away.'[22]

The pre-nuptial celebrations got off to a chequered start. The king and queen took their midday meal, as usual, in their own apartments, but the prince and princess were ordered to eat with the prince's younger siblings. Frederick, irked by years of disagreeable relations with his sisters in particular, decided to throw his weight about to impress his bride. Hervey records that 'the Prince wisely contrived to raise a thousand disputes, pretending first that his brother and sisters should sit upon stools whilst he and his bride sat in armed chairs at the head of the table; next, that they should not be served on the knee, though neither of these things had ever entered before into his head since he came into England, and that he had ate with them constantly every day'. An unseemly scrap followed, with the princesses refusing to enter the dining room until the stools were removed and chairs put in their place. 'I mention these occurrences,' adds Hervey with heavy irony, 'to show from what wise motives the irreconcilable differences in princely families often proceed, and by what important circumstances they are prudently and sensibly on both sides generally widened and kept up'.[23]

Frederick and Augusta were married later at nine o'clock in the evening in the chapel at St James's Palace, with slightly less ceremony, 'for the King's pleasure was that there should be no procession' as had been accorded to the princess royal two years earlier. An anthem had been composed in a hurry by Handel, but according to Egmont, 'was wretchedly sung by Abbot, Gates, Lee, Bird and a boy'.[24] However, the entire court seems to have been gorgeously arrayed. Augusta wore a crown set with diamonds, accompanied by four train-bearers, also wearing diamonds, 'not less in value than from 20 to 30,000*l* each,' according to *The Gentleman's Magazine*. The magazine also reported that the king was in gold brocade, the queen was decked in jewels 'of immense value', and the courtiers' suits all cost between £300 and £500 each.[25]

Having learned little from his squabble with his siblings earlier in the day, Frederick remained in a foolish mood throughout, insisting at the wedding breakfast on eating several glasses of jelly, thought then to be an aphrodisiac, and winking extravagantly at the servants as he did so. The day would have been an ordeal for the inexperienced and non-English speaking Augusta, who needed her vows translated for her during the wedding service by her new mother-in-law. It concluded, as with all royal marriages, with a very public bedding of the bride and groom. The bride was undressed by her ladies in one chamber, while Frederick was undressed and his nightshirt actually put on him by the king in another. He also donned a laughably tall nightcap, like a grenadier's bonnet, much to the indignation of his mother. Once the couple were in bed and surrounded by members of the royal family, the courtiers were admitted to the bedroom, according to the French custom. Augusta would have expected all this ceremony, but it still cannot have been easy for the young woman.

The queen wrote a full account of the wedding day in a letter to her daughter, Anne, in Holland. She was less than complimentary about the new Princess of Wales.

Heaven be praised, everything passed off wonderfully well, my dear Anne. The King behaved like an angel. Your sisters will tell you about Griff's silliness [Frederick] and the sweetness of his wife, who, far from being beautiful, has a wretched figure ... She is as anxious as a good child to please ... I felt excessively sorry for her in the chapel, which was beautifully decorated ... I told her to look at me and I would make a sign when she ought to

kneel. She clutched my skirt and said, 'For Heaven's sake, please
don't leave me,' but Griff bawled in her ear, making her repeat the
marriage sentences ... Her address was so miserable that it made
me go quite gray [Caroline's spelling] ... The bridegroom arrived
in a grenadier's bonnet and knelt before the King. She is the best
creature in the world, one puts up with her insipidity because of
her goodness. As far as one can judge her husband is perfectly
pleased with and likes her.[26]

Caroline's description hardly evokes a vision of family harmony
and happy nuptials, but one common thing that emerges from most
accounts is that Frederick was happy with his bride, and that the
marriage was to prove a successful and mutually supportive one.

So this was the nervous young bride, feted on her arrival by the
general public, yet who would eventually be hissed by that same
fickle constituency to her grave. It would be this shy innocent, fond
of her dolls and her nanny, who would come to be described as
Frederick's 'venomously loyal widow', and who would found Kew
Gardens.[27] There would be no indication in the first years of her
married life of the keen botanical interests that were to develop
after the death of her husband in 1751, but she was quickly
exposed to Frederick's commitment to gardening, as his garden at
Carlton House was already widely admired by the time of their
marriage. Frederick had also prepared with the help of William
Kent a home fit for his young wife and future family at Kew. The
White House was surrounded by a garden on which Frederick
was making a start, and which he would develop further, leaving
a charged legacy for the thirty-two year old Augusta on his death
after just fifteen years of marriage.

A pair of portraits now hanging in the State Dining Room
at Buckingham Palace gives some idea of how both prince and
princess looked in the years after their marriage. They were painted
in 1742 by Jean-Baptiste Van Loo. Frederick stands, hand on
hip, obviously a favourite pose of his, while Augusta looks out
timorously, almost wistfully, a slight woman, diminished rather
than aggrandised by the heavy embroidery and decoration on her
dress. Allowing for a certain amount of flattery (there is no hint,
for instance, of the poor complexion about which Egmont wrote),
it is nevertheless clear that Augusta was pleasant looking but no
beauty. The portrait does not hint at the redoubtable woman she

would become, whose political decisions and support for Lord Bute would even endanger her son's throne. Instead, even six years later, the painting still evokes the timid princess who prostrated herself at her in-laws' feet.

Augusta found herself joining a family perpetually at war, and indeed she was to find herself embroiled in a major disagreement little more than a year after her arrival. But to start with, the new princess needed to learn English, as Frederick recognised when he received wedding congratulations from the Lord Mayor of London and his aldermen at an official dinner hosted by one of his aides, Lord Baltimore. According to *The Gentleman's Magazine*, the prince 'received such marks of condescension and goodness as are peculiar to himself: among other obliging things, told them, that he was sorry the Princess was not so well versed in English language, as to return an answer to them in it; but that he would be answerable for her, that she should soon learn it'.[28] Frederick was as good as his word, for in 1737, the Duchess of Marlborough was recording that 'she speaks it better than any of the rest of the family who have been here so long'.[29]

Augusta faced other challenges in her first year of marriage. She insisted on taking communion at the Lutheran German chapel, and 'only wept and talked of her conscience' when Frederick pointed out that how badly her actions would be received by the clergy and by the general public. More forcefully, she was instructed that the Act of Succession required all heirs to the throne to be communicating Anglicans, a position potentially jeopardised by Augusta's remaining a Lutheran. If she continued with her Lutheran observances, she might be returned to Saxe-Gotha. 'All these arguments and conferences had their effect at last so well that the Princess dried her tears, lulled her conscience, and went no more to the Lutheran Church, but received the sacrament like the rest of the royal family.'[30]

There was also the question of her household. Queen Caroline had appointed three ladies-in-waiting for the princess ahead of her arrival: the Countess of Effingham, Lady Torrington and Lady Irwin, who went out to the Hague, along with Lord North from Frederick's household, to accompany Augusta to England.[31] Then there was the even more intimate choice of Ladies of the Bedchamber. Frederick required that one of them should be a favourite of his, Lady Archibald Hamilton. It was a contentious, if not to say unkind, choice, as Caroline pointed out to Hervey. 'The Queen said whether she believed Lady Archibald innocent or not, the Prince's behaviour to her had been so particular, and caused her to be so generally talked of as being his mistress, that it was impossible for her to put Lady Archibald about the Princess without incurring the censure of the whole world.' Frederick, however, ensured that this favourite was taken on. 'The Prince had contrived to put Lady Archibald Hamilton so well into the Princess's good graces that she was her first favourite, and always with her; and to obviate any alarms that might be given to her jealousy, he told the Princess himself that malicious people had set it about that she was his mistress.' Frederick had his way and Lady Archibald became Lady of the Bedchamber, Privy Purse and Mistress of the Robes to Augusta on a salary of £900 a year.[32]

As George II had feared, marriage put the Prince of Wales in a much stronger position politically. The Houses of Parliament addressed the king on the occasion of his son's marriage, and junior members of Lord Cobham's family, Grenville, Lyttelton and William Pitt the Elder, all made speeches in the house, paying tribute to both the character of the prince and to the princess's family. They insinuated, wrote Hervey, 'not in very covert terms, that the King had very little merit to the nation in making this match, since it had been owing to the Prince demanding it of his father, and the voice of the people calling for it too strongly not to be complied with'.[33] The future Earl of Chatham audaciously used his maiden speech implicitly to lambast the king, referring to Frederick's marriage as a 'so desirable and long-desired measure'. As a result, he lost his commission as Cornet Pitt, while Walpole struck out at this new cocky member of the opposition, saying 'we must muzzle this terrible cornet of horse'.[34] The opposition began gathering round the now-married prince, who still had cause for grievance; although he had had his allowance increased by the king on his marriage to £50,000 per annum, he still received half his Civil List allocation.[35]

Within a month of the wedding, George II set off for another prolonged visit to Hanover, once again making Caroline and not Frederick regent. Now a married man, with fluent English and having lived in England for seven and a half years, Frederick was even more incensed. Despite having a home at Kew next door to the queen's country residence at Richmond, he refused to follow her there, claiming that Augusta had measles. Caroline, alert to what she considered her son's perfidy, visited Augusta to ascertain for herself the truth or otherwise of Frederick's claim. Augusta lay in so dark a room that the queen 'returned as little informed of the true state of her daughter-in-law's health as she went'.[36]

Further trouble was to follow, despite the queen's determination not to quarrel with Frederick during the king's absence in Hanover. Both the prince and princess were seen at the same services in the chapel at St James's and were invited to dine regularly with the queen, although she reported to Hervey that she found these occasions less than diverting. 'The silly gaiety and *fade railleries* of her son, joined to the silent stupidity of her *ennuyante* daughter-in-law, had oppressed her to that degree that she was ready to cry with the fatigue of their company.'[37]

While George II was having problems with his mistress's behaviour over in Hanover, there was unrest in his British domain, with riots about corn prices in the West Country and about the employment of Irish workers in Spitalfields. Dislike of the Irish was turned on the Germans, too, with cloth workers in the City reviling their German monarch and 'huzzaing for James III'.[38] In both cases, troops were needed to restore order.

Responding to this unrest, Frederick made a rallying speech on Lord Mayor's Day in December 1736, when he was presented with the Freedom of the City. The prince replied to the Recorder's speech with a 'handsome and engaging air', assuring the twenty aldermen present that 'he should always endeavour to promote the wealth and the trade of the city ... After this they were invited to a noble dinner at Carlton House, which not being large enough to contain them all, some were carried to St James's to dine there. The city was exceedingly pleased and said to one another they now had a Prince of their own. They added that he is the first Prince of Wales who ever had this compliment, and if he would accept of being a livery man, it would complete the respect they were well able to show and greatly endear him to them.' Caroline was reported by Egmont to be choked with anger at the prince once again ingratiating himself with the general public and anyway wished that the presentation and dinner 'had at least been deferred till his Majesty's arrival and his approbation first obtained'.[39]

News reached the court the same month that the king had embarked in a storm from Helvoetsluys in the Netherlands on his way home from Hanover. Several ships were lost in the bad weather, and for a week or so it was thought that the king had perished. While the court was in this state of uncertainty, Frederick lost no time in preparing himself to take over the reins of power, further stoking the queen's rage. 'On the Prince's side,' reported Hervey, 'there was nothing to be seen but whisperers, messengers running backwards and forwards, and countenances that seemed already to belong to those who had dominion of this country in their hands, and the affairs of Europe revolving in their minds.'[40]

Eventually reports percolated through that George had set sail, but had been driven back into port, and although he had been very seasick, he had suffered nothing worse. He was detained for five weeks in Helvoetsluys, returning finally to England in mid-January. Before the king arrived back, Sir Robert Walpole took the prince to one side to point out to him that 'it could never be the interest of the Prince of Wales to quarrel with his father for private reasons, and that whoever flattered the Prince by telling him he could be a gainer by opposing his father's measures must either be the worst or the weakest of mankind'.[41] Walpole, according to Hervey, had his own views on the disaster that might befall the nation were George II to perish, believing Frederick to be 'a poor, weak, irresolute, false, lying, dishonest, contemptible wretch, that nobody loves, that nobody believes, that nobody will trust, and that will trust everybody by turns, and that everybody by turns will impose upon, betray, mislead, and plunder. And what then will become of this divided family, and this divided country, is too melancholy a prospect for one to admit conjecture to paint it.'[42]

Frederick, for his part, attempted to mend his bridges with the Prime Minister, aware that he had overplayed his hand – though he was to do so again later in the year, with fatal consequences for his relationship with his mother.

CHAPTER 8

'Under a Fool's Direction'

George II's narrow escape from death at sea in December 1736 was the closest Frederick would come to the throne. But the prince was still very much in the thick of politics and at the forefront of landscape design. The fact that both the queen and Cobham chose to employ William Kent simultaneously with Frederick was a tribute, in essence, to the genius of the designer. But it was also an indication that Frederick was a cultural force to be reckoned with.

Frederick's position as a leader of fashion is indicated by a poem written in 1737 by Richard Savage. 'Of Public Spirit In Regard to Public Works: An Epistle to His Royal Highness Frederick Prince of Wales' is a paean to the English landscape movement. It lays on flattery with a trowel, with the author making clear that Frederick, as heir to the throne, was worth wooing. Addressing Frederick as 'Great Hope of Britain', Savage speaks of his 'princely zeal! – a spirit all your own!' The poem describes his garden at Carlton House, seeing it as the most significant of his princely accomplishments and an important public work. Again, the contrast is made between the lush, landscape gardens of England and those of absolutist France. It also makes reference to England's centuries-old, peasant-led and still thriving wool industry.

> Unlike, where tyranny the rod maintains
> O'er turfless, leafless, and uncultur'd plains,
> Here herbs of food and physic plenty show'rs,
> Gives fruits to blush, and colours various flow'rs.
> Where sands or stony wilds once starv'd the year,
> Laughs the green lawn, and nods the golden ear.

> White shine the fleecy race, which fate shall doom
> The feast of life, the treasure of the loom.

Savage sees the landscape movement as representative of British freedoms, taking its authority from classical Rome.

> Thus Public Spirit, liberty and peace,
> Carve, build, and plant, and give the land increase;
> From peasant hands imperial works arise,
> And British, hence, with Roman grandeur vies;
> Not grandeur that in pompous whim appears,
> That levels hills, that vales to mountains rears;
> That alters nature's regulated grace,
> Meaning to deck, but destin'd to deface.

Savage is praising the naturalism of the English landscape movement and goes on to feature Carlton House garden in some detail, writing that

> Up yon green slope a length of terrace lies,
> Whence gradual landscape fade, in distant skies.
> Now the blue lake reflected heav'n displays;
> Now darkens regularly-wild, the maze.
> Urns, obelisks, fanes, statues, intervene,
> Now centre, now commence, now end the scene.[1]

'Regularly-wild' seems to encapsulate Kent's style. The type of landscape evoked in Savage's poem can still be seen at Stowe, and at Rousham in Oxfordshire. It's the clearest possible expression of Frederick's position at the heart of contemporary fashion and equates good gardening with moral probity.

Their mutual enthusiasm for gardening at Richmond and Kew respectively brought Queen Caroline and her son no closer. She saw slights against the authority of the king in every action of Frederick's, while he continued to battle for a larger allowance, forcing a vote in the House of Commons in February 1737. His narrow loss by thirty votes was an indication that support for the prince in Parliament and in the country in general was growing. He had been popular with the public since his arrival, having the common touch his father so obviously lacked. And George's behaviour seemed penny-pinching, as he and Caroline between them received an income in the region of a million pounds a year, against which Frederick's £59,000 looked a paltry sum. Caroline's verbal abuse continued, as she claimed that her son, who borrowed freely from a variety of sources, was completely unprincipled. According to Hervey, she launched a tirade at the time on the prince. 'The mean fool ... the poor-spirited beast! I remember you laughed at me when I told you once this avaricious and sordid monster was so little able to resist taking a guinea on any terms, if he saw it before his nose, that if the Pretender offered him £500,000 for the reversion of this Crown he would say "Give me the money".'[2] Frederick's friendship with Bolingbroke also caused waves, adding fuel to the fire of belief that the prince was a clandestine Jacobite. It seems an unlikely charge, given that Frederick had more to lose than most people were James III to win the British throne.

Frederick's enemies regarded his continual opposition to his father as impolitic weakness of character, but Dodington, himself for a period out of favour with the volatile prince, admitted in a letter to the prince written in 1749 that 'I am ready to own, that, considering the humiliating situation prepared for Your Royal Highness at your first coming to Britain, perhaps you had no means of procuring yourself a proper independency but by having recourse to the unprincely weapon of opposition'.[3]

In these continual struggles, Frederick must have looked forward to the birth of an heir. Whether or not Lady Archibald had been Frederick's mistress prior to his marriage, there is no evidence that the affair continued, or that he had any further mistresses once he was married. He seems, unlike his father and grandfather, to have been a model husband and, from the few letters that are extant, an affectionate father. It was not, as Archibald Foord suggested in his account of eighteenth-century opposition politics, 'a forlorn marriage'.[4]

Augusta held her nerve in the face of these unpleasant family disagreements. There were minor disagreements about her supposedly clambering uncomfortably past the queen in the Royal Chapel, but on the whole the young princess was observed by courtiers to behave with humility and respect to her irascible in-laws. When the king was away in Hanover, she is recorded as regularly coming to hear and play music in the queen's gallery, although unaccompanied by her husband. Caroline found her boring and mousy, her most telling complaint about Augusta being that she was under the thumb of her husband. 'Poor creature,' said Caroline on one occasion, 'if she were to spit in my face, I should only pity her for being under such a fool's direction, and wipe it off.'[5]

It was widely believed that the king and queen were anxious that a son of Frederick's would put their favourite, the Duke of Cumberland, out of the running for both the British throne and the electorship of Hanover. Caroline had already circulated stories that Frederick was impotent by claiming that Miss Vane's son was in fact Hervey's. Much, too, was made by Caroline and Hervey of Augusta's deportment on the day after her marriage. 'The Queen and Lord Hervey agreed that the bride looked extremely tired with the fatigues of the day, and so well refreshed next morning, that they concluded she had slept very sound.'[6] The obvious implication was that the marriage had not been consummated on the wedding night.

Whether or not that was the case, marital relations between the couple must have taken place at some point over the next few months, because by the spring of 1737 Augusta was pregnant. The prince, however, took his time to inform his parents, preferring to hug the secret to himself for as long as possible. He was able to keep his counsel thanks to the loose-fitting gowns of the period, which obscured Augusta's condition into the summer. There were rumours of a pregnancy, but Caroline sought to counter them, making clear her belief that her son was capable of trying to pass off another baby as his own. It wasn't, therefore, until 5 July that Frederick sent a formal notification from Kew to the queen at nearby Richmond. 'Madam,' he wrote. 'Doctor Hollings and Mrs Cannon have just told me, that there is no longer any Doubt of the Princess's being with Child. As soon as I had their Authority, I would not fail to acquaint your Majesty therewith, and beg you to inform the King of it at the same Time.'[7]

It seems hard to believe that the doctor and midwife had been unable to confirm Augusta's pregnancy until the beginning of July, given that on 31 July, she went into labour. Even assuming the Waleses first child was, say, two months premature, Augusta must have been at least six months pregnant by the time Frederick wrote to his mother. Certainly, Caroline was suspicious, cross-questioning her daughter-in-law closely about her due date when she next appeared at court. All Augusta would reply was 'I don't know', from which the queen concluded 'the Princess had received from conjugal authority absolute commands to make no other reply'.[8]

Once the fact of the pregnancy was established, George and Caroline were determined that the baby should be born at Hampton Court, where the whole royal family was spending the summer and autumn, while Frederick was equally resolved that the birth should take place in London. 'But at her labour I positively will be, let her lie-in where she will,' Hervey quotes the queen as saying. 'For she cannot be brought to bed as quick as one can blow one's nose, and I will be sure it is her child.'[9] How wrong she was proved to be.

As the royal birth didn't appear imminent, the king delayed sending a message via Sir Robert Walpole, commanding Frederick to ensure his wife gave birth at Hampton Court. According to the Duchess of Marlborough, however, 'the King and Queen both knew that she was to lie in at St James's where everything was prepared'. Had the prince actually received a direct order from the king, it would have made it harder for him to behave with such extraordinary irresponsibility when his wife did in fact go into labour, just after the couple had dined in public with the king and queen at Hampton Court.

Many accounts have been written about what happened next, some of them contradictory. The Duchess of Marlborough has it that Augusta begged Frederick to take her to St James's, 'where she had all the assistance that could be and everything prepared', rather than staying at Hampton Court where she 'might be forced to make use of a country midwife'.[10] That was indeed a defence which Frederick later made use of, but the brutal truth seems to be that he was prepared to risk the life of both his wife and his unborn child to spite his parents.

Realising that Augusta actually was in labour, Frederick hustled her quickly from Hampton Court to a waiting coach, during the process of which the princess's waters broke. According to Hervey, Augusta was lugged from the palace, her arms half-held by M. Dunoyer, the dancing master, and the rather appropriately named Mr Bloodworth, one of the prince's equerries, while Lady Archibald Hamilton and another courtier remonstrated with the prince. 'But the Prince, with an obstinacy equal to his folly, and a folly equal to his barbarity, insisted on her going, crying "Courage! courage!

ah, quelle sottise!" and telling her, with the encouragement of a tooth drawer or the consolatory tenderness of an executioner, that it would be over in a minute.'

It is all too easy to imagine the agonies endured by the princess, with her waters already broken, as she was bounced for sixteen miles over eighteenth-century roads to St James's Palace – and in a coach crowded with valets and dressers. According to Hervey's graphic account, Frederick ordered all the lights to be extinguished when the party arrived at St James's to spare Augusta's blushes, 'her clothes [being] in such a condition with the filthy inundations which attend these circumstances'. And, in contradiction of the Duchess of Marlborough's account, Hervey has it that nothing had been prepared for Augusta's lying-in at St James's. A midwife arrived shortly, but all the other necessaries for birth had to be hunted down by various emissaries from other houses in the neighbourhood, while the princess herself was put to bed between two tablecloths. Just two peers were present at the birth of a princess at a quarter to eleven. The President of the Council, Lord Wilmington, and the Lord Privy Seal, Lord Godolphin, were, however, adequate to confirm that this 'little rat of a girl, about the bigness of a good large toothpick case' was indeed the daughter of Princess Augusta. The Lord Chancellor was in the country and could not be found, but the Archbishop of Canterbury arrived fifteen minutes after the birth.

While this drama was unfolding on the road to London and at St James's Palace, the king, queen and princesses continued obliviously to play cards at Hampton Court before retiring to bed at ten o'clock. It wasn't until half past one that Mrs Titchburne, a Women of the Bedchamber, awoke the king and queen to tell them that Augusta was in labour. Caroline's immediate reaction was to put on her dressing gown and go to Augusta's side, but Mrs Titchbourne pointed out that the queen would need a coach as well, the princess now being at St James's. The king flew into a tantrum, and blamed Caroline for the prince's behaviour, pointing out the likelihood that a false child would be foisted on them. 'This has been fine care and fine management for your son, William,' he spat at her, as she dressed quickly and left for London herself with Lords Hervey, Grafton and Essex, as well as the two eldest princesses.

The party arrived at St James's at four in the morning, to be greeted by the new father, by now relaxing in a nightgown and nightcap. According to Hervey, the frosty conversation which then followed between Caroline and Frederick was their first exchange of words since the parliamentary debate about his income in February. It was also to be very nearly the last. The queen went to see Augusta, who made light of her sufferings, and kissed her new grand-daughter, also to be called Augusta. Her suspicions of malpractice evaporated when she looked at the child, whom she later described as a 'poor, little, ugly she-mouse'; 'a brave, large, fat, jolly boy' would, she felt, have been less convincing.

But although Caroline was satisfied that the child was definitely her grand-daughter, Frederick's behaviour had broken every tenet of court etiquette, and she advised him that it would be unwise for him to wait on the king that day at Hampton Court. 'The King is not well pleased with all this bustle you have made; and should you attempt coming to-day, nobody can answer what your reception may be.' Nine days after the birth, Caroline, with two of her daughters, went again to see Augusta. According to Hervey, the queen was snubbed by Frederick, who 'spoke not one single word either to her or his sisters, but was industriously civil and affectedly gay with all those of their suite who were present'.[11] When Caroline left St James's to return to Hampton Court, Frederick very publicly kissed his mother's hand and kneeled in the mud as he showed her into her carriage. 'The Prince however completely gained his point, of convincing the mob that he was the tenderest and most dutiful of sons, and the King and the Queen the most hard-hearted of parents. It is said to have enraged the Queen beyond all measure.'[12] Frederick and Augusta failed to thank the queen for coming, and she made no further visits to them. 'The King told her she was well enough served for thrusting her nose where it had been shit upon already.'[13] The result of Frederick's actions were catastrophic; mother and son would never speak again.

There was a subsequent flurry of letters between Frederick and his parents as he sought to justify his behaviour and they to impress upon him his monstrous disrespect. Copies were sent to diplomats serving overseas. Sir Benjamin Keene, British envoy to Madrid, received some of the exchanges, but was asked to keep them under wraps. But, nevertheless, like government ministers' letters of resignation today, the correspondence was effectively for public perusal, and Frederick ensured that they were also published in the October 1737 edition of *The Gentleman's Magazine*. The king, although annoyed at first, felt that they showed him in better light than his son. What the Duchess of Marlborough described as 'an extraordinary quarrel' became headline news in court circles and beyond.

The king's opening salvo was delivered by the Earl of Essex to the prince on 3 August, four days after the baby's birth. Despite its use of the royal third person and the formality of the language, George and Caroline's anger rings through.

> The King has commanded me to acquaint your Royal Highness that His Majesty most heartily rejoices at the safe delivery of the Princess; but that your carrying away Her Royal Highness from Hampton Court, the then residence of the King, the Queen & the Royal Family, under the pains & certain indications of immediate labour, to the imminent danger & hazard both of the Princess & her child, & after sufficient warnings for a week before to have made the necessary preparations for that happy event, without acquainting His Majesty, or the Queen with the circumstances the Princess was in, or giving them the least notice of your departure, & the occasion of it, is looked upon by the King to be such a deliberate indignity offered to himself, & to the Queen, that he has commanded me to acquaint your Royal Highness, that he resents it to the highest degree.[14]

In reply, Frederick wrote a long, apparently contrite and self-justifying letter, claiming that the medical professionals had thought Augusta's earlier pains to be false alarms. He also begged to be allowed to attend the king at his levee.

> It is with all the mortification imaginable, that ... my coming to town with the Princess has had the misfortune to displease your Majesty. Permit me, Sir, to represent to you, that in the pressing situation I was in on Sunday, without a midwife or any assistance, it was impossible for me to delay one moment; otherwise I should not have failed to have come myself to acquaint your Majesty with it. Besides which, the greatest expedition in the world could never have brought Mrs Cannon in less than two or three hours after the birth of the child ... I am very much concerned that

a case should happen, in which my tenderness for the Princess might seem one moment to remove, what is otherwise first in my thoughts, the desire of shewing my devotion to your Majesty. Besides this, if I may take the liberty to say so, the Princess desired so earnestly at that time to carry her to London, where all assistance was nearer at hand, that I could not resist it; for I could never have forgiven myself, if in consequence of my refusal, any accident had happened to her.

Frederick finally signs himself, 'Your Majesty's most humble and most obedient Son, Servant and Subject, FREDERICK'.[15] But his words and justifications fell on deaf ears. The king arranged for the baptism of the infant Princess Augusta on 28 August, and stipulated that he, the queen and the Dowager Duchess of Saxe-Gotha should be godparents. Neither he nor the queen, however, were to be present at the service, but would be represented by the Lord Chamberlain, while the princess was asked to find a Lady of the Bedchamber to represent the duchess.[16] Frederick responded with humble gratitude and begged again to 'take the Liberty to come and throw myself at your Feet', an honour once more flatly refused. Receiving no answer, he also wrote to the queen, but she declined to receive 'any application from the Prince upon that subject'. The last resort was to try to win over his parents through his wife, so on 15 September, Augusta wrote to the king, saying,

It is a great aggravation of my sorrow upon this occasion, to find, that by the Prince's tenderness for me, I am the innocent cause of his disgrace; and I flatter myself if I had had leave to throw myself at your Majesty's feet, I could have explained the Prince's conduct in a manner that would have softened your Majesty's resentment. How much am I to be pity'd, Sir, that an incident so grateful to me, and at the same time so agreeable to the publick, should unfortunately become the unhappy cause of a division in the family!

The king at least had the grace to reply to his daughter-in-law, although it is clear that he, like his wife, considered her 'under a fool's direction'.

It is a misfortune to you, but now owing to me, that you are involved in the consequences of your husband's inexcusable conduct; I pity you, to see you first exposed to the utmost danger, in the execution of his designs, and then made the plea for a series of repeated indignities offered to me. I wish some insinuations in your letter had been omitted, which however I do not impute to you, as I am convinced it is not from you they proceed.

A more kindly, but as intransigent, response was sent by Caroline, who told Augusta that 'I shall never fail to give you every mark of my regard and affection. I think it would be unbecoming either of us to enter into a discussion of the unhappy division between the King and my son.'[17]

It is hard at this remove to understand why Frederick behaved with such recklessness towards the wife of whom he appears to have been fond. Contemporary accounts, apart from those of Hervey, convey a picture of a clever, attractive young man, good with people, if inclined at times to be foolish and led astray. Egmont, Lady Bristol and Lord Hardwicke all spoke well of the prince, who was met with cool brutality by his parents on his arrival in England in 1728. This reception and the subsequent slights he received do much to explain some of his wilder excesses and also why he joined the Whig opposition. But the birth of a future heir to the throne would surely have been his crowning success; why then did he wish to endanger his wife and child? And why was he so determined that the child should not be born under the same roof as his parents? Did he fear that George II, like George I before him, might take his new grandchild away? This must surely have been the reason for Frederick's foolhardy actions on the night of 31 July.

The 'unhappy division' was to remain a permanent one so far as Caroline and the prince were concerned. On 10 September, Frederick received a letter from the king giving him and Augusta notice to move out of St James's Palace. 'Untill you return to your duty,' wrote the king, 'you shall not reside in my palace, which I will not suffer to be made the resort of them, who, under the appearance of an attachment to you, foment the division, which you have made in my family ... In this situation, I will receive no reply ... It is my pleasure, that you leave St. James's, with all your family, when it can be done without prejudice, or inconvenience to the Princess.' The sting here is in the tail, with the king showing himself more solicitous than her husband for the princess's well-being. George II had also learned from the fatal consequences of having his second son removed from him by his own father and is more conciliatory on one point than George I had been in 1717. He concludes that 'I shall, for the present, leave to the Princess the care of my grand daughter, until a proper time calls upon me, to consider of her education. GR.'[18]

The immediate consequences were grave not only for the Prince and Princess of Wales but for anyone who waited on them. A hurried move was made out to Kew on a Sunday, 'which gave great scandal to see that holy day so ill employed, and on so bad an occasion'.[19] They were allowed to take no furniture or even trunks from St James's, and the guards were withdrawn from Frederick's White House. The diplomatic corps was ordered to stay away from Frederick's court, and peers and privy councillors were warned that they would be banished from the king's court if they waited on the prince. Two of the princess's ladies-in-waiting, Ladies Torrington and Effingham, resigned their roles for the sake of their husbands. The Duchess of Ancaster lost her pension because her husband was in Frederick's household, while 'the king's oilman was dismissed for lighting the lamps outside the Prince's house,' wrote Egmont. 'A very poor instance of resentment.'[20]

Many people, including Lord Bolingbroke, were perplexed by the escalation of what seemed like a 'purely domestic' dispute, at which 'his father struts and storms'.[21] Egmont records that the general public, along with the City of London rallied to Frederick's side. 'When the Prince and Princess left St. James's there were many of the people who beheld it cried, and a soldier at the gate upon duty, having received order from his captain not to salute the Prince on his departure ... said afterwards ... "the tears trickled down my cheeks".'[22] Frederick, his eye on the public once again, ordered his army officers not to attend him and offend the king. He also overtly blamed his mother and expressed affection and loyalty to his father.

On leaving St James's, Augusta and Frederick removed themselves first of all to Kew, where the prince enjoyed walking each day in the lanes and fields around the White House. They also took out a £1,200 annual lease on Norfolk House in St James's Square, as Carlton House was too small as a family residence, and was used primarily for Frederick's political meetings. The same year, they acquired Cliveden in Buckinghamshire, leasing it for £600 a year. The estate, where the prince had visited Lord Orkney on a rare jaunt with his mother in April 1729, became their principal country residence for the rest of the prince's life and the focus of both their family life and their political activities. He also leased or bought Park Place, near Henley-on-Thames, from Lady Hamilton in 1738; in a series of paintings by John Wootton, Frederick is seen entertaining his friends there, and gambolling with his children and dogs.[23]

The whole dispute was a public relations disaster for George and Caroline. As his parents had done before him, Frederick with his wife set up a rival court to the monarch. Egmont recorded that the Duke of Montague thought that the king had done '*a very silly thing.* He added that he supposed that all the independent nobility and gentry would go to the Prince's Court and a number of stiff Tories who forbore waiting on him because he lived under the King's roof, and that he expected that the Princess' Court will be as numerous as the King's.'[24] The monarch's intransigence encouraged a number of political leaders, including Lords Carteret and Chesterfield, to join Frederick's cause. And while Cobham and William Pulteney (later Earl of Bath) favoured reconciliation, both remained loyal to the prince. Lyttelton, Cobham's nephew, who had spoken on Frederick's behalf in the allowance debate in February, became the prince's secretary, although Frederick was warned by Lords Baltimore and Carnarvon that such a move would harden his father's attitude to him. For the next five years, until Walpole's fall, Frederick would be actively involved in the opposition to the Prime Minister.

Within a few weeks of Frederick's quitting St James's Palace, Queen Caroline became dangerously ill. In early November, while at St James's Palace visiting her new library, designed by William Kent, she experienced severe abdominal pains. She struggled through an afternoon social engagement, before going to bed and calling Hervey to her side. A ruptured navel hernia, suffered when she gave birth to her youngest child, Princess Louisa, in 1724, had been left untreated for thirteen years. The queen was initially weakened by the customary blooding and vomiting induced by a particularly unpleasant concoction called Daffy's Elixir, a mixture of mint-water, usquebaugh and snake-root. The doctors then decided to operate, attempting an incision to push the gut back into the body, and instead causing septicaemia. Caroline lingered on for eleven days, suffering acute agonies, surrounded by her family. The king was constantly at her side, prepared even to sleep on the floor rather than leave her, while the stress of watching night after night by her mother caused Princess Caroline to have nosebleeds. Frederick was notable by his absence, although he repeatedly asked to visit. Lord Hervey was commissioned by the king to tell Lord North, the prince's courtier, that 'in the present situation and circumstances His Majesty does not think fit that the Prince should see the Queen, and therefore expects he should not come to St. James's'. The queen was unaware of Frederick's requests, remarking to her husband that 'sooner or later I am sure one shall be plagued with some message of that sort, because he will think it will have a good air in the world to ask to see me; and perhaps hopes I shall be fool enough to let him come, and give him the pleasure of seeing my last breath go out of my body, by which means he would have the joy of knowing I was dead five minutes sooner than he could know it in Pall Mall'.[25]

Again, even in such extremity, Frederick seems to have won the publicity battle, with Egmont noting that 'people speak hardly of her for not yielding to the Prince's repeated desire to see her. She was otherwise a tender mother, beloved of her children, who with watching and sitting up with her have been quite worn down.'[26]

One of the queen's anxieties was that her garden at Richmond would pass to her eldest son, who might indeed have been happy to complete the work there; after all the thought that had gone into its conception, the queen did not live to see the terracotta busts of every king of England from Alfred to George II put in place in Merlin's Cave. The king was able to reassure her that it would remain his property for his lifetime. Indeed, although he scorned Caroline's horticultural efforts while she was alive, he continued to pay for a separate gardener for each palace after her death. He also appeared to accept that Caroline's enthusiasm for gardening had added a further 188 acres to the royal gardens and doubled the cost of their maintenance.[27]

Queen Caroline died on 20 November, without having seen her eldest son again. She was buried in Westminster Abbey on 17 December, deeply mourned by her daughters and younger son, if not by Frederick. Others, too, praised her intelligence and her political and cultural interests; Walpole, who had worked closely and effectively with her for over a decade, described her as 'the sole mover of this court', while Voltaire spoke of her as 'this princess [who] was born to encourage the whole circle of arts, and to do good to mankind'.[28]

The king's grief was real. As his wife died, he vowed that he might have mistresses but he would never remarry, a promise he kept for the remaining twenty-three years of his life. On Christmas Day, he refused to take communion and ordered that the preacher, the Dean of Exeter, should make Caroline and not Christ's birth the subject of his sermon.[29] Egmont, ever the watchful observer, like Hervey, noted that at court the following month, 'the King spoke to me. He stayed not two minutes out, and had grief still fixed on his face'.[30]

CHAPTER 9

'A Declared Head to Range Themselves Under'

So what role did Augusta take while her husband quarrelled with his father and watched his mother die from a distance? Egmont, a partisan for the Waleses, described Augusta as having 'a peculiar affability of behaviour, and a very great sweetness of countenance, mixed with innocence, cheerfulness and sense'.[1] Others, however, believed that she coped more than well with Frederick and with the unfortunate family circumstances in which she found herself after her marriage. She entered 'into all his little tricks to gain popularity, and [offered] herself a ready instrument in all his plans of falsehood and deception'. These are the words of the Earl of Shelburne, afterwards the 1st Marquess of Lansdowne, and Prime Minister from 1782 to 1783, who wrote extensively and unflatteringly in his memoirs about both Frederick and Augusta.

Shelburne took the Hervey line about Frederick, describing him as having 'a strange mixture of cunning, incessant activity, and habits such complete hypocrisy as would seem to have required more talent and force of character'. The earl notes Frederick's fondness for having his portrait painted. 'His pictures, of which there are many, give a very exact representation of his character. His characteristic was activity, which continues to be that of the family to this hour: a great misfortune where there is not a very good head to conduct it.' Shelburne has no doubt that Lady Archibald Hamilton was Frederick's mistress, and indeed suggests that he planned to marry her on the death of her husband. Forced into Augusta's circle, she ruled 'as before with absolute sway, the Princess appearing to submit to everything'.

The future Prime Minister was as cutting about Augusta as about

Frederick, arguing that 'it seems to have been her fate through life to have been neglected and undervalued, and under cover of that neglect to have compassed all her points and obtained more power than would fall to the lot even of an ambitious person in her situation'. Far from accepting the Duke of Montague's view that Augusta's court would be at least as glittering as the king's, Shelburne writes that she was 'neglected by her husband, kept down by Lady Archibald, and suffering all the mortifications attendant upon great and insignificant situations in all Courts'.[2] It was also suggested by Lord Wentworth that Frederick's court was poorly attended, with observers remarking that few coaches stopped at his door.[3] Shelburne claims in his memoirs that Augusta was 'naturally given to dissimulation and intrigue' and 'had both time and opportunity to improve these important qualifications'. He also believed her to be two-faced, colourfully describing her as having 'an eye which almost turned in the socket, and carried a great deal of insinuation, and if attentively examined a great deal of observation. She had resolution equal to any enterprise, and had a perfect command of temper ... [and was] a ready instrument in all [Frederick's] plans of falsehood and deception.'[4]

Factual inaccuracies in Shelburne's account suggest that he may not be an entirely trustworthy observer, although much of what he says about Augusta was later echoed by Horace Walpole, who disliked her as much as Hervey had disliked Frederick. Shelburne's view of Augusta is markedly different from that formed by Caroline, who was advised by Sir Robert Walpole to handle the young princess carefully in the early days of her marriage. Walpole possibly spotted that Augusta was shrewder than she appeared, and that she might in time become a formidable opponent – or indeed ally. 'It would only give the Prince a jealousy, and prevent his ever suffering his wife to have any interest with him or any influence at all over his conduct.' Caroline took the point, but decided on closer acquaintance with Augusta that she was never likely to be much of a player. The queen 'thought there was no sort of harm in her, that she never meant to offend, was very modest and respectful, and that for her want of understanding it was what to be sure fatigued one when one was obliged to be with her'.[5]

Whether Shelburne is right about Augusta hiding her guile under a mousey appearance, there is evidence to suggest that she was a woman of character, who grew into her job, and was later determined not only to continue but to surpass the work that Frederick had started at Kew. Frederick was to involve her closely in planning his succession towards the end of his life, indicative of his faith and confidence in her understanding and discretion. The marriage was fecund, too, despite all Caroline's insinuations about her son's impotency; a son, the future George III, was born at Norfolk House in the summer of 1738, and given his grandfather's rather than his father's name, a rare conciliatory gesture on the part of Frederick. Seven other children followed; the last, a daughter, Caroline Matilda, was born posthumously in July 1751.

The couple divided their time between their several homes: Kew, Cliveden and Park Place in the country, and in town, Norfolk House, Carlton House and Leicester House, which Frederick leased from 1743. They also made visits and progresses, during which they continued to be well received by the general public, to the irritation of the king. The autumn season of 1738 was spent in Bath, where they were waited on by the local corporation, and balls and fetes were held in their honour, supervised by Beau Nash. Nash also erected a seventy-foot high obelisk to commemorate the visit, and asked Pope for an inscription. The poet reluctantly provided less than resonant lines which, you feel, Nash could have penned for himself.

> In memory of honours bestow'd
> And in gratitude for benefits conferr'd on this city
> By His Royal Highness
> Frederick, Prince of Wales
> And his Royal Consort
> In the year 1738
> This obelisk is erected by
> Richard Nash Esqre.

Before his marriage, Frederick had marble busts erected at Kew, made by sculptors Peter Rubens and Peter Scheemakers, and set on decorated, carved plinths, while preparing the White House to be a family home. He did little other work at Kew until the late 1740s as he began to plan his succession in detail, the two activities seemingly interwoven.

Throughout the period from 1737 to the late 1740s, Cliveden was the couple's main country residence. They leased the estate from Lady Anne Inchiquin, daughter of Earl of Orkney, and second in command at Blenheim. The gardens had been redesigned in 1713 by Claude Desgots, a nephew of Le Notre and his successor as Louis XIV's designer, a late example of French influence on English gardening at a time when landowners such as Cobham and Burlington were already creating a new and distinctive English style. Lord Orkney was a friend of both Cobham and Pope, with whom he corresponded about garden design. He subsequently redesigned the garden in a simpler fashion, more in the new English style. In a letter to his brother, he wrote that 'I call it a quaker parter for it is very plain and yet I believe you will think it noble'.[6] He also built 'a very pretty Octagon Temple of Portland stone,' which was admired by Jeremiah Miles, a visitor to the garden in 1742. 'Before the grand front of the house is a fine platform planted round with a double row of fine elms: this spot commands a most glorious prospect of the Thames, & of Berkshire on the other side of it. The great beauty of the gardens is their situation, & the hanging wood before mentioned wch is cutt out in walks, & vistos.'[7]

According to Sarah, Duchess of Marlborough, in 1738, Frederick incurred 'a good deal of expense at Cliveden in building and furniture'.[8] Outside, he made fewer changes; the planting of an ilex grove is one of the few additions the prince is thought to have made.[9] He did, however, fill the existing beds with plants he bought from nurserymen such as Peter Collinson, who imported rare treasures from America and elsewhere. It was these planting schemes he wished Lord Bute to admire when they met a decade after Caroline's death.

The fact that an ordinary man on a tour of England was able to visit Cliveden during the prince's tenancy indicates that Frederick was aware of the power of the visual image, and wanted, like Cobham, to show off his estate to the travelling public for political reasons. Cliveden was very much a home for him and Augusta, where they played cricket and put on amateur theatricals with their young family, but it was also the place where he gathered together his political supporters.

After his wife's death, George II remained true to his word; he never remarried, but he did bring his mistress, Countess Wallmoden, over from Hanover in June 1738 and installed her in apartments occupied by a previous mistress, Henrietta Howard.[10] In February 1740, Wallmoden was naturalised and then the following month made Countess of Yarmouth, to the fury of his unmarried daughters, Princesses Amelia and Caroline, and of the general public, who disliked the monarch's continued predilection for all things German.

Relations with Frederick also remained distant, although less combustible than when Caroline was alive, suggesting that the queen had been the prime mover in the discord between father and son. The prince continued short of money, but with war brewing against Spain, he decided it was politic not to force the issue of his allowance in the 1738 parliamentary session, although his opposition to the king and Walpole bubbled on. Once again, he won the approbation of the Duchess of Marlborough, who wrote, 'The Prince of Wales has done, I think, a very right thing for he has declared to everybody, that though he did design to bring the business of his revenue into the House, he is now resolved not to do it, it being but a trifle and what could not succeed after losing a question of so much consequence for the preservation of the nation.'[11]

In the words of Horace Walpole, Frederick over the next few years 'went all lengths of opposition and popularity till the fall of Sir Robert Walpole, when he was reconciled to, though never after spoken to by the King'.[12] International events were to play into Frederick's hands over the next three years.

Walpole tried to prevent the war that broke out with Spain in 1739 and grumbled on until 1748. The conflict became known as the War of Jenkins' Ear, after a merchant navy officer who had part of his ear cut off when his ship was boarded by the Spanish in April 1731. During his long premiership, Walpole always attempted to keep Britain out of wars, but, by 1738, there was a swell of public opinion that the government was failing to support British seamen. It also seemed that Walpole's anti-war views were contributing to Britain's decline as a European power, and George was heckled in public. Frederick was the obvious figurehead for the pro-war party, supported in the Commons by Cobham's Boy Patriots, such as William Pitt, already a thorn in the side of the monarch.[13] When war was declared in October 1739, the Prince of Wales stood on the steps of a city tavern, toasting the health of the mob as they rejoiced in the streets.[14] The people, along with the opposition to

Walpole, had 'a declared head, the heir apparent of the Crown, to range under'.[15]

While George disappeared to Hanover, Frederick continued to appear with his wife in public, revisiting Bath, attending the races at Banbury and going on a number of well-received progresses through England – activities perhaps lacking in seriousness when the country was at war, but at least English-based, unlike his father's.

In August 1740, Frederick sponsored the Anglo-Scots poet James Thomson to compose *Rule Britannia*, a patriotic anthem for a people at war, expressing their hopes for naval supremacy. It was written for *The Masque of Alfred*, set to music by the London-born Thomas Arne and performed in an outdoor amphitheatre at Cliveden, designed by Charles Bridgeman for Lord Orkney. The occasion was ostensibly the third birthday of Princess Augusta, but there are resounding political overtones in the choice of subject matter; five years earlier, both Cobham and Frederick had erected busts in their gardens of Alfred, the legendary founder of the British constitution.[16]

It was a good moment for Frederick to mobilise against Walpole, who had attempted to act as a brake on the prince's activities for over a decade. In power since April 1721, Walpole had split the Whigs in the 1730s, found himself the butt of the literary world and increasingly unpopular with the nation at large. Much of the opposition to Walpole in parliament and opposition circles was caused by envy of his undoubted abilities, his success and his close association with the monarch, as much as genuine disagreement with the principles on which he ran his government. Walpole had seen it as politic to side with the king and queen rather than their son, but, by so doing, he had created other problems for himself, and pushed the prince into the arms of Cobham, Bolingbroke, Carteret and Pulteney. The latter two were effective parliamentary operators, who used Frederick as figurehead as they attacked ministerial corruption and Walpole's manipulation of the monarch.

Ironically, it was the Spanish war that Walpole had resisted which was to be his downfall. By the early 1740s, the conflict was going badly for Britain, with Walpole being blamed for a succession of military and naval blunders. In February 1741, Carteret requested that the king should 'dismiss Sir Robert from his presences and councils for ever'.[17] Over the next year, parliamentary pressure

'The Music Party': Frederick, Prince of Wales, with his Three Eldest Sisters, Anne, Caroline and Amelia by Philippe Mercier (1733). (Royal Collection Trust / © Her Majesty Queen Elizabeth II 2015)

The Family of Frederick, Prince of Wales by George Knapton (1751).
(Royal Collection Trust / © Her Majesty Queen Elizabeth II 2015)

St James's Park and the Mall, British School (*c.*1745). (Royal Collection Trust / ©
Her Majesty Queen Elizabeth II 2015)

The Royal Barge designed by William Kent (1731). (Royal Collection / © Her Majesty Queen Elizabeth II 2015)

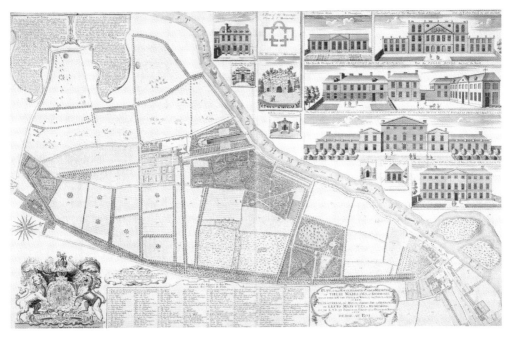

Plan of the House, Gardens, Park & Hermitage of their Majesties at Richmond by John Rocque (1734). (Royal Collection Trust / © Her Majesty Queen Elizabeth II 2015)

Plans, elevations, sections and perspective views of the gardens and buildings at Kew in Surry, the seat of Her Royal Highness the Princess Dowager of Wales by William Chambers (1763). A view of the lake and island, with the Orangerie, the Temples of Bolus and Bellona, and the House of Confucius. (Royal Collection Trust / © Her Majesty Queen Elizabeth II 2015)

The White House, Kew by Johan Jacob Schalch (*c*.1760). (Royal Collection Trust / © Her Majesty Queen Elizabeth II 2015)

A View of the Garden at Carlton House in Pall Mall, a Palace of Her Royal Highness, the Princess Dowager of Wales by William Woollett (1760). (Royal Collection Trust / © Her Majesty Queen Elizabeth II 2015)

Alexander Pope's classically inspired garden at Twickenham influenced Frederick's work at Carlton House. The poet himself is seen here in this drawing by William Kent with the artist himself and Pope's dog Bounce. (Courtesy of the British Museum)

View from the Portico of Stowe House to the Park by Jacques Rigaud. (By kind permission of Stowe House Preservation Trust/Stowe School)

View from Nelson's Seat at Stowe by Jacques Rigaud (By kind permission of Stowe House Preservation Trust/Stowe School)

Richard Temple, Viscount Cobham, the creator of the landscape garden at Stowe, by Jean-Baptiste Van Loo. (By kind permission of Stowe House Preservation Trust/ Hall Bequest Trust)

John Stuart, 3rd Earl of Bute, with his secretary, Charles Jenkinson by Sir Joshua Reynolds (*c.*1762). (© Bute Collection @ Mount Stuart, photographer Keith Hunter)

John Stuart, 3rd Earl of Bute by Sir Joshua Reynolds (*c*.1777). (© Bute Collection@Mount Stuart)

Mary, Countess of Bute by Sir Joshua Reynolds (1777). (© Bute Collection@Mount Stuart)

George, Prince of Wales, later King George III by Allan Ramsay (*c.*1758). (© Bute Collection@ Mount Stuart)

Augusta, Dowager Princess of Wales by Allan Ramsay (1758). (© Bute Collection@ Mount Stuart)

The Triumphal Arch: a sarcastic take on Bute's treaty concluding the Seven Years War. London: E. Sumpter (1763). (Courtesy of The Lewis Walpole Library, Yale University)

Richard Grenville-
Temple, Earl Temple
in an engraving by
William Dickinson
after Sir Joshua
Reynolds. (By kind
permission of Stowe
House Preservation
Trust/Stowe School)

An hieroglyphic letter from the [Princess of Wales] to the [Earl of Bute]: reports
of an improper relationship with Bute and Augusta were bandied about the streets
of London. London: E. Sumpter (1763). (Courtesy of The Lewis Walpole Library,
Yale University)

RESIGNATION.

Resignation: beaten down by the fierce onslaughts on his personal probity, Bute resigned as prime minister after less than a year in office. London: E. Sumpter (1763). (Courtesy of The Lewis Walpole Library, Yale University)

A Snug Place: a Scottish bonnet and royal insignia more than hint at the supposed affair between Bute and Augusta. London: E. Sumpter (1763). (Courtesy of The Lewis Walpole Library, Yale University)

The Temple of Ancient Virtue (©National Trust Images/Andrew Butler)

The Temple of the British Worthies (©National Trust Images/Andrew Butler)

The Temple of Concord and Victory (©National Trust Images/Andrew Butler)

was stepped up on Walpole; a debate on the war in January 1742 resulted in a ministerial majority of just three votes.[18] Walpole realised that he needed Frederick's support to win back the parliamentary support that was ebbing away, and was prepared to buy it. Dr Secker, the Bishop of Oxford and future Archbishop of Canterbury, was commissioned to offer Frederick the £100,000 per annum he had been requesting for the last decade. On top of that, if Frederick could mobilise votes in the House for Walpole, he would also be paid arrears of £200,000 for the last four underpaid years.[19]

The king and Walpole between them tried a two-pincered attack. George wrote directly to Augusta, asking her to intercede with Frederick on the question of Walpole's impeachment. Whether or not it was the princess's words which swayed Frederick, the idea of impeaching Walpole was dropped, although his resignation was forced. The loss of his first minister was a blow to the authority of the king who had relied on Walpole for more than fourteen years, and was a coup for Frederick. His guard, which had been withheld since 1737, was restored, and Frederick and Augusta made a triumphant tour of the City and a much-publicised trip to Greenwich, flags flying on Kent's magnificent barge.[20] Yet the Prime Minister's defeat proved a hollow victory for Frederick; although he finally gained the extra £50,000 a year, the arrears were not paid, nor was any money forthcoming from parliamentary funds to pay his debts. Walpole was replaced by a nonentity, Lord Wilmington, the former Spencer Compton for whom Walpole had had to draft George II's first speech to the council on his accession to the throne in 1727. Without such a powerful figure to fight against, the opposition's sting was drawn, making Frederick less necessary to them.[21]

The fall of Walpole did bring about a reconciliation of sorts between Frederick and the king, who had not spoken to each other for almost five years. Augusta, decked in £40,000 worth of borrowed diamonds, attended the Duchess of Norfolk's ball, while Frederick was at last admitted to the king's levee. George had sworn he wouldn't speak to his son, but was prevailed upon to do so, abruptly asking Frederick about the health of his wife. The prince replied by kissing the king's hand, which was smartly withdrawn. It was a chilly rather than cordial encounter, but an important step had been taken.

There was also a rapprochement between the siblings, with Frederick and Augusta accompanying Amelia, Caroline, Cumberland and Louisa to the opening of the Ranelagh Gardens. These pleasure gardens were planned to be more exclusive than the raffish Vauxhall Gardens and charged an entrance fee of two shillings and sixpence rather than a shilling.

The following year, George once more departed for Hanover, on this occasion taking with him his younger son, the Duke of Cumberland, his sights set on involving himself militarily in the War of the Austrian Succession (1740–8). Frederick was left behind and again not even accorded a place on the regency council in his father's absence. George and Cumberland spent the spring in Hanover, before fighting together against the French at the Battle of Dettingen in June 1743, the last time that a British monarch would take to the field in war. Dettingen averted disaster rather than being a famous victory, but the king's courageous action, at the head of the British infantry, did much to restore his popularity at home. Mr Kendal of Lord Albemarle's Troop reported that 'His Majesty is certainly the bravest man I ever saw. I saw the balls go within a yard of his head and when he was desired to go out of danger he answered, "Don't talk to me of danger, I'll be even with them."' Cumberland also acquitted himself bravely and was reluctant to leave the field of battle even after he was injured in the leg, a wound which would plague him for the rest of his life.[22]

The return home of the king and Cumberland was triumphant, as Horace Walpole wrote to Horace Mann. 'We were in great fears of his coming through the city, after the treason that has been publishing for these two months: but it is incredible how well his reception was … They almost carried him into the palace on their shoulders; and at night the whole town was illuminated and bonfire. He looks much better than he has these five years, and is in great spirits.'

Frederick seems to have accepted with remarkable good humour Cumberland's success on the battlefield. He greeted both father and brother in person on their return from Dettingen, although, added Walpole, 'the King's reception of the Prince … was not so gracious … though the Princess was brought to bed the day before, and Prince George is ill of the smallpox'.[23] But Frederick called his new son William, after Cumberland, and even commissioned a painting of the duke at Dettingen. The brothers seemed to have remained on good terms throughout their lives, spending time together at Kew and walking around the plantations which Frederick was laying out there.[24]

The next half decade or so would be desert years for Frederick. After the reconciliation with his father, Frederick managed to get two of his own men, Lord Baltimore and Lord Archibald Hamilton (husband of Augusta's lady-in-waiting) positions in the Admiralty. These placemen did nothing, however, for the prince, who initially allied himself again with disaffected Whigs, no happier with Wilmington than with Walpole, and Cobham's Boy Patriots, Pitt, Lyttelton and the Grenvilles.

Frederick's close alliance with Cobham, and their shared opposition to the government of Walpole, had been commemorated by the Temple of Friendship at Stowe. Designed by James Gibbs, it was built in the early 1740s and stands significantly in the Path of Liberty, balancing William Kent's 1731 Temple of Venus on the other side of the garden; erected in the Path of Vice, it was dedicated to the goddess of sex and of gardening. The Temple of Friendship was damaged by fire in the 1840s and is now a roofless ruin, but it originally had a ceiling decorated by murals symbolising male friendship, justice and liberty – all the things which, it was implied, were threatened by Walpole. The building was used by Cobham for political supper parties, and busts of his close friends and family, including Pitt the Elder, Lord Chesterfield and George Lyttelton, were commissioned to stand on pedestals around the wall. Peter Scheemakers sculpted busts of Cobham, now in the Victoria & Albert Museum in London, and of Frederick. The latter was bought for the Royal Collection by the Queen Mother from the Temple family at Sotheby's in 1941. It shows Frederick as he would surely have liked to have been seen: in Roman armour, with his Garter badge conspicuously displayed, a furrowed brow and a firm expression on his lips.[25] Wigless, his hair cropped, he looks the very model of a Roman military leader, the kind of guise in which Julius Caesar was so often displayed.

It was a flattering tribute by Cobham to the prince, especially as Frederick was never allowed to play any military role, or indeed as significant a political role as he would have liked. After a short premiership, Wilmington died in July 1743, ushering in the age of the Pelhams; Henry Pelham and his brother, the Duke of Newcastle, would between them head the government for much of the next eighteen and a half years. Frederick was ensnared by subsequent political manoeuvrings; Pelham initially found a place for Lord Middlesex, another of the prince's favourites, with the intention of winning the prince to his side. In a brief and rare alliance, George and his son both supported Carteret, the secretary of state, whose pro-war policy was becoming increasingly unpopular. In November 1744, Pelham and Newcastle presented the king with the alternative of dismissing the government or Carteret, by then the Earl of Granville. The king's hand was forced, and Frederick was powerless to save his friend. Pitt was still left out in the cold but Lyttelton was given Lordship of the Treasury. There were rumours and counter-rumours about why Frederick's secretary had joined the triumphant government, but the upshot was that the prince dismissed Lyttelton, thus completing his own political isolation. Frederick was perhaps fortunate that Hervey had died the previous August, otherwise the diarist might well have had much to say about Frederick's apparent disloyalty to a friend who had served him long and well – and who had powerful connections, too. Lyttelton's letter to Frederick hints at the depth of his disappointment in his former master.

> In obedience to your commands, I return your Royal Highness these papers which you did me the honour to leave in my hands, and which I should have been happy and proud to have retained as memorials of your former favour to me, which I endeavoured to merit by the most faithful services, and which my conscience assures me I never did anything to deserve the loss of … But it has been my misfortune to have my conduct much misrepresented to your Royal Highness, but, however, I may suffer under your unmerited anger, I shall always continue to preserve the most grateful sense of your past goodness to me, and the most sincere, disinterested zeal for your service.[26]

Frederick appeared routed and was again out in the cold. Although for once he had sided with the king, it had not proved to his advantage and George continued to exclude his eldest son from his political counsels. Frederick was supported wholeheartedly by his wife, described by Carteret as 'as sensible & deserving a person as ever lived'. Augusta managed to borrow money through the offices of her brother, the Duke of Saxe-Gotha, to pay the debts not covered by Frederick's new increased allowance.[27] Frederick continued to work on the White House, building an expansive and separate set of fine kitchens, now open to the public and located just in front of Kew Palace. Theirs was a domestic rather than political existence for the middle years of the 1740s. An example is a story of Augusta having been given a turtle as a present and having to send to a clergyman to come over the river to advise on how best to prepare it.

The Temple of Friendship was to be Cobham's last tribute to the prince he had encouraged and backed. In the 1740s, his style at Stowe remained just as political as the landscape movement shifted into its naturalistic stage, dominated by Lancelot 'Capability' Brown. Brown, who was so-called because he saw the 'capabilities' in any landscape he was called upon to design, became head gardener at Stowe in 1741 and began work on the Grecian Valley. Cobham's interest at this period was in emphasising the importance of his own family's role in national life. In 1747, his nephew, Captain Thomas Grenville, was fatally wounded in command of HMS *Defiance* in a battle with the French off Cape Finisterre. In his memory, Cobham erected a column decorated with the prows of ships and surmounted by a statue of Heroic Poetry holding a scroll inscribed *Non nisi grandia canto* ('Of none but heroic deeds I sing').[28] The column was later moved by Grenville's brother, Earl Temple, to its present position in the Elysian Fields, facing the Temple of British Worthies.

The other significant memorial of the 1740s was the Cobham Monument, a soaring octagonal column built by Brown to a design of James Gibbs. On the top, master of all he surveys, is an over-lifesize statue of Lord Cobham in Roman armour, which was commissioned after his death in 1749 by his widow. There are clear echoes of Trajan's Column in Rome and of the Victory Column of the Duke of Marlborough at Blenheim, heroic national soldiers with whom Cobham wanted to associate himself. The message is again transparent; it is the liberty-loving Whigs, such as Cobham and his Cubs, who command both land and sea, making Britain great in the face of encircling enemies.

By contrast, Frederick never wielded a sword. His weakened position indeed was thought to have given heart to the Old

Pretender, who believed that 'the utter contempt into which Prince Frederick is fallen at this time, so that nobody for the future will have any recourse to him or dependence upon him, but in case of discontent will naturally look for redress from another quarter'.[29] There had been rumours of a potential Jacobite invasion for some time when Prince Charles Edward Stuart, Bonnie Prince Charlie, landed with a small French invasion force in Scotland in July 1745.

Frederick asked to be allowed to command English troops to counter the invasion, but was peremptorily refused by his father, many historians believe to stop Frederick supplanting Cumberland as a popular idol. So Cumberland went north, ultimately to defeat the Jacobites at the Battle of Culloden in April 1745, and subsequently to earn himself the title of the Butcher by massacring the Highlanders. In the meantime, Frederick was left in southern England, kicking his heels and behaving with apparently childish indifference to the battles being fought across northern England and Scotland. As the royal troops retook Carlisle from the Jacobites in a bloody assault, Frederick was seen pelting a model of the city with sugar plums at his dining table.

Cumberland was once again hailed as a victor by the general public. He was voted £25,000 per annum by parliament as a reward for his endeavours, and, in his honour, Handel composed 'See the conquering hero comes' for the oratorio *Judas Maccabeus*. Although Frederick greeted his brother on his triumphant return from Dettingen, he offered no such congratulations after Culloden. Royal historian Frances Vivian argues that this refusal has mistakenly been attributed to envy. 'On the contrary,' she writes, 'it is in my view of a piece with his humanity to his servants and his numerous contributions to relieve small debtors.'[30] Another historian has it that Frederick empathised with Prince Charles, his younger contemporary whom he somewhat resembled. He may have seen in Charles's desire for a throne something of his own frustrations.[31]

It is also possible that the barbaric treatment meted out to the rebels offended Frederick, as it did many others both at the time and since. A glimpse of the mood in London is offered in a letter from Horace Walpole to Horace Mann. He wrote of Lord Kilmarnock, whose 'head was cut off at once only hanging by a bit of skin', and of Lord Balmerino, who 'certainly died with the intrepidity of a hero'. He added that 'My Lady Townshend, who fell in love with

Lord Kilmarnock at his trial, will go nowhere to dinner, for fear of meeting with a rebel-pie; she says everybody is so bloody-minded that they eat rebels!'

Frederick could do little for the Highlanders, but he did intercede on behalf of several peers and opposed harsh anti-Highlands legislation in Parliament, to the annoyance of both his father and brother. Walpole doubted that the prince's actions were entirely distinterested. 'The Prince of Wales, whose intercession saved Lord Cromartie, says he did it in return for Old Sir W. (Lady Cromartie's father) coming down out of his death-bed to vote against my father in the Chippenham election. If his Royal Highness had not countenanced inveteracy like that of Sir Gordon, he would have no occasion to exert his gratitude now in favour of rebels.'[32]

Flora Macdonald, the legendary heroine of the 'Skye Boat Song', who helped Bonnie Prince Charlie escape to the island of Skye after Culloden, was captured and imprisoned in the Tower of London. Frederick secured her release after visiting her in the Tower, where he was impressed by Flora's courage and resilience. He went against the advice of Augusta, who was strongly critical of what she regarded as Flora's unseemly behaviour.

But these were small successes for Frederick. Throughout 1746, he remained on the political periphery, during a period of relative calm in government. The following year, with his father approaching his mid-sixties, the prince began once again to plan actively for his succession, re-employing Dodington as his political secretary and involving Lord Egmont, son of the diarist, as well. It was at this point that he first encountered the man who would profoundly affect the lives of his wife and eldest son, and to help bring about the foundation of Kew Gardens.

PART III

CHAPTER 10

'An Odd Accident'

In the summer of 1747, John Stuart, 3rd Earl of Bute, decided to spend the day at the Maidenhead races. Too hard up to keep his own carriage, the impecunious Scottish peer was driven by a local Twickenham apothecary to the event, where he probably hoped to improve his fortunes with a few well-placed bets. Bute's fortunes were to be changed that day, and with them the shape of eighteenth-century politics and horticulture, not by a successful flutter, but by what the diarist Horace Walpole would describe as 'an odd accident'. For also enjoying the sport of kings on that summer morning were Frederick, Prince of Wales, and his wife, Augusta. Although not then moving in court circles, Bute was thought noble enough to make up a four at 'whisk' with the royal couple when it came on to rain. By the time the weather had cleared, the apothecary, tired of waiting for his passenger, had returned home to attend to his own affairs, so the lift-less Bute was invited by Frederick to spend the night at Cliveden, his riverside house nearby. That might have been that had the earl not dazzled Frederick with his rare knowledge of plants when the prince proudly showed Bute round his extensive gardens the following morning. Bute 'pleased his R.H. so much', recorded Walpole, 'that he kept the Earl two or three days; and not long after, appointed him a Lord of his Bedchamber'.[1]

On such moments does history turn. For this chance meeting and Bute's subsequent appointment were to have far-reaching consequences. Had he not been an amateur botanist of some distinction, the earl might never have found a place in the prince's entourage nor exerted such influence after his death on Augusta, as Dowager Princess of Wales, and on her son, the future George III. Bute would go on to become Prime Minister and effectively the last royal favourite to hold executive power without a political constituency. He would also assist Augusta in establishing Kew Gardens.

Bute's career had been chequered up to that point, and he had spent several years in the political cold at his family's home on the Isle of Bute shortly before the encounter with Frederick. Described by one biographer as 'a man of wide interests and unbounded curiosity', Bute nevertheless had the gift of making enemies.[2] The third member of the trio with which this book is concerned is perhaps the most intriguing, if also the most traduced. Cultivated and scholarly, Bute was a man of the Enlightenment, whose patronage within the universities of Scotland played an important part in defining Scottish culture in the late eighteenth century.[3] Yet his considerable abilities were decried by observers such as Shelburne, another of the scintillating but savage diarists who abounded in the eighteenth century. Shelburne wrote,

> It is not easy to give a just idea of the character of the Earl of Bute, as it consisted of several real contradictions and more apparent ones, with no small mixture of madness in it. His bottom was that of any Scotch nobleman, proud, aristocratical, pompous, imposing, with a great deal of superficial knowledge such as commonly to be met with in France and Scotland, chiefly upon matters of Natural Philosophy, Mines, Fossils, a smattering of Mechanicks, a little Metaphysicks, and a very false taste in everything ... He could be pleasant in company when he let, and did not want for some good points, so much as for resolution and knowledge of the world to bring them into action.[4]

The sting in the tail of that damning judgement on Bute echoes many of the criticisms made of Frederick, a further indication of the poor esteem in which both men were held by their courtly contemporaries. It also brings up again the subject of taste – 'a very false taste' hints at lack of judgement. No prophet is without honour, save in his own country, however; Bute earned the respect of scientists and plant-collectors across Europe and America for his wide-ranging knowledge of botany and natural history.

To get a sense of how the man himself wanted to be seen, let us

look forward a few years at two portraits he commissioned. The
first was probably painted in 1762 when he succeeded the Duke of
Newcastle, becoming George III's first appointed Prime Minister. It
is a double portrait, with his secretary, Charles Jenkinson (later 1st
Earl of Liverpool), by Sir Joshua Reynolds. The portrait is intriguing
for several reasons, not the least being that Bute should have picked
Reynolds rather than Allan Ramsay, the Scottish portrait painter
whom he himself had introduced to the royal court. This, argues
Francis Russell, was 'because he doubted Ramsay's ability to
achieve so compelling an historical and psychological statement'.[5]
Almost certainly the case and a good enough reason in itself, but
it may also have been that Bute was canny enough to choose an
English rather than a Scottish painter to puff his gaining the highest
office in the land.

In constructing an image of himself, Bute was aided by Reynolds,
for the painting is a masterpiece and of far greater artistic merit than
any commissioned by either Frederick or Augusta. Bute, wearing his
Garter star, stands slightly to the left of the picture, by an ornately
carved table piled with books and manuscripts representing the
affairs of state he now directs. He looks to his left at Jenkinson,
from whom he accepts a paper with a faint, gracious bow. The
secretary, however, glances back over his left shoulder, a conduit
from the onlooker to the black-clad minister. It is a portrait of court
rather than cabinet government and there are echoes of another
great painting, of which both Reynolds and Bute must have been
conscious – Van Dyck's mesmeric portrait of Thomas Wentworth,
Earl of Strafford, with his secretary, Sir Philip Mainwaring. It is
a classic pose; there are earlier, Italian examples by artists such
as Sebastiano del Piombo of cardinals and their secretaries. The
fact of having a secretary in itself emphasises the status of the
individual depicted and invokes a professional world. The effete
Bute perhaps also wanted to borrow some of the bull-neck strength
visible in Van Dyck's portrait of Charles I's adviser; Strafford glares
at the viewer while the secretary looks nervously over his shoulder.
There is some distortion of Van Dyck by Reynolds, a considered
distancing from Strafford, who was sacrificed by Charles I and
executed by parliament. Bute's portrait is altogether more benign,
and, significantly, full-length and designed to show off the elegant
legs of which he was inordinately proud. He is seen in the round,
as a man at ease in his political surroundings. Nevertheless, it was

as unwise for Bute to borrow authority from Strafford, given his terrible end, as it was for Frederick to align himself with the Black Prince who never inherited the throne. Although, unlike Strafford, Bute escaped with his life, his political career was also shipwrecked to save the king.

Reynolds painted Bute again, some ten years later, in 1773. The portrait, now in the National Portrait Gallery in London, shows the earl in full Garter regalia: over an embroidered doublet, he wears blue velvet robes lined with cream silk, a red sash and the Garter crest on his left shoulder and carries a plumed hat. Once more the legs take centre stage, their shapely elegance all the more impressive given that their owner was then sixty. By the time this portrait was painted, Augusta was dead and Bute was estranged from the king. He was devoting himself to his estates at Luton Hoo – where he employed 'Capability' Brown – and in Dorset, both hinted at by parkland trees in the background of the picture, and to his work as a trustee of the British Museum. As in the earlier portrait, Bute scans away to his left, with a weary, yet slightly complacent smile, not meeting the viewer's eye; Lord Chesterfield complained that he never made eye contact.[6] A fluted column, Grecian urn and elbow-high wall stretching the width of the picture give solidity to the slightly insubstantial figure of Bute. A similar version of the portrait painted in about 1777 is at Mount Stuart.

Both paintings are extraordinary psychological studies of an elusive historical figure, suggesting that Bute was at the centre of events, and yet detached. That he was vain is unmistakable (by contrast, there is pomposity, but less vanity, I think, in Frederick's portraits) and eager to be liked. 'It was my father's foible, I must confess,' wrote his daughter, Lady Louisa Stuart, 'to be too open to flattery, especially that kind of it which consists in professions of devoted attachment.'[7] This wish to be acknowledged and respected was almost certainly the result of the extended political exile early in his career. Those years heightened his near craven desire for acceptance and made him less clear-sighted as a politician, fatally hampering his dealings with the more skilful Pitt, among others.

John Stuart, 3rd Earl of Bute, was born in Edinburgh in May 1713, the son of the second earl. His grandfather, the first earl, had not welcomed the political union of England and Scotland and left Parliament in 1707 after the Act of Union was enacted. His younger son joined the Pretender's entourage in Rome, but his elder son and heir, the second earl, accepted both the union and the Hanoverian succession; he was elected as a representative peer for Scotland in 1715, and despite his Tory views, became a lord of the bedchamber to George I. He remained in Parliament until his death in January 1723, when Bute was only nine years old.

Through his mother, Lady Anne Campbell, Bute was connected with one of the most powerful families in Scotland. His uncles, the 2nd Duke of Argyll and the Earl of Islay, were both pro-Hanoverian, political managers for George I in Scotland. The duke was charged with defending both Stirling and Edinburgh from the forces of Lord Mar during the Jacobite rebellion in 1715. Argyll opposed Mar at the Battle of Sheriffmuir in November, and although the outcome was indecisive, it effectively put an end to Mar's challenge and to the campaign of the Old Pretender.

Bute's formidable uncles took charge of his education after his father's death, and the boy spent his school holidays on their English estates, being nurtured as a member of the English rather than the Scottish aristocracy. He was at Eton from 1724 to 1730, a near contemporary of William Pitt, two of the Grenville brothers (one the future Earl Temple of Stowe) and Horace Walpole, all of whom would eventually become his political enemies. While at Eton, Bute struck up a friendship with Thomas Worsley of Hovingham in Yorkshire; both men would later work closely with Sir William Chambers. He built on this classical foundation, not at Oxford or Cambridge, as might have been expected, but at the University of Leiden in the Netherlands. He initially studied law, but was increasingly interested in natural sciences, a specialism of the university where Linnaeus would subsequently work. A fellow Scottish student of Bute's, Isaac Lawson, became a friend of Linnaeus, and financed the printing of Linnaeus's *Systema Naturae* with Jan Frederick Gronovius. Bute corresponded with both Lawson and Gronovius on botanical matters, and remained in contact with this influential centre of botany for years after leaving university. In July 1745, for instance, Bute wrote to Gronovius saying that Linnaeus 'has really in a very short time done more to embellish that lovely science than all the united pens of his forerunners'.[8]

Bute's lifelong interest in botany and horticulture had been encouraged in boyhood by both his father and his uncles. The Crichton-Stuart family, former stewards to the kings of Scotland, had lived on the Isle of Bute off the west coast of Scotland since the thirteenth century, but it was while Cobham and Bridgeman were gardening at Stowe that the 2nd Earl of Bute built Mount Stuart between 1716 and 1721 (it was subsequently destroyed by fire in 1877 and replaced by the present Victorian mansion). He also began laying out the 'Policies', a Scottish word for pleasure grounds, planting elms, hornbeam and elders in a network of rides not dissimilar to the avenues at Stowe, as can be seen from a bird's-eye view of Bridgeman's 1720 layout. The earl worked on a grand scale, requiring 4,000 'allars' (or alders) to be imported from Holland.[9]

On his return from his European travels, Bute put a toe into the political world, becoming Commissioner of the Police for Scotland and a Scottish representative peer, like his father before him; in 1738, he was nominated to the Order of the Thistle. He was sufficiently entrenched in court circles by 1737 to be present at the funeral of Queen Caroline.

More significantly, both for his future happiness and eventually for his financial security, he married the heiress Mary Wortley Montagu in August 1736, just a few months after Frederick wed Augusta. Bute's new wife was the daughter of the celebrated writer, traveller and medical pioneer Lady Mary Wortley Montagu. She had her children inoculated against smallpox, having observed the success of preventative doses during her travels in Turkey, and it was her example that inspired Queen Caroline to follow suit. A renowned wit and beauty, she eloped in August 1712 with Sir Edward Wortley Montagu, and was friendly with Hervey, the Duchess of Marlborough and Alexander Pope. For a few years, she was a prominent figure at the courts of George I and the then Prince of Wales until Caroline took offence at a satirical poem written by Lady Mary. She lived an irregular life, separating from her husband in 1739 to live in Italy with her lover, Francesco Algarotti.

Charmed by Frederick when she visited him in Hanover, she was less impressed when they met again in England. In the summer of 1732, she wrote a ballad satirising Frederick as a puppy who has a broken bottle (Miss Anne Vane) tied to his tail. A well-intentioned bystander, Lady Mary's friend, Hervey, tries to untie the bottle but is well and truly bitten in the process.[10] She also ridiculed the Whig opposition in another poem, written in 1734, for setting up Frederick as a golden calf.[11]

Despite her elopement as a young woman, and the irregularities in her own life, Lady Mary and her husband opposed their daughter marrying Bute, as they didn't regard the impoverished young peer as sparkling enough a match. It was, however, to be a successful marriage, which produced a large family. That Mary, Countess of Bute, was a woman of character can be seen from another Reynolds portrait in the family's collection at Mount Stuart. Painted in 1777, it shows the countess, by then a woman in her sixties, out on a walk in the park at Luton Hoo, again with mature trees in the background. A small spaniel plays about the feet of the countess, who wears a rich cream silk gown, half hidden with a black net cloak. She is turned three-quarters towards the onlooker, her hands clasped in business-like fashion at her waist and a firm, appraising look on her face. This, you sense, was a woman who was very much Bute's equal. She also brought him enormous wealth from her father's coal-mining concerns on his death in 1761, as described by Horace Walpole. It was, he said, 'a fortune, that ... was estimated at one million three hundred and forty thousand pounds'.[12]

The first phase of Bute's political career was to be short-lived, when he made the mistake of backing the Duke of Argyll rather than his younger uncle, the Earl of Islay, in a dispute with Sir Robert Walpole. Walpole's son, Horace, gives a customarily sharp description of the brothers in his *Memoirs of King George II*, claiming that they had 'little in common, but the love of command. The elder brother was graceful in his figure, ostentatious in his behaviour, impetuous in his passions, prompt to insult, even where he had wit to wound and eloquence to confound; and what is seldom seen, a miser as early as a hero.' By contrast, Walpole adds that the much-praised gardener Islay was, nevertheless, 'slovenly in his person, mysterious, not to say with an air of guilt in his deportment, slow, steady where suppleness did not better answer his purpose, revengeful, and if artful, at least, not ingratiating. He loved power too well to hazard it by ostentation, and money so little, that he neither spared it to gain friends or to serve them.'[13] Much of Bute's later troubles may be intelligible, if Walpole is indeed correct in his summing up of the uncles who had so much influence over the young Scot. Matters came to a head between Argyll, Islay and Walpole when the latter proposed draconian legislation to deal with rioting and the lynch-mob murder of a British captain,

Porteous, in Edinburgh in 1736. Ultimately, Walpole was forced to back down on the severe measures planned, with Argyll, unlike Islay, taking the view that Walpole's stock was falling.[14] Argyll was more outspoken than Islay in his opposition to Walpole, over the next few years withdrawing his support and criticising the Prime Minister's pacific foreign policy over the Spanish war. Islay, writes Walpole, 'attained the sole authority in Scotland by making himself useful to Sir Robert Walpole, and preserved it by being formidable to the Pelhams. The former had disgusted the zealous Whigs in Scotland by throwing himself into the arms of a man of such equivocal principles; the Earl pretended to return to it, by breaking with his brother when that Duke quarrelled with Sir Robert.'[15] Bute backed Argyll, incurred Walpole's wrath and failed to be re-elected in 1741.

Out of political favour and short of cash (it would be another twenty years before his money problems were relieved), Bute retired with his wife and growing family to his ancestral home on the Isle of Bute. He returned to his botanical studies, corresponding with other botanists in Europe, including Peter Collinson. The American shrub *Stuartia*, which first bloomed in England in 1742, was named after Bute. He also put his considerable knowledge into practice on his estate; his journals between 1739 and 1744 reveal how much time and thought he gave to the gardens, as he continued planting ash, oak and sycamore through the Policies during the 1730s and 1740s, and created the Lime Tree Avenue which runs down to the Clyde.[16]

But Bute remained an ambitious man, and neither he nor his wife wanted to remain indefinitely out of public affairs. The 1745 rebellion gave him the spur he needed; to avoid being accused of Jacobite sympathies, he sailed with his family back across the Clyde, and travelled south, never to return to Scotland.

He had neither the money nor the influence to live in central London, nor to rejoin the royal court. Initially, he rented a house at Twickenham, where he was to be seen looking for botanical specimens among the hedges and paths alongside the River Thames. Despite their political differences over Walpole, Bute's younger uncle, 3rd Duke of Argyll since the death of his older brother in 1743, made over to Bute Caen Wood (now called Kenwood), on Hampstead Heath. The estate was admired by Bute's mother-in-law, who wrote to her daughter in August 1749, 'I very well remember Caen Wood House, and cannot wish you in a more agreeable place. It would be a great pleasure to me to see my grand children run about in the gardens. I do not question Lord Bute's good taste in the improvements round it.'[17] It was, however, from the rented property in Twickenham that Bute set out to the Egham races in the summer of 1747.

As well as being six years Frederick's junior, Bute had been out of political life since before the fall of Walpole, and so must have seemed pleasantly untarnished by the world-weariness of many of the prince's courtiers. The fact that Bute had lost office partly as a result of his opposition to Frederick's old aggressor would also have been in his favour.

The two men found that they had much in common, and it is no coincidence that Frederick began to work more intensively on Kew shortly after meeting Bute. Their budding friendship and shared taste for amateur dramatics was surveyed acidly by both Horace Walpole and Lord Chesterfield, the latter writing that Bute 'soon got to be at the head of the little, idle, frivolous and dissipated Court. He was the Intendant of balls, the Coryphaeus of plays, in which he acted himself, and so grew into a sort of favourite of that merry Prince'.[18] Walpole, as ever, was able to cap most observers in spite, claiming that by 1748 Bute 'had fallen in love with his own figure, which he produced at masquerades in becoming dresses, and in plays which he acted in private companies with a set of his own relations'.[19]

One such entertainment was performed by the prince's children in 1749 at Cliveden. The masque was Joseph Addison's *Cato*, about the Roman republican statesman, and was highly political. The prologue, thought to have been written either by Frederick or Bute, contains significant lines that were recited by Frederick's son, Prince George (the future George III).

> A boy in *England* born – in England bred;
> Where freedom well becomes the earliest state,
> For there the love of liberty's innate.[20]

'England', 'freedom', 'liberty' – these were words intended to strike a chord with Whigs and Tories alike, showing that Frederick wanted both parties on side as he planned his succession and contended with his father, helped by men such as Bute.

The importance of the close friendship of the two men was recognised by Bute's mother-in-law. Lady Mary Wortley Montagu, once against her daughter marrying Bute, began to take a different tack as, twelve years later, she saw her son-in-law making headway in royal circles. She wrote to Lady Bute in July 1748, saying, 'I am very glad you are admitted into the conversation of the Prince and Princess. It is a favour that you ought to cultivate for the good of your family, which is now numerous, and it may one day be of great advantage. I think Lord Bute much in the right to endeavour the continuance of it, and it would be imprudent of you to neglect what may be of great use to your children.' She ends the letter, significantly, with a reference to Bute's knowledge of gardening. 'I wish … Lord Bute would be so good to chuse me the best book of practical gardening extant.' Lady Mary's letters complain frequently that she never hears from Lady Bute, borne out by the fact that she makes the same request for 'a book of practical gardening' on Christmas Day 1748 and again in March 1749.[21]

The Bute marriage was proving more fruitful than she had expected, both personally and politically, and her letters suggest that she now applauded her daughter's decision. Moreover, with King George II past his mid-sixties, Frederick was once again looking like the horse to back, as she wrote to her husband in May 1749. 'I am very glad my daughter's conduct answers the opinion I ever had of her understanding. I do not say it to lessen the praise she deserves, but I realy [sic] think here is some due to Lord Bute. It is seldom that the affections of a man of his age continue so many years. I think her much in the right to cultivate the Princess's favour, but in general have no great faith in court friendships.' The latter comment may spring from her having been expelled from court circles for the unwise satire on Caroline. Nevertheless, the letter concludes that she remembers 'Lord Bathurst's epigram, that Princes are the sons of Kings'.[22]

By the late 1740s, Frederick was gathering around him a new court. After a period of arm's-length harmony, he went back into open opposition to the king from 1747. In preparing to reign, the prince chose men who shared his interests in buildings and their estates. Bute was a horticulturalist, who had done much to improve Mount Stuart. Others included Sir Thomas Robinson of Rokeby, architect of the west wing of Castle Howard, which was owned by his father-in-law, the Earl of Carlisle. Robinson's appreciation of what the prince had achieved at Carlton House has been quoted in a previous chapter. Frederick also appointed to his council Lord Bathurst, the creator of the park and gardens at Cirencester, and significantly a Tory. In his garden, Bathurst had erected a statue of Queen Anne in 1741 in line with the house and the parish church, indicative of his support for the Stuarts, and the close relationship between Church and State, an aspect played down by the Whigs.[23] The inclusion of Bathurst in his inner coterie was a clear shift away from the Whig position on the part of Frederick. George Bubb Dodington, who had completed Vanbrugh's Eastbury, was also reappointed, this time becoming the Treasurer of the Chamber. Dodington, the man who had lent Frederick the money to buy Carlton House, had been sacked as his political secretary back in 1733. The prince's letter to Dodington is a rare survival of his correspondence, most of which was burned by Augusta on his death. As in the case of Lyttelton, Frederick proved himself too willing to listen to malicious rumours, a fact he admits himself in this rather poignant letter.

> My good Dodington ... What an ungrateful part am I to play. I wish a man well, I think him an honest man, and I must tell him the stories that publickly are told here of him ... I mean publickly are whispered about him ... But as one can't in this wicked age be sure of anything, or anybody ... I should acquaint you with it ... for I should always tell a man what is told to me behind his back...They report confidently about town that everything is easy since you are gone, and therefore you as the disturber are to be cut ... If you was wicked enough to intend to hurt anybody you are too wise to do it so grossly; therefore if I do not see it writ by your own hand I'll never believe it. This was an attempt to make me disgrace you, which I take to be my own disgracing, if upon a little tattle of some few people a prince will give up a friend, or servant. Any prince may be cheated by people they have confidence in ... but weak is the prince, and can never be well served, if he believes too quick ...[24]

This curious mixture of self-criticism and self-justification, which does more to diminish Frederick's standing than any amount of Hervey's vitriol, didn't prevent a rupture between Dodington and the prince at the time. It must, however, have served to appease

Dodington, who was prepared to rejoin the prince's entourage in 1749; he was promised a salary of £2,000 a year, plus 'a Peerage and the Seals of the southern province' on Frederick's accession to the throne. In July, Dodington wrote in his diary that 'this day I arrived at Kew about eleven o'clock. The Prince received me most kindly, and told me he desired me to come into his service upon any terms, and by any title I pleased: that he meant to put the principal direction of his affairs into my hands: and what he could not do for me in his present situation, must be made up to me in futurity. All this in a manner so noble and frank, and with expressions so full of affection and regard, that I ought not to remember them but as a debt, and to perpetuate my gratitude.'[25]

Dodington was no doubt looking over his shoulder as he wrote this diary entry, but he was to prove a faithful friend to the prince, before and after his death. The prince's closest political councillors would be Dodington and also the 2nd Earl of Egmont, son of the Egmont whose memoirs provide such a colourful picture of the court of George II. It is clear, however, from Dodington's diary that Bute was a constant presence throughout the next two years; whenever Dodington dined with the prince at Kew, Cliveden or Carlton House, Bute was also sure to be there. In particular, Frederick turned his attention to his garden at Kew, where he would start to embody his vision of Britain for the future. In this, Bute would be deeply involved.

CHAPTER 11

'Gardening and Planting Have Lost Their Best Friend'

As he set about appointing a new team of advisors, the men likely to be his ministers once he ascended the throne, Frederick also started work again in earnest at Kew. Previously, he had been less bold there than at Carlton House, devoting himself to the house rather than to the garden. He had been content to lay out wide lawns and avenues, but now he wanted to create a country estate suitable for a king, where he could express complex philosophical and political ideas. Frederick chose to involve his associates in his horticultural efforts, purposefully to emphasise that the garden had a political message; those who would serve also had to understand that connection. Courtiers called to Kew were expected to work outside, as Dodington wrote in two diary entries in February 1750. 'Worked in the new walk at Kew,' he says one day, and then, on the next, with all the despair of a fat man and a bon viveur, 'All of us, men, women, and children, worked at the same place – a cold dinner.' On another occasion, Dodington spent a whole week with Frederick at Kew.[1]

Frederick went back to the drawing board in the late 1740s at Kew, virtually over-riding what he had previously done there, and creating an ethos very different from that of Carlton House. Leasing the adjacent property to his mother's garden at Richmond had always had its problems. Despite his fierce competition with Caroline in both horticultural as well as personal terms, he had curiously chosen so far to display his alternative iconography not next door at Kew, but in London at Carlton House.

Separated from the Richmond garden by the ironically named Love Lane, Frederick's Kew was the more challenging. Caroline had benefited from a broader site, and the added advantage of a view across the river to the Duke of Northumberland's Syon House and gardens. Consulting the genius of the place was harder for the prince whose long, narrow garden overlooked undistinguished meadowland. Sir William Chambers, Augusta's Scottish architect, subsequently outlined the difficulties the gardens posed and Frederick's achievement there.

> The gardens of Kew are not very large. Nor is their situation by any means advantageous; as it is low, and commands no prospects. Originally the ground was one continued dead flat: the soil was in general barren, and without wood or water. With so many disadvantages it was not easy to produce any thing even tolerable in gardening: but princely munificence, guided by a director, equally skilled in cultivating the earth, and in the politer arts, overcame all difficulties.[2]

Although much of what Frederick planned was still in its infancy at his death, his aims for Kew, as Chambers suggested, were elaborate and expensive. He bought or leased another forty-two acres, and laid out and planted an additional thirty-two acres by his death in 1751.[3] Augusta would eventually garden an estate of 110 acres. The garden was intended to be cosmopolitan, with wide-ranging cultural references, reflecting both the prince's interests and Britain's emerging role as an international power.

The antiquary and engraver, George Vertue, employed by Frederick from 1748 to catalogue Charles I's scattered picture collection, is a source of information about Frederick's thinking and ambitions at the period. Vertue hints at the prince's frustration at his exclusion from the military excursions in which his younger brother played a part in the 1740s; he tries to make up for a lack of practical experience by learning about military history. George II's success at Dettingen may also have made Frederick realise that a king needed to be a man of action, and not just a man of culture. Vertue records that 'in a long conference with his Royal Highness – the Pr.of Wales – ... he gave me a relation of his own attachment and desire of knowledge of all late. & former actions in the armyes abroad in Germany now in this late warrs as also in former warrs in Queen Anns time. [He] amuses his time & mind in knowledge and study & says this he proposes for not only his present use but for his son or posterity when ever warrs should happen. To be ready for their use.'

In October 1750, Vertue travelled from Leicester House, the prince's London headquarters, to Kew by coach, and described his visit, using his singular punctuation and spelling. It gives an impression of the scope of Frederick's work on the gardens and also of his active involvement in what his gardeners were doing.

> There when wee, had done to come into the gardens. where he was directing the plantations of trees exotics with the workmen – adviseing & assisting. where wee were receivd gratiously and freely walking and attend the Prince from place to place – for 2 or three hours. Seeing his plantations told his contrivances designs of his improvemts in his Gardens. water works. canal &c great numbers of people labouring there his new Chinesia summer hous. Painted in their stile & ornaments the story of Confusius and his doctrines &c.[4]

The House of Confucius was one of several major building projects that Frederick had in train during the last years of his life, and was a considerably more solid structure than the Chinese Temple at Stowe, which was later removed by Earl Temple.[5] In his 1763 account of the buildings of Kew, Chambers describes it as an octagonal building of two stories, and attributes its design to Joseph Goupy, who submitted a bill to Frederick in 1750 for several designs, including a Chinese arch. Some art historians believe it to have been a youthful work by Chambers, who subsequently denied it, embarrassed by an example of his youthful enthusiasm for the rococo style.[6]

Invoking the life and work of Confucius was meaningful. The Chinese philosopher's teachings on political morality were well-known and admired by the educated classes in the eighteenth century.[7] The House of Confucius equates with Cobham's Temple of Ancient Virtue at Stowe and shows the prince displaying knowledge of philosophy and political thought, and assigning the philosopher's moral virtue to himself. Although Chambers' *Dissertation on Oriental Gardening* was not published until 1773, over twenty years after Frederick's death, the prince would have been familiar with the ideas expressed by the architect. Based on Chambers's own experiences of travelling in China, it encapsulates the virtues of Chinese thought and gardening. 'Amongst the Chinese,' he wrote, 'gardening is held in much higher esteem, than it is in Europe: they rank a perfect work in that art, with the great productions of the human understanding; and say, that is efficacy in moving the passions, yields to that of few other arts whatever. Their gardeners are not only botanists, but also painters and philosophers; having a thorough knowledge of the human mind, and of the arts by which its strongest feelings are excited.'[8] In building the House of Confucius, Frederick was endorsing this view.

The most ambitious of his projects, sadly never realised, was a Mount Parnassus. This would have been adorned with statues of ancient and modern heroes and philosophers, and would have been Frederick's interpretation of Cobham's Temple of British Worthies, while simultaneously evoking the Temple of Ancient Virtue. Vertue was commissioned by the prince to find or make drawings himself of ancient and modern philosophers who were to have been paired, such as Edward III with Arminius, a German chieftain who fought the Romans, and King Alfred with Lycurgus, who also features in the Temple of Ancient Virtue at Stowe. Archimedes was to be put with Newton and Horace with Pope. Lord Cobham, Frederick's long-term ally, had died in 1749; he, too, found a place in Frederick's pantheon, beside the Roman general, Lucullus.[9]

The iconography of Stowe was in Frederick's mind as he planned these buildings. Mount Parnassus would have complemented the House of Confucius as the Temple of British Worthies did the Temple of Ancient Virtue. This scheme was devised by Frederick shortly after the construction of the Gothic Temple of Liberty at Stowe. The temple, one of Cobham's last contributions, symbolised the imagined British liberties of Saxon legend, overturned by the Normans, threatened again by the Stuarts, and, at the time of its construction, by the government corruption against which the prince himself had also stood.[10] It would, however, be the last positive allusion to Stowe at Kew, for within a few years the political landscape and alliances shifted again. Augusta's work on Kew, while paying tribute to her husband's founding involvement, was to have a very different iconography, and would directly conflict with that of Cobham's nephew, Earl Temple.

The third of Frederick's major projects was the purchase, through the British resident in Florence, of thirteen late sixteenth-century life-sized marble statues by Pietro Francavilla. The figures included Apollo, Zephyr, Pan, Ceres, Flora and Proteus, between them symbolising Frederick's vision for Kew as a garden which would combine the artistic (Apollo/Pan) with the botanic (Flora) and the agricultural (Ceres). Proteus represented the Nature's own energy. The statues arrived after Frederick's death in March 1751 and were never taken out of their crates at Kew.[11]

Frederick planted at Kew and simultaneously increased the size of his household; it grew from forty senior people (that is, on a salary of over £100 per annum) in 1736 to sixty-four in 1747 and seventy-one in 1751. The source of payment and the salaries varied; half of Dodington's generous £2,000 a year was paid out of Frederick's own pocket rather than from his Civil List allowance. Frederick always borrowed heavily; in 1738, for instance, he took out a £30,000 loan from three London bankers on tin revenue securities. He repaid the loan in 1742, but he wasn't always so punctilious. Thirty years after the prince's death, a Berkshire gentleman wrote to William Pitt the Younger that he estimated himself 'a loser of £20,000 by my father's connection with the late Prince of Wales to whom he was a fixed and great associate'. This hefty debt was incurred while Frederick was living at Cliveden.[12]

His plans for his succession would eventually cause problems for his son, the future George III, especially when implemented by the Scot, Lord Bute. Frederick, like Cobham, had hated the inherent corruption of Walpole's government, which he believed to be lining its own pockets. But what Frederick envisaged was not what Walpole's enemies had favoured in the 1730s and 1740s; they sought still to keep the monarch answerable to the Whig aristocracy, and contested the Tory belief in the divine right of kings. The fluidity of the Tory and Whig positions was revealed in the aftermath of the Excise Crisis of 1733, when both Tories and Whigs espoused the ideas expressed by Bolingbroke in *The Idea of the Patriot King*. Frederick made it the basis of his eldest son's education, impressed by Bolingbroke's emphasis on the public good in opposition to the pursuit of private interest. The prince contrasted his own approachability with his father's remoteness, which was compounded by George's frequent visits to Hanover, and enshrined the importance of his role as a British prince in both his gardens at Carlton House and at Kew.

Frederick now visualised a monarchy that would present itself as above party, rather than kow-tow, as he believed his father and grandfather had done, to the Whig oligarchy. He began negotiating with the Tories, and during a meeting with a group of them at Leicester House in 1747, he promised 'totally to abolish for the future all distinction of party, and so far as it lies in his power, (and when it does lie in his power), to take away all proscriptions from any set of men whatever, who are friends to the constitution'.[13] Frederick wanted to make the king master in his own house, devising policy as he would lay out a garden, by preparing fresh soil. But his ideas, influenced by Bolingbroke, also echo the words of Robert Filmer's *Patriarcha*, which was originally written in 1628. It was published by the Tories in 1680 to reinforce the case for the divine right of kings at a time when the newly formed Whigs were attempting to exclude the future James II from the succession on the grounds of his Catholicism. Filmer wrote 'in defence of Kingly Government, and of his … Majesties lawful and just rights … trampled upon by a domineering faction', and said he reverenced 'Monarchy above all other forms of government'.[14]

Frederick used political patronage to build up a solid core of supporters. Many of his appointments were of people closely related to MPs who might therefore be expected to give the prince their vote in any conflict with the government.[15] Henry Pelham's government was believed by Frederick to control all his father's political decisions, as Walpole had previously done. Frederick feared that, like his father in 1727, he would have to continue with the previous monarch's Prime Minister. And indeed that was what did happen in due course; the Duke of Newcastle remained at the helm for two years after George II's death in 1760. The nomination of Newcastle as godfather to George and Caroline's second son had caused the breach between George I and the then Prince of Wales in 1717. Yet the two were later reconciled; when George II died, Newcastle wrote that he had 'lost the best … master and the best friend that subject ever had'.[16]

Frederick's somewhat motley band of followers was described by Walpole as being 'composed of the refuse of every party'.[17] At the end of the 1740s, the cohort consisted mainly of those who were out of office, including both Tories and disaffected Whigs such as Lord Granville who had fallen out with the Pelham brothers. In 1750, Lord Bute was made a gentleman of the bedchamber, believed to be an over-promotion by both Dodington and Egmont, neither of whom had any idea of the power that Bute would wield within a few years. But it was the canny Scottish peer who helped to set the prince on a sounder financial footing by placing his affairs in the hands of the banker Thomas Coutts. Egmont was Frederick's intended Prime Minister, while the trimmer Dodington recorded in his diary his efforts at bringing the Tories on board.

> I had set on foot, by means of the Earl of Shaftesbury, a project for a union between the independent Whigs and Tories, by a writing, renouncing all tincture of Jacobitism, and affirming short, but constitutional and revolutional principles. I had given his Lordship the paper: his good heart and understanding made him indefatigable, and so far successful, that there were good grounds to hope for a happy issue.[18]

Other horse-trading included a proposed bill, accepted by the Tories and drafted by Egmont, that Frederick would accept a fixed allowance of £800,000 a year rather than the varying amount given to George II. Egmont was also concerned to work out a detailed timetable for the first fortnight of Frederick's reign. Because virtually all Frederick's papers were destroyed on his death by Augusta, it is hard to be entirely certain about his intentions. There are, however, insights to be gained from copies of correspondence and minutes of meetings kept by Egmont. These scraps of conversations, together with Dodington's diary and a letter from Frederick to his eldest son (the only paper not destroyed by Augusta), provide insight into what Frederick was trying to achieve in the months before his death.

It can be seen from Egmont's papers that Bolingbroke, now an old man, still had the ear of the prince. Egmont records discussions in October 1750 at Cliveden, during which 'the Prince said he would lay aside the Duke [of Cumberland] in the command of the Army as soon as he came to the Crown, and that Lord Bolingbroke had advised him strongly to do it ... That he intended to put his second son Edward in his place. Against this I remonstrated to the utmost, and told him that it was dangerous to make a second son of the Crown head of the army.'

There are intriguing glimpses of the prince's thinking. The final of four drafts of Frederick's succession speech to parliament refers to the fact that 'the distinguished wealth and power of the British Empire are apparently derived from the peculiar privileges you enjoy'. This early use of the phrase 'British Empire' shows Frederick looking beyond aristocratic privilege at home to the wider world, as he was doing in his garden at Kew. He talks of separating Britain from Hanover and considers sending one of his sons to the West Indies with the title Duke of Virginia, to bind the colonies closer to the monarchy. He also looks at pragmatic monarchs abroad, such as the early-seventeenth-century French king, Henry IV, for whom Paris was worth a Mass. Henry's conversion to Catholicism was equated in Frederick's mind with his own accommodations with the Tories; he considered the latter a worthwhile price to pay to secure an easy passage on his succession. 'Let us remember both Henry IV and Sulli [*sic*], in all times these are our models,' wrote Frederick to Egmont. 'Let us follow 'em in most all, except their extravagencys.'

There seems to have been thinly veiled hostility between Dodington and Egmont, Frederick's chief lieutenants in the year before his death. Egmont records that Dodington's job as Treasurer of the Chamber is 'a new created place about the Prince – [Dodington's] manner cool and false to me – presumes a great deal – and hints of measures of quiet contrary to our system – afraid of his being abused – of our getting before him in opinion'.[19]

Indeed, Egmont's diary notes and correspondence hint at a less than happy ship, although Walpole records that the Cobham cousins (Sir George Lyttelton and the Grenvilles) 'had just patched up their peace with the Prince'.[20] It is hard to know whether King Frederick I would have been a significantly superior king to George II. Impetuous and at times irresponsible, he was, however, a more artistic and cultured man than his father, more intelligent than his son and less of a reprobate than his grandson, George IV. He was frustrated at every turn by his father and by the role of Prince of Wales, which remains to this day a difficult anomaly. Nevertheless, there is a sense in reading about Frederick and his wide cultural interests that he might have grown into the job as his son would do.

But that was not to be, for in March 1751, the prince, in Egmont's words, 'was taken ill at Kew. After staying all day in the garden til night, in the damp rain and hail to look at his workmen.'[21] An entry in Dodington's diary on 6 March recorded, like Egmont, that the prince had caught cold at Kew, and added that he was subsequently blooded – a less than helpful medical treatment that for centuries laid waste to Europe's royal families and resulted in Louis XIV, for instance, being succeeded by his great-grandson.[22] Walpole reported that after catching cold, the prince recovered sufficiently to attend the House of Lords on 12 March. 'He went to Carlton House to unrobe, put on only a light frock, and went to Kew, where he walked some time; and returning to Carlton House, laid down upon a couch for three hours in a ground room next to the garden, caught a fresh cold and relapsed that night.' Frederick's death was attributed by physicians to a burst abscess, incurred by being hit on the chest by a tennis ball, according to Walpole, three years before.[23] Other accounts have it that the offending ball struck during a game of cricket.

During Frederick's two-week illness, the king sent to enquire after his health. Augusta, pregnant with the couple's ninth child, sat up with him over several nights. He was also attended by his eldest son, George, to whom he was devoted, as is clear from affectionate, paternal letters he sent the boy over the years. On 20 March, Dodington wrote in his diary that 'I was told at Leicester House, at three o'clock, that the Prince was much better, and had slept eight hours in the night before, while, I suppose, the mortification was forming; for he died this evening a quarter before ten o'clock'. Graphically, another diary entry noted that 'his physicians, Wilmot, and Lee … either would not see or did not know the consequences of the black thrush, which appeared in his mouth, and quite down his throat. Their ignorance, or their knowledge of his distemper render them equally inexcusable for not calling in more assistance.'[24]

Frederick's mother, Queen Caroline, had once said to Hervey that her first born was 'the greatest beast, in the whole world, and … I most heartily wish he was out of it'.[25] Now the prince was indeed dead, and, at forty-four, ten years younger than his mother had been at her death. 'Thus died Frederick Prince of Wales! having resembled his pattern the Black Prince in nothing but dying before his father,' wrote Horace Walpole.

As soon as he was dead, Lord North was sent to notify it to the King who was playing at cards: he immediately went down to Lady Yarmouth [his mistress en titre at the time], looking extremely pale and shocked, and only said, "Il est mort!" He sent a very kind message to the Princess, and another the next morning in writing by the Lord in Waiting, Lord Lincoln. She received him alone; sitting with her eyes fixed; thanked the King much, and said she would write as soon as she was able; in the meantime, recommended her miserable self and children to him.[26]

Frederick's funeral took place in April, 'performed with the usual state', according to Walpole.[27] There was little precedent for such an occasion as it was the first death of a Prince of Wales since that of Prince Henry, son of Charles I, in 1612, so the ceremonial used for Prince George of Denmark, husband to Queen Anne, was selected. The body was embalmed and placed within a coffin of wood lined with lead, covered in crimson velvet and decorated with gilt hinges and nails. The prince's bowels were placed in a velvet-covered box and buried in Henry VII's Chapel in Westminster Abbey. Changes were authorised to morning and evening prayers in the royal chapels, and a railed walkway was constructed from the House of Lords to the abbey door. The court went into mourning from the end of March to September, although Egmont believed the English court 'to be utterly lacking in even the semblance of grief'. Warrant books from the Lord Chamberlain's department show that £12,080 6s 7d was spent on the funeral for Queen Caroline, while a bare £3,000 went on Frederick's obsequies, plus a further £2,250 for six yards of black satin and two yards of white for eight escutcheons of the prince's arms.[28]

The occasion was marred by disputes over a number of issues, including who should accompany the prince's coffin to the abbey. 'Lord Limerick consulted with me about walking at the funeral. By the Earl Marshal's order, published in the common newspaper of the day ... neither he as an Irish Peer, nor I as a Privy Counsellor, could walk,' wrote Dodington.[29] There was a further, indecorous argument between the abbey clergy and the College of Arms officers as to who should have the funeral furniture after service, a dispute which was settled by the Privy Council to the satisfaction of neither body.[30]

Dodington, disappointed of a political future by Frederick's death, was the chief, if perhaps not the most reliable witness to his master's funeral; he regarded the occasion as a succession of slights, which 'sunk me so low, that, for the first hour, I was incapable of making any observation'. The bedchamber attendants who were ordered to attend the corpse and bowels in the Prince's Lodging in the Lords overnight before the funeral were not fed, but at their own expense 'were forc'd to bespeak a great cold dinner from a common tavern in the neighbourhood'. The day itself went hardly better, in Dodington's view.

> The procession began, and except the Lords appointed ... to hold the pall and attend the chief mourner, and those of his own domestics when they were called in their ranks, there was not one English lord, not one Bishop, and there was but one Irish Lord (Viscount Limerick), two sons of Dukes (Earl of Drumlanrig and Lord Robert Bertie), one Baron's son (Mr Edgecumbe), and two Privy Counsellors (Sir John Rushout and myself), out of their great bodies, to make a show of duty to a Prince, so great in rank and expectation.
>
> While we were in the House of Lords, it rain'd very hard ... when we came into Palace Yard the way to the abbey was lined with soldiers, but the [managers] had not afforded a covering of rough deals overhead ... We went in at the S. E. door, and turned short into Henry the VIIth's chapel. The service was perform'd without either anthem or organ. So ended the sad day.

And, he added, 'The Duke of Somerset was chief mourner, notwithstanding the flourishing state of the Royal family'.[31] This may, however, have been down to royal protocol rather than an intended affront to the prince's memory; the Duchess of Somerset was chief mourner at Queen Mary's funeral in 1695 (accompanied by celebrated music by Henry Purcell). Yet Prince Charles, the future Charles II, did lead the mourning at his older brother's funeral in 1612, and it is surprising that neither the Duke of Cumberland nor Frederick's eldest sons, by then almost in their teens, were present. According to *The Gentleman's Magazine*, more peers, including Lords Egmont and Bute, attended the funeral than were listed by Dodington. Nevertheless, it does seem that Frederick was treated in death by his father much as he had been in life. In December 1751, Frederick's youngest sister, Louisa, by then Queen of Denmark, also died, and also of a parturition hernia like her mother. On receiving his daughter's final letter to him, the king broke out, recalled Walpole, 'into warm expressions of passion and tenderness. He said, "This has been a fatal year to my family! I lost my eldest son – but I am glad of it."'[32]

Frederick's obituaries gave him the same kind of mixed press he had received in life, although most stressed that he was good natured and a kindly father. Lord Chesterfield wrote to his son that 'the prince of Wales ... was more beloved for his affability and good nature, than esteemed for his steadiness and conduct'.[33] Pitt, for some years estranged from the prince, lauded him in the Commons and praised the king for the courage with which he had shouldered the death of his son. An unknown London preacher claimed that Frederick 'had no great parts, but he had great virtues; and indeed, they degenerated into vices; he was very generous, but I hear his generosity has ruined a great many people: and then his condescension was such that he kept very bad company.' Tobias Smollett, writing six years later in his 1757 *History of England*, claimed that 'this excellent Prince ... was possessed of very amiable quality which could engage the affection of the people – a tender and obliging husband, a fond parent, a kind master, liberal, generous, candid and humane; a munificent patron of the arts, an unwearied friend to merit; well disposed to assert the rights of mankind in general and warmly attached to the interest of Great Britain'.[34]

Frederick's most famous epitaph is a bleak poem, thought to have been composed by a Jacobite.

Here lies poor Fred, who was alive and is dead;
Had it been his father, I had much rather;
Had it been his brother, still better than another;
Had it been his sister, nobody would have missed her;
Had it been the whole generation, so much the better for the
   nation.
But since it is Fred, who was alive and is dead,
There is no more to be said.

The most enthusiastic encomiums for the prince came from the horticultural community, by whom he was regarded with far greater respect. Frederick was mourned by Peter Collinson, who for over forty years supplied the British aristocracy and botanic gardens with rare seeds and plants from an American nurseryman, John Bartram. Collinson wrote to Bartram, 'The death of our late excellent Prince of Wales has cast a great damp over the nation. Gardening and planting have lost their best friend and encourager; for the Prince had delighted in that rational amusement a long while; but lately he had a laudable and princely ambition to excel all others.'[35] Another leading horticulturalist, Dr John Mitchell, echoed Collinson, asserting that 'Planting and Botany in England would be poorer for his passing'.[36]

It was not only gardening and botany which would be 'poorer for passing'; John Stuart, 3rd Earl of Bute, stood to lose all that he had gained by that 'odd accident' at the Egham Races. Only recently admitted to the prince's inner circle, and with no English constituency of interest, he must have believed his hopes of political preferment, and of regular income, dashed by Frederick's death. This was certainly the opinion of his mother-in-law, Lady Mary Wortley Montagu, who wrote in a letter that 'Bute's career had rested solely on his personal favour. It now seemed to be over.'[37]

This was a reasonable view to take in the spring of 1751. But Bute had done enough to impress his patron's wife, now Dowager Princess of Wales. In time, she would find a significant place for him in her household and counsels, with major consequences for both British horticulture and politics.

CHAPTER 12

'To Play What Game She Pleased Without Observation'

By all accounts, Augusta, now Dowager Princess of Wales, soon to give birth her ninth child, was deeply shocked by her husband's death. She admitted no one 'above the degree of a Valet de Chambre' in the last days of Frederick's life and then, according to Walpole, she 'stayed four hours in the room after he was dead, before she could be convinced of it'.[1] That she had changed from a shy, mouse-like teenager into a forceful, shrewd woman is revealed by Egmont. He took the view that Augusta had excluded himself and Dodington from Frederick in his last hours to break their influence over the prince. He recorded that Augusta 'made the rest withdraw and told us that – she did not know but the King might seize the Prince's papers ... and that we might be ruined by these papers ... she pulled off the silk cover of the pillow of a couch in the Prince's dressing room to serve as a bag to put them in'. Egmont's last duty was to smuggle the offending papers out of Carlton House for Augusta, who then burned them all.[2] Egmont's account attributes Augusta's behaviour to panic, but it was a decisive gesture, demonstrating her grasp of political reality. It also suggests that Frederick had admitted her to his counsels, making her well aware that much of what he had been planning would be considered treasonable by the king.

Although a party system began to emerge from the late seventeenth century onwards, there was still no concept of a loyal opposition; opposition as a means of holding government to account for its actions remained an idea for the future. The monarchy itself was in transition from having near-absolute executive power to maintaining just a constitutional role. The animosity between the Hanoverians and their eldest sons was part and parcel of this transition, and the role of the Prince of Wales became all the more anomalous as the policy-making power of the monarch dwindled, yet in the eighteenth century political opposition from the Prince of Wales was anticipated if unwelcome. By contrast, consider the outcry if the present Prince of Wales were obviously to support the opposition party against the government. Frederick's plan to replace the government with his own placemen on his father's death, as would have happened in previous centuries, was already a questionable course of action by the 1750s, representing a break with the continuity between the reigns of his two predecessors. All the more so as Frederick appeared to consider a return to a monarchy which would hold power above party, not in the constitutional sense we understand it today, but more as his artistic role model, Charles I, had done; what, in fact, we should now see, and was feared then, as dictatorship. In planning for his succession, Frederick wanted an end to ministerial corruption, greater economy in government, the reduction of taxes and payment of the national debt.[3] All these ideas would have been anathema to George II and certainly to his ministers.

Augusta feared that the discovery of Frederick's plans, and her association with them, might well lead the king to remove her children from her, as George I had done in 1717 from her parents-in-law. She also wished to ensure that she would be made regent if George II died before her son George's eighteenth birthday. She dreaded Cumberland's appointment to the role, believing that he might then try to usurp the British throne from such a position, and exile young George to the throne of Hanover. Not only did she burn Frederick's papers, she distanced herself immediately from Egmont and Dodington, and made her peace with the Pelhams and, even more importantly, with the king, who visited her several times after Frederick's death. A mourning widow, she threw herself on George's mercies, as recounted by Walpole. At the end of March, 'the King went to see the Princess. A chair of state was placed for him, but he refused it, and sat by her on the couch, embraced and wept with her. He would not suffer the Lady Augusta to kiss his hand, but embraced her and gave it to her brothers, and told them they must be brave boys, obedient to their mother, and deserve the fortune to which they were born.'[4]

The princess carried her point; the children remained with her at Leicester House, although the king appointed Prince George's tutors and governors. Egmont was manifestly disappointed by his abrupt dismissal from Augusta's confidence. 'I now plainly see she has been flattered into a total reliance on the King,' he wrote, 'and has thought it necessary for her own purpose to abandon all the Prince's friends – which is not impolitic in her circumstances – The only fault she might have broke it decently to those who were so near her husband, and were so much concerned in it as I am, and so faithful to her and her children's interest.'[5]

Her anxiety about how the king might jump is reflected in a conversation with Augusta recorded by Dodington. '"You know," says she, "the Crown has a power of resumption of Carlton House, and gardens, for a certain sum: the King had not long since, a mind to see them ... we walk'd in the gardens and he seem'd mightily pleased with them, commended them much, and told me that he was extreme glad that I had got so very pretty a place: I said that it was a pretty place, but that the prettiness of a place was an objection to it, when one was sure not to keep it."'[6]

The only paper that Augusta didn't burn was a letter drawn up by Frederick in January 1749 to his eldest son. Her forbearance was presumably out of a sense of duty to both her husband and her child, for the contents were less than flattering to the king, and illuminate the prince's political thinking. The superscription to the letter is 'Instructions for my Son George, drawn by my-self, for his good, that of my family, and for that of his people, according to the ideas of my grand-father, and best friend, George I'. It is a letter full of affection and hints at a warm relationship between Frederick and his son, but it makes no attempt to disguise Frederick's contempt for his own father, at whom he takes several side swipes. He warns the future George III that 'flatterers, courtiers or ministers are easy to be got, but a true friend is difficult to be found'. He goes on,

If you cannot be without war, let not your ambition draw you into it ... a wise and brave prince, may often times, without armies put a stop to the confusion, which the ambitious neighbours endeavour to create. 'Tis not allways armies or fleets, that will do this. Many times 'tis done only by the weight of his authority, which can be got no other way, than by a wise settled and steady conduct.

The unsteady measures, you see, my son, have sullied and hurt the reign of your grandfather. Let your steadiness retrieve the glory of the Throne.

He exhorts George to 'convince this nation that you are not only an Englishman born and bred, but that you are also this by inclination'. Most significantly, he wants his son 'to read over carefully & often the will' of George I, the very will which George II suppressed on his accession to throne, and which envisaged the separation of Hanover from Britain. 'From that moment, Jacobitism will be in a manner rooted out [another horticultural metaphor], and you will not be forced then, to court your ministers for one job or another; as unfortunately your predecessors have been forced to do.'

The letter is a clarion call for a powerful British king, ruling in his own way. 'Remember, that Great Britain is the head of the Protestant powers, and that from the Crown alone.'[7] Power, in other words, is invested in the throne, and not in the aristocratic oligarchy which had held sway throughout his father's and grandfather's reigns. Bute's programme for George II cannot be definitively linked with Frederick's plans, largely because of the loss of his papers. There is, however, evidence in both Egmont's and Dodington's diaries that the machinations at Frederick's political headquarters, Leicester House, influenced the young Prince of Wales and Bute – and, in Lord Egmont's papers, that initially George fulfilled many of his father's wishes.[8] Frederick's letter to his son was contentious stuff, and it is surprising that Augusta left the document out of the flames that consumed the rest of the prince's papers. She presumably had some sympathy at least for Frederick's point of view, and her subsequent support for Bute's political position would seem to reinforce that.

Two months after her husband's death, Augusta gave birth to their last child, a daughter, Caroline Matilda. This is this baby whom the princess holds in her arms in a painting, *The Family of Frederick, Prince of Wales*, which she commissioned later the same year from George Knapton. The recently widowed yet assured princess is at the centre of the family group, no longer the pathetic, dependent figure caricatured by Queen Caroline in Hervey's memoirs; this is a woman pitching to be made regent should the king die during her eldest son's minority (Prince George was then thirteen). Wearing a black mantilla to indicate she is in mourning, Augusta sits as if enthroned on a raised dais, flanked by solid classical columns supporting rich velvet drapes, and with the Prince of Wales's portrait and coat of arms on the wall behind. She is surrounded by her nine children, proof both of her fertility and the strength of her fifteen-year marriage. Beside her stands her eldest daughter, Princess Augusta, a poised young woman in blue silk who stares directly, if not defiantly, at the onlooker; she has metamorphosed from the 'little rat of a girl' or the 'poor, little, ugly she-mouse' she was termed by her grandmother as a baby. The two eldest princes sit affectionately together to one side, a map of the gardens at Kew open on Prince George's knee, signifying interest in his father's legacy. The younger children play with toys, pets and musical instruments in a carefully composed picture of family harmony, presided over by a portrait of the late Prince Frederick.

Here Augusta is setting out her stall with deliberate calculation, aware that her first priority for both herself and her children was to shore up her position with the ageing, irascible king. In a way, it is surprising that she allowed such an unflattering depiction of Frederick to be included behind the family group; the prince looks bloated, self-regarding and with eyes bulging even by Hanoverian standards. It is a far cry from the romantic figure that he cut in the portraits that he himself commissioned. Was it malice aforethought, perhaps? Her over-riding aim at this point must have been to sell herself to the king, above all as a suitable mother, particularly in view of the unpleasant family precedents.

In this highly political portrait, Augusta looks confident, yet demure, with a slight blush playing about her face. Fully in control of the situation, she turns a fond gaze on her two sons and tenderly nurses Frederick's posthumous baby. And, to point the message of the picture, balancing the portrait of Frederick on the left is a statue of Britannia on the right. Augusta is underlining that she, not George II, is now unquestionably the parent of the next king, having provided four sons. She knows how to nurture a seed which will grow; no wonder she proved in time to be such an effective gardener.

There is another code in the painting. In his portrait on the wall, Frederick points with his left hand towards the White House and Kew Gardens. It almost seems that Augusta was suggesting here that she would continue what her husband began there as part of her overall strategy for herself and for her eldest son.

Augusta's tactics seem to have worked, as Dodington, quoted by Shelburne, recounted.

> The Princess acted her part with singular propriety. She lived retired without the least ostentation. The Publick supposed her occupied and attached to her numerous family. The Court was old; the Ministry was old; there was a long generation between them and the heir-apparent and his brothers and sisters. The old King, who had always been violent against his son, sought to prove himself in the right by his tenderness for the Princess. She knew admirably how to improve the appearance if not the reality of this to her advantage.

Shelburne admitted that Augusta 'had a difficult part to act', and describes her, in effect, as the model of dullness, spending her evenings 'with a very small party of select people of a certain race, more distinguished for their propriety and correctness of conduct than for their wit, and out of any political line, so as to give no offence to any party'. Under the guise of extreme decorum and submissiveness to the king, Augusta was able, believed Shelburne, 'to play what game she pleased without observation.' By being overlooked, the peer said, Augusta 'compassed all her points and gained more power than would have fallen to the lot even of an ambitious person in her situation'.[9]

Shelburne saw her as the powerful and manipulative woman who would be jeered by the crowds at her funeral in 1772. She was undoubtedly politically astute; in the years immediately following her husband's death, she kept in with the king and accepted his appointments for her eldest son. However, the king remained wary, according to Walpole. George II 'told Mr Pelham soon after [the] Prince of Wales's death: "You none of you know this woman, and you none of you will know her till I am dead." Lord Cobham told L[ady] S[uffolk] he had studied [Princess Augusta] but could not find her out. "All I know is," said he, "that those she is most civil to, she hates the most."'[10]

Cobham's suspicions of Augusta are an indication that the princess was already drawing away from all the Whig factions, even those supported at one time by her husband. This division would deepen in the late 1750s when her support for Bute ranged her against the government, which by then included one of Cobham's 'cubs', William Pitt the Elder. The effects of this dispute would be felt in the gardens at Kew.

Augusta's other major project was to continue Frederick's work there and the gardens prospered under her direction. The year after Frederick's death, the head gardener at Kew, John Dillman, was commissioned 'to compleat all that part of the garden at Kew that is not yet finished in the manner proposed by the plan and to keep all that is now finished, which together is computed at 35 acres'.[11] This included the realisation of Frederick's Elysium, designed to match the Elysian Fields at Stowe, by creating a landscape with lawns, lake, woodlands and fields and adorning it with symbolic ornamentation. It was a construction programme to match Lord Cobham's at Stowe. Within a dozen years, Augusta erected almost twenty buildings at Kew, including a Palladian Bridge, similar to those at Stowe and at Wilton House near Salisbury in Wiltshire. No building was specifically dedicated to her husband, perhaps because Augusta saw the whole garden as his memorial. Many of the twenty or more structures were designed by Sir William Chambers. He was introduced to the princess by Bute, who also appointed him as tutor in architecture to the Prince of Wales. He was kept busy, if not well rewarded, by the royal family, as he wrote in a letter to Robert Wood in 1757.

My hands are full of work, but my pockets are not full of money. The prince employs me three mornings in a week to teach him architecture; the building [and] other decorations at Kew fill up the remaining time. The princess has the rest of the week, which is scarcely sufficient as she is forever adding new embellishments at Kew.[12]

Only four of Chambers' buildings are now extant: the Ruined Arch (1759), Orangery (1761), the Pagoda (1762) – still the icon of Kew to this day – and an 1845 copy of the Temple of Aeolus (1763). His other work which has since been swept away included an Alhambra, a mosque, a Gothic cathedral and several other classically inspired temples, all of them intended to demonstrate Britain as the centre of a new global trading empire to match that of ancient Rome. And yet, as at Stowe, amid all this political glamour, there was a consciousness that Kew was also a working estate, where sheep grazed on the lawns, and cattle were driven along the paths, as Chambers wrote of his ruined arch; 'It was designed and built by me in the year 1759, in order to make a passage for carriages and cattle, over one of the principal walks of the garden'.[13] All this was done in the spirit of the Enlightenment, combining an aesthetically pleasing vision of the countryside with an awareness of practical economics.[14]

Chambers gives a picture of how the garden would have looked in the early 1760s in his book of plans and elevations drawn up for Augusta in 1763. 'The upper part of the garden composes a large wilderness; on the border of which stands a moresque building, commonly called the Alhambra. It consists of a salon, fronted with a portico of coupled columns, and crowned with a lantern. On an open space, near the center of the same wilderness, is erected the tower, commonly called the Great Pagoda ... Near the Great Pagoda, on a rising ground, backed with thickets, stands the mosque ... The minarets are placed at each end of the principal building. In my design of them ... I have endeavoured to collect the principal particularities of the Turkish architecture.'[15]

As a keen amateur botanist, Frederick had already contemplated outstripping Stowe by creating a botanical garden within the landscape at Kew. George Vertue recorded after a visit to Kew that the prince 'was planting about his Gardens also many curious and forain Trees exotic'. In a letter of November 1750, Sir Thomas Knowlton had written that 'The Prince of Wales is now about preparation for building a stove three hundred feet in length, for plants and not pines: and my Lord Bute has already seatled a correspondance in Asia, Africa, America, Europe, and every where he can; as, to be shure, my Lord is the most knowing of any in this kingdome by much of any in it; such is his great abilitys therein; and he is the person as has prompted the young prince; and from such, what may not be expected? And next spring it will rise and grow apase, as all glasse and frams will be ready.'[16]

That next spring, the prince died and his greenhouse was not erected, but by the end of the decade, Augusta was planning something similar. If not quite as large as Frederick's intended plant house, it was equally ambitious, as is recorded in a letter to Linnaeus in the late 1750s. Its author, Dr Stephen Hales, perpetual curate at Teddington for over fifty years and Augusta's private chaplain from 1751, was another knowledgeable botanist. He wrote to the eminent Swede that 'the Princess will build a hot greenhouse 120 feet long next spring at Kew with a view to have exotics of the hottest climates in which my pipes to convey incessantly warm air will probably be very serviceable ... the rooms will be covered with shutters in winter to keep the cold out which will make a perpetual spring and summer. What a scene is here opened in greenhouse vegetation.'[17]

It was a daring move, and the princess was prepared to spend freely to realise her vision at Kew, causing her to be widely accused of extravagance; one newspaper claimed she 'expended, first and last, upon her elegant gardens at Kew, not less than 100,000*l*. exclusive of wages to Gardeners, &c'.[18] Chambers pays tribute to the princess and suggests that her achievement was well worth the cost, even if his earlier letter implies that he didn't benefit himself from the 'liberal hand'.

> What was once a desart is now an Eden. The judgement with which art hath been employed, to supply the defects of nature, and to cover its deformities, hath very justly gained universal admiration, and reflects uncommon lustre on the refined taste of the noble contriver; as the vast sums which have been expended to bring this arduous undertaking to perfection do infinite honour to the generosity and benevolence of the illustrious possessor, who with so liberal a hand distributes the superfluity of her treasures in works which serve at once to adorn the country, and to nourish its industrious inhabitants.[19]

Dodington wrote in his journal in 1752 that the dowager princess's special concern was to isolate her son from 'the young people of quality [who] were so ill educated and so very vicious, that they frightened her'.[20] She was determined to keep George away from the jaundiced and louche Whig aristocrats who surrounded the king, and groom him herself for kingship in a contrasting atmosphere of piety and moral rectitude. The prince was prevented by his mother from having the same kind of relationship with his grandfather that Frederick had enjoyed with George I. Nevertheless, once George had been made Prince of Wales, it was initially the king and not Augusta who selected his new household. Walpole wrote scathingly about George II's decisions,

> The Pelhams, who had now laid a plan of perpetuating that power, which by so many accidents had dropped into their

hands, determined to beset the young Prince entirely with their own creatures. Lord North was removed to make way for Lord Harcourt, who wanted a governor himself, as much as the Duke of Newcastle was likely to do, by parting with Stone [Newcastle's secretary], who was to be the real engine of their policy, while Lord Harcourt, was civil and sheepish, did not threaten them with traversing their scheme, or teaching the young prince other arts than what he knew himself, hunting and drinking. Stone, lately grown a personal favourite with the King during the journeys to Hanover, was a dark, proud man, very able and very mercenary. The other preceptor was Hayter Bishop of Norwich, a sensible well-bred man.[21]

Andrew Stone, according to Walpole, managed to ingratiate himself with Augusta, even though she was initially suspicious of him, given that Frederick had thought him a Jacobite. Internecine strife broke out within the household, so that when George II returned from a trip to Hanover in late 1752, affairs 'were ripe for his interposition'.[22] Harcourt sought an audience with the king and accused Stone, the sub-preceptor George Scott, and James Cresset, the dowager princess's secretary, of 'Jacobite connections, instilling Tory Principles' and atheism.[23]

Despite these accusations, Stone, Scott and Cresset all remained in post, Stone and Scott until 1756, and Cresset until Augusta's death in 1772. But Harcourt was removed to be replaced in December 1752 by a somewhat reluctant James, 2nd Earl of Waldegrave. 'The Earl was very averse to it: he was a man of pleasure, understood the court, was firm in the King's favour, easy in his circumstances, and at once undesirous of rising, and afraid to fall.'[24] Waldegrave himself wrote, 'In this respect I fully answer'd their purpose, for tho none of their dependants, I had a very sincere esteem and friendship for Mr Pelham, and was at least a well wisher to the Duke of Newcastle'.[25]

Waldegrave found the prince difficult to teach, in part because George had been cloistered at Leicester Square. He was, wrote Waldegrave, 'uncommonly full of princely prejudices, contracted in the nursery, and improved by the society of bed chamber women and pages of the back stairs ... I soon perceived that the best which could be hoped for, was to give him right notions of common things, to instruct him by conversation rather than by books;

and sometimes, under the disguise of amusement, to entice him into the persuit of more serious studies.' A worldy wise courtier, Waldegrave was concerned mainly to educate the prince as a king in his grandfather's mould, and to maintain the status quo. 'The Princess and her son seem'd fully satisfied with my zeal, diligence, and faithful services: and I was treated with so much civility, that sometimes I thought myself almost a favorite.'[26]

This, however, was far from being the case. Augusta was unhappy with her son's academic progress and personal development, confiding in Dodington that 'she wish'd he were a little more forward, and less childish, at his age'.[27] She also disliked his exposure to the Whig agenda rather than to the more radical, effectively Tory, programme drawn up by her husband.

The dowager princess turned, therefore, to her longstanding confidant, Lord Bute, to help her prepare her son for kingship. The Scottish earl's chief attraction was that he came from outside the closed world of the court and belonged to no particular faction. His views were not those of a courtier, but were informed by a wider concern for what he saw as the necessary moral reformation of Britain from the now corrupt control of the Whigs. Although losing his official role in the prince's household on his death, Bute had remained personally close to the princess; Bute's secretary, Charles Jenkinson, later the 1st Earl of Liverpool, believed that Augusta was fond of Bute because he was the only individual in her husband's entourage who actually liked her for herself.[28] Waldegrave, for obvious reasons, was slighting about Bute, describing him as having 'a good person, fine legs, and a theatrical air of the greatest importance'. He added in his journal that he doubted Bute's abilities, claiming that Frederick himself had said that 'Bute was a fine showy man, who would make an excellent embassador in a court where there was no business', adding that 'the sagacity of the Princess Dowager has discover'd other accomplishments, of which the Prince her husband may not perhaps have been the most competent judge'.[29] Walpole was even more explicit about the claims that would mar the early years of George III's reign; when Frederick wanted to be alone with his latest conquest, Walpole said, he would 'bid the Princess walk with Lord Bute. As soon as the Prince was dead, they walked more and more, in his memory.'[30]

Bute's friendship with Frederick, and their shared botanical interest and political ideals were important to Augusta, who continued to use the garden at Kew to express Frederick's broad vision of Britain's place in the world. Brought up herself in an authoritarian German court, and having been influenced, like her husband, by the writings of Lord Bolingbroke, she wanted to educate her son to exercise power for himself. George II, she believed, had become a cipher, with the government overseeing a system of bribery and corruption.[31] She also disliked the influence that George II's fondness for Hanover still had on British politics, and 'wished Hanover at the bottom of the sea as the cause of all our misfortunes'.[32]

After long and difficult negotiations with the king, Augusta carried her point and Bute became Groom of the Stole, an ancient role which gave him the dubious honour of emptying the prince's pisspot, by then more honoured in the breach than the observance. The position, however, made Bute the prince's closest courtier and the effective head of his household. It was a significant moment in the young prince's life. From the beginning, Bute realised that he and his charge would encounter criticism from the Whig oligarchy. There is even an early foreshadowing of the trouble that all three would face over the nature of Bute's relationship with Augusta. 'It will sooner or later be whispered in your ear,' wrote Bute to the prince, 'don't you know Lord Bute was your fathers friend and is strongly attached to the Princess, he only means to bring you under your mothers government, sure you are too much a man to bear that.' He added, however, that 'the prospect of serving you and forming your young mind is exquisitely pleasing to a heart like mine ... I glory in my attachment to the Princess, in being called your fathers friend, but I glory in being yours too; I have not a wish, a thought but what points to your happiness alone.'[33] George responded to Bute's tutelage, perhaps in part because both had lost their fathers as children. Whether the prince looked upon his new governor as a surrogate father, a mentor or just a link with his dead father, he called the earl his 'dearest friend' in the substantial body of letters he wrote to Bute over the next ten years, until political forces drove them apart. All demonstrate a dependence which would lead, after his accession, to his being accused of favouritism and of manipulation by Bute.

George reacted well to the more systematic and serious course of study on which his new mentor insisted. His published letters to the earl indicate that he understood that personal reformation was needed, while Bute began to nurture in the prince what he described as a 'quality perhaps unknown to his predecessors; I mean manly firmness, unshaken resolution'.[34]

Having gained the firm support of both the Prince of Wales and his mother, Bute began quickly to flex his political muscles, negotiating an alliance between William Pitt, now an influential member of the government, and Augusta at his town house in South Audley Street. Pitt, a Groom of the Bedchamber to Frederick from 1737 until 1745, fell out with the prince when he offered his support to the Pelham ministry. Pitt recognised by the mid-1750s that he needed to make overtures to the prince and his advisors at Leicester House, for that was where power would lie on George II's death. After a period out of office, he rejoined the government, and, partly as result of brief, opportunist support from Leicester House, pulled off a deal with Newcastle and became minister for war. A series of glacially polite letters written by Pitt to Bute between 1755 and 1758 make clear the fragile nature of the relations between the two. A letter, for instance, written in July 1758, indicates Pitt's awareness that Bute is the conduit to Augusta and the Prince of Wales. Pitt is, he says, 'truely penetrat'd with the sense of their Royal Highnesses gracious acceptance of my entire devotion to their commands, let me entreat your Lordship to lay me at the feet of the Prince and Princess of Wales and to express for me the most respectful and gratefull sentiments of my heart'. He also praised Bute's moral curriculum for the young prince, saying, 'May my noble friend's honest labours in planting the seeds of moral virtue never be frustrated! and may the reviving country reap the happy fruits of a Prince train'd to love his people enough to wish generously to reform them!'

The friendship between Bute and Pitt was never one between like-minded men and it foundered within three years. There were many areas of disagreement, not least the necessary inclusion of the Duke of Newcastle in any future government, a move to which Bute was implacably opposed. And both objected to a lack of openness in the other, as Pitt reported to Newcastle (describing himself in the third person). Bute had, he wrote, 'complained of Mr. P's reservedness in not having acquainted him with the occurrences as they happened. Mr. P. said that the reason was that most things that had passed were immaterial, but that as to others, when he informed his Lordship of any material news, he had found that my Lord Bute had been informed of them before (viz. by my Lord Holdernesse).'[35] By 1760, as Walpole would write, Pitt 'had for some time been on the coldest terms with Lord Bute; for possession of power, and reversion of power, could not fail to make two natures so haughty, incompatible'.[36]

Other, more serious disputes between Bute and Pitt concerned the conduct, particularly after George III's accession, of the Seven Years War. This global conflict, which would define the future of Britain, would be commemorated at both Stowe and Kew.

CHAPTER 13

'The Paradise of Our World, Where All Plants Are Found'

In 1759, at the height of the Seven Years War, a plump, apple-cheeked Scotsman with a quizzical smile arrived at the royal gardens at Kew to take up his new position. William Aiton, just twenty-eight years old, had been appointed as the first curator of the royal physic garden by the Dowager Princess of Wales on the advice of the Scottish Lord Bute. It was a major role, for the princess had further, greater ambitions for the gardens which she had already furnished with a dazzling array of buildings, designed by yet another Scot, Sir William Chambers. It is from Aiton's arrival at Kew that the Royal Botanic Gardens date their foundation.

For Aiton, born and trained on a farm in Lanarkshire, this lofty appointment must have been something of a coup, especially as he had spent the previous five years at the Chelsea Physic Garden recorded as no more than an anonymous 'Apprentice'. His boss there had been the redoubtable Philip Miller, author of the influential *Gardeners Dictionary*. Published in 1731, the dictionary had become essential reading for eighteenth-century horticulturalists, helping to shape, among others, the gardens of George Washington at Mount Vernon and Thomas Jefferson at Monticello.[1]

Aiton could hardly have been taken on in a more momentous year, for 1759 was Britain's *annus mirabilis* when, in Frank McLynn's phrase, 'Britain became master of the world', mid-way through the conflict known as the Seven Years War.[2] This war had its roots in Europe, but its battles were fought on several continents, including the American mainland, in the Caribbean and in India. Although other countries were involved, it was, in essence, a fight for world supremacy between Britain and France; in 1759, Britain effectively won that battle, in the process establishing an empire on which the sun would not set for almost 200 years. That year, Britain captured Quebec from France and, with the support of its Prussian allies, crushed the French on mainland Europe at the Battle of Minden. This battle was commemorated, but with different emphases, by a Temple of Victory at Kew, built by Chambers, and a Temple of Concord and Victory at Stowe, designed to publicise the triumph of William Pitt the Elder, kinsman to the Temple family.

Defending his country threatened by invasion, Admiral Sir Edward Hawke destroyed the French fleet at the Battle of Quiberon Bay, thereby confirming British naval superiority. France's Caribbean sugar islands also fell to Britain, and further headway was made in India; within two years all France's possessions there would come under British control.

Against the backdrop of the Seven Years War, and what amounted to a worldwide conflict, the appointment of Aiton might have been small beer. Yet this and a number of other events seem curiously appropriate for the year in which Britain established herself not only as a naval and military power, but as an international economic, industrial and cultural force. 1759 is arguably the year that finally saw the last vestiges of feudalism and ushered in the era of capitalism.

These other events included the opening in January of the British Museum, based on the collection of Sir Hans Sloane, patron of the Chelsea Physic Garden. The great Scottish architect Robert Adam designed Kedleston Hall in Derbyshire, home of the Curzon family since the twelfth century and of the future Viceroy of India, Lord Curzon. That role was hewn out in the nineteenth century after the eighteenth-century British victories in India over the French. In 1759, the twenty-nine-year-old Josiah Wedgwood started the Ivy Works, launching the ceramics business which epitomised the success of British trade and industry in the late eighteenth century. Partly through his efforts, the great network of canals was created, binding together the industrial cities of England and increasing Britain's prosperity. This was the cradle of the Industrial Revolution. And, resonating with this story, one of his legendary pieces of work, the 'Frog Service', subsequently made in

Stoke-on-Trent for Catherine the Great, Empress of Russia, would feature more views of Stowe than of any other English estate.

Handel died in 1759, the composer favoured by George II and wilfully disregarded by Frederick. There were notable births, too, of Mary Wollstonecraft, William Pitt the Younger and William Wilberforce, all three destined to make their mark on their own time and on the future. John Wilkes, Bute's chief antagonist in the following decade, was appointed an officer in the Buckinghamshire militia – close to the home of Earl Temple, successor to Lord Cobham at Stowe, and subsequently Wilkes's patron in the fight against Bute.

In the eighteenth century, the Thames had relatively few bridges; people made their way across by ferry or stayed on their side of the river. In June 1759, however, Kew Bridge opened, making it easier for those living on the north bank of the river to visit the royal pleasure grounds and physic garden which were regularly open to the public.

The appointment of Aiton and the foundation of Kew came at a time of expansion and rapid political, social and industrial change in Britain. The Royal Botanic Gardens would be part of that process; in the hands of Sir Joseph Banks, the vast plant collections became the embodiment at home of British power overseas and an instrument of economic power.

Much had already been done by the time that Aiton arrived at Kew. 110 acres had been walled or fenced, with Bute being closely consulted on the sourcing of plants and tree-planting. From 1759, the care of such extensive acreage would be divided between Aiton, who took responsibility for the nine-acre physic garden, and John Haverfield, who looked after the pleasure grounds, kitchen garden, melon ground and orangery.[3]

Bute's was the organising mind at Kew over the next thirteen years. He worked as *ex officio* director until Augusta's death, but never managed to gain the kind of recognition for the gardens that Banks was able to achieve, nor to be accepted himself by the British cultural establishment. He was intolerant of those he thought less gifted than himself and was incapable of bonhomie. Despite his interests, he never joined the Royal Society or the Society of Antiquaries and was constantly offending other aristocrats because of his outspoken advancement of his own views. In a letter of 1751 to Gronovius, for example, he claimed that botany in England was not flourishing because 'tho' the nobility and gentry are at present mad with planting American Trees the science is absolutely neglected, both by them and gentlemen of the Aesculapian faculty'.[4] Bute's fellow aristocratic botanists may not have read his letters to Gronovius, but his perception of them as dilettantes was no doubt crystal clear. He was more admired by those he patronised, such as Chambers and Peter Collinson. Collinson imported plants from the American collector John Bartram for patrons who included the dukes of Norfolk, Richmond, Bedford and Argyll (Bute's uncle), Charles Hamilton at Painshill Park in Surrey and Philip Miller at the Chelsea Physic Garden. Correspondence was clearly already established between Collinson and Bute by early 1745 when Bute was still living at Mount Stuart. A letter written at that time describes a collection of shells which Bute has gathered on the Isle of Bute and is sending to Collinson, apologising that 'they are so few, so common & trifling, I am asham'd to send so poor a collection, but as I believe there are few others to be met with on the west coast of Scotland'. Bute details the colours and shapes of the shells, before going on to tell Collinson of the 'infinite obligation all lovers of planting have to your good name. I can't really express how much it delights me; to see so generous an ardour for encreasing [*sic*] the knowledge of nature, a knowledge that infallibly brings a good man to that of His Great Maker.' The next year, from his rented home in Twickenham, Bute thanked him 'for procuring me the Reeds'. He also wrote of his plans to make a *hortus siccus* (a collection of dried specimens), according to method used by Gronovius. Interestingly, Bute always addresses Collinson as 'Sir' or 'Mr Collinson' in their correspondence, while the more clubbable Duke of Richmond writes to the nurseryman on at least one occasion as 'Honest Peter'.[5]

Through their long acquaintance, Collinson saw Bute as standing head and shoulders above his peers in the breadth and depth of his knowledge, as he wrote to Linnaeus in April 1755. 'You desire to know our botanical people. The first in rank is the Right Hon. the Earl of Bute. He is a perfect master of your method ... But we have great numbers of nobility and gentry that know plants very well but yet do not make botanic science their peculiar study.'[6]

Collinson refers elsewhere to Bute as the 'Maecenas of Gardening'. He describes Bute's tutelage of the Prince of Wales in the same breath as he praises the former's work at Kew, suggesting in his Commonplace book that the same moral sense and wide understanding informed both activities. 'Lord Bute's influence and example and advice have had a happy effect on the King's uniform conduct while Prince of Wales. From his Lordship's great knowledge in the science of botany, the gardens at Kew have been furnished with all the rare exotick trees and flowers that could be procured.' Writing to Bartram on another occasion, he adds that 'Lord Bute ... is the only great man that encourages ingenious men in planting botanical rarities'. He regarded Kew as 'the Paradise of our world, where all plants are found, that money or interest can procure. When I am there, I am transported with the novelty and variety; and don't know which to admire first or most.'[7]

Plants ordered from Bartram and Collinson helped to build up the unparalleled collection at Kew, and at the expense of the Chelsea Physic Garden, which declined during this period, although plant material continued to be exchanged between the two gardens. The work of Aiton and Haverfield, both employed on Bute's recommendation, was admired by Collinson, who told Bartram that at Kew, 'all vegetables are treated with the utmost care and all that art can do to bring them to perfection in our climate'.[8]

The gardens became a mecca for plants and seeds, helped, of course, by their high-profile royal ownership. Bute wrote to the Governor of Georgia that 'the Exotic Garden at Kew is by far the richest in Europe ... getting plants and seeds from every corner of the habitable world'. When amateur botanist John Ellis was appointed London agent for West Florida in 1763, he told the President of the Board and Trade and Plantations that 'all the pay I demand ... is to be in rare plants and seeds for the Royal Garden at Kew'. He presented a tea plant to Kew and later bragged to the Governor of New York that he had 'introduced many rare & valuable plants into the Royal Gardens at Kew'. Ellis also wrote that he had sent 'Mr Aiton, her Royal Highness the Princess Dowager of Wales's Botanic Gard'ner at Kew, a parcel of seeds and dont doubt but that he will raise them; as he is a perfect master of his business'.

Plants were also brought to the garden from nearer at home. One carrier's invoice between February 1768 and March 1769 shows that consignments came from various nurserymen as well as the Chelsea Physic Garden, while private gardens in Cambridgeshire, Dorset, Lancashire, Oxfordshire, Yorkshire and Wales also supplied plants to Kew.[9]

By November 1763, the *St. James's Chronicle* was reporting that Kew had 'become so highly celebrated abroad, that the Empress of Russia has sent an eminent architect, and some of her best gardeners, to take a survey of those elegant gardens, which her Imperial Majesty intended to imitate at her Palace of Peterhoff'.[10]

Bute's own commitment to Kew is manifest from a generous donation he made to the gardens after the death of his maternal uncle and guardian, the 3rd Duke of Argyll, in April 1761. Formerly the Earl of Islay, Archibald Campbell was one of the leading plant collectors of the day and had developed his estate on Hounslow Heath out of unpromising territory. His large plantation of trees and shrubs included many new introductions to this country, such as Cedars of Lebanon grown from seed and a grove of North American conifers. Argyll's work and generosity were admired by Collinson, who, he wrote, 'began planting by raising all sorts of trees and shrubs from seeds from our northern colonies and all other parts of the world; he had the largest collection in England, and ... gave to every one to encourage planting, and raised plants on purpose to oblige the curious at this seat of his called Whitton. He had a fine collection of rare birds and beasts ... his library was scarce to be equalled.'[11] Bute inherited Argyll's estate on his death, and generously – or ambitiously – decided to transplant many of the Whitton trees to Kew in the spring of 1762. The towering *Ginkgo biloba*, near Chambers' Orangery, a *Robinia pseudoacacia* and a *Sophora japonica* from the duke's collection still survive there, although now aged, under stress and in need of support.[12]

Although styled by Horace Walpole as a man of 'little reading, and affected learning', Bute was a hard-working scholar, whose methodical procedures gave Kew the sound footing on which Banks would be able to build later in the century.[13] In retirement, Bute applied himself to compiling nine volumes of *Botanical Tables*. Published in 1785, only twelve copies of the book were produced, at the eye-watering cost of £12,000. Other recipients of the book included Catherine the Great of Russia and Bute's replacement at Kew, Sir Joseph Banks. What rings through the book's introduction is the pleasure given to Bute by the natural world. 'The Book of Nature is a sacred writing, and a proper perusal of it becomes an act of religion.' It was her appreciation of this kind of moral sense which encouraged Augusta to ask Bute to tutor Prince George. Bute writes about the 'amazing variety of brilliant colours, and wild fantastic forms – which ever way we turn, to the hill or valley, the forest or the brook, every step affords a new object, while, air, exercise and health, attend the pleasing pursuit'.

The clearest clue to Bute's intellectual self-confidence is his willingness to take on Linnaeus by suggesting his own slightly different system of classification, validated, he claims, by other contemporary scientists. He admits that 'the celebrated Linnaeus stands the unrivalled author. Before him the descriptions of the genera were everywhere imperfect; and those of the species quite unintelligible.' But he adds that Linnaeus's system is also imperfect. 'There are more exceptions to his classical characters; more plants ranged under heads they do not suit; than in any one method I am acquainted with.'[14]

Bute's plans for Kew were as bold as those of Augusta; he wanted the gardens to become a centre of botanical excellence and research, and recognised that it was necessary to be systematic about recording plant material acquired. To help him, Bute ill-advisedly befriended a naturalist on the make to whom he was probably introduced by the Duke of Northumberland in about 1757. A vicar's son from Peterborough, John Hill had been apprenticed to a London apothecary, worked for a while as an actor, before turning his attention to the study of botany and medicine with the aim of being accepted by the Royal Society. He had worked since the early 1740s as a plant collector for, among others, the Duke of Richmond. The duke was not much impressed, judging by two letters sent to Collinson. In the first, written in November 1741, the duke says, 'Hill the apothecary is now with me. He's a well behaved fellow, butt between you & I is not he what we call a puppy?' In December the following year, he wrote again in similar vein, tacitly accusing him of obsequiousness. 'Hill the Bothanist, apothecary, poet or stage player, whatever you please to call him is here, & much your humble servant.'[15]

Hill flourished initially under Bute's patronage, and began working at Whitton with Argyll, whom he described as 'a distinguished botanist [who] has shewn his protection to all who have followed the same path'. In 1758, Hill himself wrote a paper, dedicated to the Duke of Devonshire, promoting the foundation of a botanical garden in England and stressing its commercial potential.

Nor is the use of botany limited to one article: beside medicine, the useful arts, and commerce may owe to it the greatest obligations ... The want of botanical knowledge robs our country of these advantages: and beside these, it offers many more. 'Tis not, as they have thought, who did not understand it, a frivolous employment for the idle ... but in these higher lights becomes a force of health and prosperity; and is worthy the attention of a patriot.[16]

Patriotism and horticulture; the two activities were aligned in Hill's view, which chimed with Bute's. Employed at Kew, his role was described rather vaguely by his widow as 'the disposing and superintending a part of the Princess of Wales's Garden at Kew, destined for Botany. In order to do this, he formed a correspondence with men of distinguished learning every where; receiving and giving seeds.' She also explained how the economic possibilities of Britain's new colonies were also explored by Hill on Bute's behalf. 'Those islands which were conquered during the administration of the *immortal* [Lady Hill's italics] Pitt, wanted Governors, and those were appointed by Lord Bute ... That those conquests might become profitable, Lord Bute desired Sir John Hill to direct their cultivation; which he did, and gave each of those Governors in writing, his separate instructions; and according to their transmitted accounts, when there, wrote back what should be dismissed, and what encouraged.' Even more ambitious was Bute's suggestions that Hill should draw up 'the most voluminous, magnificent and costly work that ever man attempted ... *The Vegetable System*'.[17]

This detailed catalogue of the plant world eventually ran to twenty volumes, the first of which was published in 1759. In 1768, Hill also compiled the first catalogue of plants at Kew, *Hortus Kewensis*. Listing some 3,400 species under their Linnaean names, it reveals that Kew was already a storehouse of international flora.[18]

Hill, however, had a poor reputation among the scientific community, and Bute himself later had his doubts about him, writing to John Strange in January 1774 that 'I have heard so much of his vanity and imprudence that I keep him at the greatest distance'.[19] Not at such a distance, however, but that Bute was also tarred with Hill's brush. For Bute's Whiggish enemies, the maverick Hill was yet another stick with which to beat the earl. Both *The Vegetable System* and *Hortus Kewensis* were extensively criticised, on political grounds as much as for any botanical errors which may have slipped in. When Hill died in 1775, according to Hill's widow, Bute refused to pay the debts incurred by her husband in compiling *The Vegetable System*, and failed to organise a pension for her. The result was Lady Hill's splenetic address 'to the Public', in which she claimed that Hill's part work with the colonies went unrewarded. The italics are hers. '*Those the stores of merchandise, which England has received from those quarters, rose from the labours of him who never was requited.*' Her final appeal beseeched the public to recognise that 'my enemy is theirs: the same Lord Bute who lost them a world, has poorly stooped to heap oppression upon an object, whom our religion tells us, is the peculiar care of Heaven – a widow'.[20]

Whether or not Lady Hill is right that Bute effectively discarded Hill when he ceased to be useful to him, her vitriol draws attention to Bute's widespread unpopularity in the 1760s; by the late 1770s, at the time of Lady Hill's address, Bute was even being blamed for the loss of the American colonies.

Horace Walpole visited Kew in 1761, and it appears from his commentary that he went as a member of the public and not by private invitation from either Bute or Augusta. His comments on the garden were considerably less complimentary than, say, they had been about William Kent's Rousham, which he had found the previous year 'the best thing I have seen of Kent ... the whole, sweet'. Walpole alluded in his journal to one of the lesser events of 1759 – the problems Augusta had experienced with the lease on Kew taken out by her husband, causing her to believe she might have to abandon the estate. He is also clear about the extent of Bute's influence and the expense of the dowager princess's projects, and is not overwhelmed.

> Frederic Prince of Wales enlarged & ornamented the house, & began great works in the garden. The Princess Dowager continued the improvements, & Lord Bute had the disposition of the ground. In 1759 the lease, held of Lord Essex, was near

expiring; they paid £800 a year for it – Lord Essex did not care
to sell it; the Princess was piqued, & was on the point of leaving
it. At last Lord Essex consented to sell it for £17,000, & the
Princess continued the improvements & laid out great sums here;
it is said £30000. There is little invention or taste shown. Being
on a flat, Lord Bute raised hillocs to diversify the ground, &
carried Chambers the architect thither, who built some temples,
but they are all of wood & very small. Of his design was the
round Temple in the middle, with a circular portico, called the
Temple of Victory on the battle of Minden ... The bridge & the
round temple were each erected in a night's time to surprize the
Princess – this was in imitation of parallel strokes of flattery to
Louis 14.[21]

The invocation of Louis XIV was not innocent and would have
been intended to ring alarm bells early in George III's reign, when
Lord Bute's undisguised 'predilection for the Tories' threatened
'to break up the Whig party', the people whom Walpole would
have continued to see as guardians of political liberty – whatever
his father's differences with the Cobham faction in the 1730s
and 1740s.[22] So it is important that Walpole also again mentions
'taste', with its invocation of morality as well as aesthetics; Bute
has no taste in laying out a landscape, nor moral rectitude in his
political behaviour, is the easily interpreted sub-text of Walpole's
remarks.

Walpole makes no mention of Kew's acquisition of rare plant
material, his interest being more tweaked by the architecture and the
landscape. Yet it was these acquisitions, and the Temples' constant
revision of their garden designs at Stowe, which exemplified the
growth in a new type of luxury consumption, generated by overseas
trade and thriving in a period of relative internal stability.[23] As
tourism at home developed among the 'middling sort', as well as
among people such as Walpole and his friends, it spawned, as we
have seen, the guidebooks produced for the gardens at Richmond
and Stowe.

Although no such guidebook appears to have been written
for Kew, Augusta would have known she was gardening for the
general public, and that her gardens would have been a port of
call on many a tourist itinerary. *London and Its Environs* (1761),
for example, contains a travel-guide description. 'The gardens are

extremely fine, and are formed with an agreeable wilderness and pleasing irregularity, that cannot fail to charm all who are in love with nature.'[24]

Already quoted, Chambers's 1763 account of the gardens and buildings, a 'very expensive publication ... nobly paid for by Royal Bounty', reads like a tour guide. 'On entering the garden from the palace, and turning towards the left, the first building which appears is the Orangery, or green house ... The design is mine, and it was built under my inspection in the year 1761.'[25]

Accounts in newspapers and other periodicals flag up the importance of tourism in the late eighteenth century and paint lively pictures of the actions of both the tourists and the people detailed to show them round. Visitors would be escorted by servants, inclined at times to throw their weight about, as shown by occasional angry complaints. In August 1765, a gentleman wrote to a newspaper about being 'impertinently denied admittance' to Kew gardens by a door porter.

> I went to Kew on purpose to see the gardens ... a short thin man of fifty appeared ... having the appearance of gentlemen, we desired entrance, to which he immediately shut the door ... he chose rather to wait on a group of his own stamp ... composed of house-maids, cooks, grooms, &c. ... which did not a little discompose us, especially upon recollecting the orders given out at Richmond and Kensington for the indulgence of the genteelest part of his Majesty's loving subjects ... therefore, 'tis hoped and prayed, that those door-keepers who have not the capacity of knowing the genteel part from the mob, will be replaced by those who do ... Unless these people are humbled, I do despair of ever seeing Kew-gardens.[26]

The agricultural writer and observer Arthur Young witnessed a similar incident of 'excessive insolence' at Blenheim in 1768. He watched the park-gate porters 'abusing a single gentleman in a very scurrilous manner, for not seeing them after giving the house-porter half a crown for seeing it ... I hint these circumstances as a proof, that noblemen of the most amiable character, like the Duke of Marlborough, have, unknown to them, the real magnificence of their feats tarnished by the scoundrel insolence of the lowest of their servants. The vile custom of not being able to view a house, without paying for the sight, as if it was exhibited by a showman, is detestable.'[27]

Accounts such as these reveal both the snobbery of the 'middling sort' of visitors (both use the word 'gentleman'), and the fact that, eager to embrace that elite world, they are blinded by what they perceive as aristocratic virtues. What they fail to register is that the servants themselves may well be reflecting their masters' ambivalence about admitting visitors to these grand enclosures.

This was because garden-opening was not without its dangers. The *Middlesex Journal* in June 1772 reported that local magistrate Sir John Fielding, brother of the novelist, Henry, had been called to deal with a 'Capt. Cunningham, who some time since cut the trees, and pasted up papers in Kew-garden, for which he was secured, and placed in a mad-house, where, it is supposed, he made his escape'.[28] In view of such incidents (others reported include the theft of melons from Kew, then sold in Covent Garden), the king appears to have become less happy about public openings after the death of his mother.[29] *St James's Chronicle* in September 1773 announced 'that that day was the last the Public would be ever indulged in walking there', inspiring a sarcastic rejoinder.

> A correspondent recommends to a great personage the shutting up of St. James's and Hyde-Parks, together with Kensington Gardens, Kew and Richmond, and that a covered road be made from Buckingham-House to Kew that the Sanctum Sanctorum of Majesty may no longer be violated by the profane eyes of the people.[30]

Perhaps stung by such comments, George III relented, giving orders the following July 'that the gate in the road near Richmond be opened, for admission of the inhabitants of Richmond, and parts adjacent, into the Royal gardens at Kew'.[31] Most estate owners would probably have shared the king's view when he opened Kew in 1772, 'every Thursday, for the Reception of such Persons as chuse to walk in them; and none are to be refused admission who make a decent appearance'.[32]

Doubtful though the grandees might have been about opening to the public, open they did, for gardens continued to be a crucial political tool throughout the eighteenth century. The very fact that ordinary people were able to look at the work of Bute and Augusta at Kew and at that of Cobham and Earl Temple, at Stowe, meant that political argument took place in the full glare of the public eye, rather like a television debate today. At the dawning of the new reign, the symbolism at Kew and at Stowe took on a new urgency. This time, it was not just an internecine family quarrel, but another round in the battle about British identity, with implications that threatened the monarchy itself in the early 1760s.

CHAPTER 14

'A Passionate Domineering Woman and a Favourite Without Talents'

George II died suddenly in October 1760 at the age of seventy-seven, struck down by a fatal heart attack while straining one morning in his water closet. It was somehow an appropriate admixture of the tragic and the absurd which had dogged the life of the man who was pulling on his trousers when told he had become king.

He had survived to see Britain triumph at the battles of Minden and Quiberon Bay, but, by his death, he was reigning over a war-weary nation, and left his grandson to bring the conflict to a conclusion. The Prime Minister, the Duke of Newcastle, was Whig old guard. His government had been prepared to scapegoat Admiral Byng for naval and military failures in the early days of the Seven Years War, but it had over the last year achieved significant military and naval victories.* As a result, Pitt was a much feted secretary of state for war, with support both in the House of Commons and in the country. Pitt had seen that Tories would have to be included in future administrations, perhaps in the true sense enabling the king to rule above party, as Frederick had envisaged. Indeed, Walpole suggests that the distinction of party had already been eroded by the time that George III came to the throne, and that it was George III and Bute who created new divisions, potentially endangering all the political gains made since the Glorious Revolution seventy years earlier.[1] At the very least, there was a major difference in emphasis between Pitt on the one hand and the king and his former tutor on the other as to how the war and the peace negotiations should be conducted.

Nevertheless, the future looked promising for the new, British-born George III. 'No British monarch had ascended the throne with so many advantages as George the Third,' wrote Horace Walpole. 'In the flower and bloom of youth George had a handsome, open, and honest countenance, and with the favour that attends the outward accomplishments of his age, he had none of those vices that fall under the censure of those who are past enjoying them themselves ... The administration was firm, in good harmony with one another, and headed by the most successful genius [Pitt] that ever presided over our councils.' But, according to Walpole, 'A passionate domineering woman, and a favourite without talents, soon drew a cloud over this shining prospect'.[2]

Augusta continued to cut the new George III off from the court. 'As the King passed in his chair to visit his mother in an evening, the mob asked him, if he was going to suck?'[3] And Bute was firmly at the young king's side on his accession when Newcastle arrived at Leicester House to kiss hands. Two days after George II's death, Bute was sworn in as a privy councillor and all dealings between the government and the new king were transacted through him, although he only actually joined the government in 1761, as Secretary of State for the Northern Department. Confident that Britain was by then strong enough to defeat both France and Spain, Pitt resigned when Bute and George refused to widen the conflict by declaring war on Spain. Newcastle was also effectively forced to resign in 1762 over the projected peace terms, making way for Bute, who became a Knight of the Garter, First Lord of the Treasury and Prime Minister. In alienating Newcastle, George and Bute made dangerous enemies of many leading Whig families, causing half a generation of ministerial instability.

Mob attacks began on Bute immediately, even before he became Prime Minister. In November 1761, Pitt, the hero of the Seven Years War, and his brother-in-law, Earl Temple, were greeted triumphantly when they attended the annual banquet hosted by the new Lord Mayor of London. Not so Bute. 'A party of bruisers, with George Stephenson, the one-eyed fighting coachman, at their head, had been hired to attend the chariot which contained the blazing comet [Bute] ... and to procure shouts and acclamations from the mob.' Instead, however, the mob turned on Bute, and 'before they arrived at Guildhall, the bruisers were almost bruised to death themselves'. He received a similar reception on his way to the banquet the following year. 'As soon as it was known who he was, he was entertain'd with a general hiss.'[4]

Bute professed reluctance for front-line office, and claimed in a letter to his Eton friend, Thomas Worsley, that he only took it because of 'the certain knowledge of the general corruption that has taken possession of this country'.[5] He wrote in 1761 to Lord Holdernesse, whom he replaced in the Northern Office, that 'the King too partial to my poor services insisted for several weeks upon my taking the Secretary's office, I then used every argument to shew in how much better hands the seals were placed; how much more useful I could be in a private line, how infinitely more agreeable to myself'.[6] Later the same month, Bute also wrote to the king, 'I take up the pen at a very serious minute of my life. I have ... taken my farewell ... of ease, comfort, and (what to a mind like mine the world cannot make up) of having part of my time at least in my own disposal.' He regarded his new position as 'an awful change'. The letter turns into a personal declaration of what he had tried to achieve over the previous five years.

> I have had the honor of being nearest to your person many years and to instil into your Royal Mind, whatever virtue honor or public spirit could suggest to me, ever looking up to your glory and happiness, my every thought has been pointed to that alone; nor can I accuse myself of having once entertained a selfish view; one interested thought since the Princess first entreated me to apply my life to your education ... some think I have a little merit in his education, and that I enjoy his friendship and favour, these have been acquired by honest noble means and not the wretched arts thro' which minions have too often fascinated their Prince; and rendered the very name of favourite odious to every worthy man.[7]

The word 'favourite' was indeed 'odious to every worthy man', and odious is how Bute's influence over the new king was seen, especially as the earl owed his promotion entirely to the king's affection for him and their close relationship since 1756. Bute's lack of experience was only one of the charges laid against him. 'The favourite was unknown, ungracious, and a Scot,' wrote Walpole. 'His connection with the Princess, an object of scandal.' In the early days of the reign, posters were stuck up at the Royal Exchange and in Westminster Hall, demanding, 'No *petticoat government, no Scotch favourite*'.[8]

To take Walpole's second criticism first, in the decadent world of George II's court, it was believed that a warm friendship between a man and a woman could have only one basis. 'I am as much convinced of an amorous connexion between B. and the P.D. [Princess Dowager] as if I had seen them together,' recorded Walpole years later.[9] The rumours of a sexual relationship between Augusta and Bute had long been bruited, particularly in view of their collaboration on the gardens at Kew. The pair would be taunted unrelentingly, year after year. In 1754, when Bute gave up Caen Wood, he took a town house in South Audley Street and also a house on Kew Green, where he built extensions for his botanical library and study.[10] One cartoon, for instance, shows how Bute could have snuck unseen from the gate of this house into Kew gardens to visit Augusta in the White House. The general, outraged perception was that a man, thought to be the Princess Dowager's lover, had now been propelled, mainly on that account, into the highest office by her son. 'The Princess herself was obliged to discontinue frequenting the theatre, so gross and insulting were the apostrophes with which she was saluted from the galleries.'[11]

The fact that Bute was an outsider, a Scot and, unfortunately, a Stuart by name, united the Whig factions against him. His appointment, Richard Pares has written, 'was an affront to the political class, and so badly did George III think of that class that it must probably have been meant as such'.[12] 'He was connected neither by blood or familiar intercourse with the leading families of England,' wrote an early historian of the period. 'He was not versed in the arts of popularity or used to the struggles of parliamentary opposition; and his manners were cold, reserved and unconciliating. Prejudices were easily exerted against him as a native of Scotland.'[13] At a time when the people of England were still coming to terms with difficulty with the idea of being 'British', there was an all-pervasive suspicion of the Scots, who 'especially in London, enjoyed the dubious distinction of being marginally more unpopular than the Jews', according to John Brewer.[14] Bute's hand was seen behind George III's first speech to parliament, which caused major offence. When the new king proclaimed, 'I glory in the name of Briton,' many would have preferred him to call himself an Englishman. Fears grew of a Scottish pincer movement on government, when Bute, along with several other of his countrymen, took leading roles in the new ministry. Scots were also conspicuous in London business and professional life, among them Philip Miller, a botanist of Scottish descent, who had run the Chelsea Physic Garden for over forty years. Universities in Scotland specialised in training doctors, many of whom found employment in England, tending to the needs of the increasingly affluent middle class.[15] The appointment in 1761 of the Scot Robert Adam alongside Chambers to the new positions of Architects of Works was attributed to Bute's influence. The fact that he had also employed Scots, Chambers and Aiton in the royal gardens at Kew added fuel to the fire.

By the early summer of 1762, an all-out publicity battle had broken out, involving weekly magazines, cartoons and even poetry. In an incautious move, which would help to destroy his own career, Bute himself triggered the press war in May with the launch of the government-sponsored *Briton*, edited by the Scottish novelist and journalist Tobias Smollett. A month later, the ironically entitled *North Briton* sprung into the attack. Edited by the radical polemicist and MP John Wilkes, and financed by Earl Temple, the magazine mounted wave after wave of verbal strikes on Bute. Wilkites depicted themselves as patriotic Englishmen, resisting an 'alien' assault on parliamentary liberties by Britain's first Scots-born Prime Minister.[16] 'And oh! how the rabble would laugh and would hoot/Could they once set a-swinging this John Earl of Bute,' wrote Wilkes.[17] Robert Walpole's son, Horace, wrote to his friend, Horace Mann, shortly after Bute became Prime Minister. 'The new administration begins tempestuously,' he said. 'My father was not more abused after twenty years than Lord Bute is in twenty days. Weekly papers swarm, and like other swarms of insects, sting.'[18]

Against this blanket assault, the beleaguered royal favourite attempted to bring the Seven Years War to an end. During his short-lived premiership, from May 1762 to April 1763, he succeeded, with the help of the Duke of Bedford in Paris, in negotiating the Treaty of Paris in February 1763, which finally concluded hostilities. Bute's letters during the negotiations are often angry and fretful, as he struggled with political problems at home. The Duke of Devonshire, for instance, refused to attend 'the council that was to settle finally the terms on which we were to make peace', causing Bute to write furiously to the Marquis of Granby of 'the very strange and disrespectful conduct of people of great names'.[19]

Points at issue included possessions of the French in the West Indies and their fishing rights in Canadian waters, both of which were restored to France under the treaty. The islands of Guadeloupe were one bone of contention; in the International Slavery Museum in Liverpool, there is a portrait of the beleaguered British governor of Guadeloupe writing a letter to his government at home begging for the islands to remain British. The painting is instructive about public and colonial opinion at the time. In letters to Bedford, negotiating with the French in Paris, Bute declared that the French were exhausted and humiliated; intelligence suggested that they couldn't continue the war. But, with a degree of realism, he accepted that some concessions were needed in order to effect a treaty and restore some *amour propre* to Britain's defeated enemies.

His secretary, Charles Jenkinson, wrote in 1763 that 'Great Britain has no ancient claim to the Island of Guadeloupe ... it is particularly valuable to France.' He goes on to suggest that it is in Britain's commercial interests that her former enemies are able to recoup their losses and begin trading again. 'The proper force of Great Britain is maritime; It is the most consistent with the nature of her government, & best fitted for the defence of her territory; & consequently the natural object of her ambition must always be the increase of her commerce ... is she should retain at the peace no more of that continent [North America and the Caribbean islands], than what of ancient right belongs to her, she would yet have extent of country sufficient & situated under a sufficient variety of climates to answer all the ends of commerce.'[20]

The often prickly relationship between Bute and Bedford is revealed by their correspondence in the autumn of 1762. Bedford at times complained that Bute's dispatches were contradictory, and objected that every drafting point had to be sent to London for approval. 'I assure you, that I gave way to this,' wrote Bute, 'purely out of friendship & regard for you. I thought that in the dangerous & responsible situation you stand, I could not have rendered you more effectual service.' Even with British concessions, the negotiations were never plain sailing; letters from Bedford and Egremont in Paris painted 'the conduct of the French Court, in a very unpleasant light, and consequently the peace in a most declining way'.[21]

Eventually, the treaty was signed, although Bute's political opponents believed that he had made too many concessions to Spain as well as to France. In returning several Caribbean islands to France, Bute had, it was later argued, left a back door open to the French through which they were able to supply the Americans during the revolutionary war. Bute also approved the stationing of twenty-one battalions of soldiers in the American colonies, to support colonists formerly under French control. The cost was initially to be paid by Britain, but, in order to meet economic targets in the long term, the Americans would be charged the price of their own security. This display of military power did nothing to allay the American fears that the end of the Seven Years War would mean more, rather than less, interference from Britain. The Stamp Act of 1765, enacted by Grenville's ministry after Bute's resignation as Prime Minister, but believed to have his handwriting all over it, imposed high customs duties on the American colonists. Put these various actions together, and, in John Bullion's words, 'it is fair to say that the revolution began with the plan formulated by the King and Bute'.

Bullion also believes, however, that George III and Bute planned 'conscientiously and boldly'.[22] Bute's letters written during the peace negotiations were often self-justifying and even peevish in tone, but also give the sense of a man who, if somewhat at sea in uncharted waters, was determined to do the best for his king and for his country. He wrote to the Marquis of Granby, saying, 'I will be bold enough to affirm, that this country has not made so great, so safe, & so permanent a peace ... as this, for some hundred years past'.[23]

There were indeed those who were not critical of the peace terms, whether or not they had time for Bute himself. Among them was the American polymath Benjamin Franklin if the implications of a letter from his correspondent William Strahan are to be believed. Strahan, an Edinburgh-born printer who worked for Edmund Burke, Adam Smith, Edward Gibbon and Samuel Johnson, was appointed King's Printer in 1770 and was an MP from 1774 to 1784. He and Franklin maintained a correspondence for over forty years. In a letter of August 1763, he wrote to Franklin that he would 'have seen, in general, by the public papers, what a cry is raised against the peace, and how unpopular it has rendered Lord Bute. I wish I cou'd say, that making this peace was Lord B's only fault, for I agree with you in thinking it a very good one. But I am sorry to tell you, that my countryman has shewn himself altogether unequal to his high station.'[24]

An unpopular cider tax, reminiscent of Walpole's excise tax, hastened Bute's departure, and under increasing pressure, he resigned as Prime Minister in April 1763.[25] Having failed to win the public relations battle, he wrote somewhat peevishly to a friend, 'The peace once sign'd, ratified and debated ... the helm that demanded a bold and venturous hand, may at this peace, be manag'd by a child'.[26] To General Townshend he wrote, 'I dislike too much a ministerial life, to wish by any measure to settle myself permanently in office ... I have hardly met with any thing but cruel abuse & base ingratitude.'[27] Apart from personal disinclination for the vicissitudes of public life, Bute contended that his main intention in stepping down was to protect the king. In a long letter of self-justification to the Duke of Bedford, he explained his reasons initially for accepting the premiership. 'I did it with the utmost reluctance, & nothing but the King's safety & independancy, could have made me acquiesce in a way of life so opposite to every feeling.' He believed his departure from office would draw the poison of press attacks away from George and make his government stronger. 'I am firmly of the opinion, that my retirement will remove the only unpopular part of the government ... I fondly hope therefore, I shall by my retiring, do my Royal Master much more service than I could have performed by continuing in office.' And, with a last snipe at the old Whig guard, he added that the king remains determined 'never upon any account to suffer those ministers of the late reign, who have attempted to fetter, and ensnare him, ever to come into his service while he lives to hold the scepter'.[28]

In Wilfrid Blunt's memorable phrase, politically, Bute was 'a mountaineer with no head for heights'. According to Bishop Warburton, a writer and editor who held the office of Bishop of Gloucester from 1759 to 1779, Bute was unsuitable to be Prime Minister for three reasons: he was a Scot, a royal favourite, and an honest man.[29] If Bute hoped to stop the press attacks on himself and on Augusta, he was to be sorely mistaken. Just a week after he left office, the King's Speech, setting out the peace terms at the opening of Parliament, infuriated Wilkes, Pitt and Temple. The speech, written by a ministry then headed by George Grenville, was nevertheless almost certainly the work of Bute. Six days later, the infamous edition No.45 of the *North Briton* was published, with a lacerating attack on the speech, to which was added the suggestion that Bute had bribed Parliament to vote acceptance. 'The *Minister's speech* of last Tuesday,' ran the editorial,

> is not to be paralleled in the annals of this country. I am in doubt whether the imposition is greater on the Sovereign, or on the nation. Every friend of this country must lament that a prince of so many great and admirable qualities, whom England truly reveres, can be brought to give the sanction of his sacred name to the most odious measures and the most unjustifiable public declarations from a throne ever renowned for truth, honour, and an unsullied virtue.[30]

The reaction was instantaneous; the *North Briton* was closed down, the original manuscript of No. 45 destroyed, and edition No. 46 was removed from the presses. Wilkes himself was arrested, imprisoned and put on trial, announcing in a letter from prison that 'as an Englishman I must lament that my Liberty is so wickedly taken from me'. He claimed privilege of Parliament and was therefore discharged to reap substantial damages, to the cry of 'Liberty! Liberty! Wilkes for ever!'. He also had the continued support of Earl Temple, who was dismissed as Lord Lieutenant of Buckinghamshire as a result. Unrepentant, Temple would later erect a new statue of *Liberty* at Stowe in the 1770s to represent Wilkes.[31]

Although Bute no longer headed the government, his resignation was seen by many, spurred on by Wilkes, as a piece of political pantomime; the earl would continue to advise the king as 'minister behind the curtain', making his way to meetings with George at St James's through the gardens of Augusta's home at Carlton House. The violent criticism of the trio was augmented rather than diminished and now had multiple targets: the weakness of the king, controlled by an inconsequential, yet dangerous Scottish peer, and the supposed adultery of Bute and Augusta. That the latter two were confidential is clear from a number of Bute's letters, including one from the 1750s, written to the then Prince of

Wales, in which Bute spoke of Augusta as 'the tenderest mother, who to the endearing softness of her sex, unites the firmness and the noblest virtues of the best of ours ... happy has it been for this nation that the young Royal Family were left under her wing'. In a letter to Augusta from about the same time, Bute spoke of 'all the warmth that duty, gratitude and friendship can inspire. How great the confidence she is pleased to place in him [Bute was writing in the third person], how immense the obligation laid upon him.'[32]

These are florid but essentially formal commendations, and it is generally agreed that there is no evidence that Bute and Augusta were ever lovers. Her apparently willingness to jeopardise her reputation was rather to ensure that their trusted counsellor continued to have access to her son even after his resignation, than because of romantic ardour for the Scottish earl.

Nevertheless, Bute's enemies continued to stoke the flames. Over the next few years, some 400 or more cartoons and savaging broadsheets viciously satirised the supposed affair between Augusta and Bute, the 'Petticoat' and the 'Jack-boot'. The images were sexually explicit; Augusta carries the jackboot on her back in one cartoon, fondling its spur, while an obelisk nearby is topped with an inflamed thistle. In a second, Bute stands astride two jackboots while the Princess of Wales looks up his kilt.[33] In another, Bute, tartan testicles dangling down, stands astride two boxes, one decorated with a picture of a goat and entitled 'Lust' and the other with a snake, captioned 'Fraud'. The image of the snake also evokes Eve's seduction by the snake in the Garden of Eden. The couple were compared to Roger Mortimer and Isabella, queen to Edward II, who was thought to have been murdered by his wife and her lover in Berkeley Castle by the insertion of a red-hot poker in his rectum. Jackboots and petticoats were paraded through the streets to be either burned or hung on gibbets. The antipathy was nationwide, for Bute was seen by the mob who loved Pitt as the political executioner of their great war hero. Bute's effigy was hung on the city gates or defaced in Exeter, Monmouth, Taunton and Plymouth, and as far away as New York. In 1771, years after Bute's resignation, effigies of Bute and Augusta were taken in a ceremonial procession to Tower Hill, where they were beheaded and then burned by a London chimney-sweep dressed as a cleric. Even the coinage was defaced; for example, a George III half-penny was intricately modified with a coffin and an axe fused to the side with the king's head, and a jackboot and a woman's figure hung from gallows on the other.

Such violent expression of political opposition was a fact of eighteenth-century life, and Sir Robert Walpole had himself endured public pillory. But the attacks on Bute were concerted, sustained and permeated every level of the 'public sphere'. Bute feared for his life. The windows of his London house were broken by rioters on more than one occasion and he travelled incognito, even when abroad. Having been hissed at, insulted and pelted with refuse to the opening of Parliament one year, he attempted to hide his identity by taking a hackney cab for the return journey. He was discovered by the mob, who 'by threats and menaces, put him very reasonably in great fear ... [for] if they had once overturned the chair, he might very soon have been demolished'. The attacks did not abate even when, in 1766, his decade-long relationship with George III cooled. Two years later, as he went abroad to convalesce after illness, a crowd armed with pebbles and stones turned up at Dover to see him on his way. As late as 1783, he was continuing to receive poison-pen letters.[34]

Pitt eventually became Prime Minister in July 1766, choosing unwisely to abandon the Commons, where he had had so much success, to join the Lords as the Earl of Chatham. Lord Chesterfield wrote to his son that 'the joke here is, that [Pitt] has had *a fall upstairs*, and has done himself so much hurt, that he will never be able to stand upon his legs again. Everybody is puzzled how to account for this step; and in my mind it can have but two causes; either he means to retire from business, or he has been the dupe of Lord Bute and a great lady.' The 'great lady', of course, is a reference to Augusta. A year later, government was disrupted when Chatham was laid low by gout, from which he often suffered. Chesterfield wrote again to his son, 'Here is at present an interregnum. We must soon see what order will be produced from this chaos. It will be what Lord Bute pleases.'[35] Over four years after his retirement as Prime Minister, Bute was still seen as the *eminence grise*.

But by 1767, Bute had been sidelined, consulted by no one on political events. 'You know me well enough to be certain that I could not read your letter without being hurt to a great degree at many parts of it ... My heart is half broke and my health

ruined with the unmerited barbarous treatment I have received,'
he wrote to George III, begging the king to be permitted 'in this
most humiliated situation to possess your friendship independent
of your power'.[36] Bute might have been able to retain his influence
over and friendship with the king had he never become embroiled
in politics, but, as Chesterfield's letter suggests, he would always
be suspected of harbouring a desire for power.[37] And the king
himself had tired of the abuse to which his association with Bute
had exposed him. 'Destitute' of worldly knowledge, Bute, although
an honest man, had rendered the 'young, virtuous, *British* King ...
in the beginning of his reign, singularly unpopular; and a minister,
hating corruption, abhorring hypocrisy, and having the prosperity
of his country really at heart, the object of universal disgust'. It
was Bute's 'ignorance of the world, with a timidity altogether
inexcusable', which had 'encouraged the Opposition to go lengths
hitherto unprecedented'. This is the belief of Strahan, who had
little time for Pitt, 'of whose honesty I entertain no good opinion',
or for Wilkes. 'What are we to expect, think you, if we again come
under the dominion of this imperious tribune of the people. His
Clodius Wilkes, the most profligate of men, is in high spirits since
the trial of the messengers, which I was not present at. I expected
no pleasure from that Transaction, having no desire to be a Witness
of that Incendiary's temporary triumph.' Far from establishing
the monarch above party, as Frederick had hoped, Bute had
instead made George more vulnerable than his grandfather had
been, implies Strahan. 'In this situation, are you not under some
apprehensions for the King, unless some able and honest men step
forth ... and rescue him from the jaws of faction?'[38]

As George matured into his role as king, he gradually distanced
himself from Bute, sacrificing him as Charles I had Strafford for
the good of his throne (though with less draconian results). Charles
Jenkinson, Bute's former political secretary, concluded that George
finally became 'disgusted with the sort of loftiness and huffy manner
of Lord Bute.'[39] Although they continued to correspond for some
years, the pair never saw each other after about 1767. Accounts
differ as to their final meeting. George Greville had it from the
Duke of York, George III's son, that they met for the last time when
Augusta arranged for Bute to see George at Kew. The encounter
was acrimonious, with Bute accusing George of abandoning and
neglecting him. 'The King replied that he could not, in justice to

his ministers, hold any communication with him unknown to them, when Lord Bute said that he would never see the King again. The King became angry in his turn, and said, "Then, my Lord, be it so, and remember from henceforth we never meet again'."[40]

When Bute died in 1792, the king he had served so tenderly and well responded, in the words of Jeremy Black, 'with scant interest and largely formal courtesy'. 'Breaking with Bute was a key aspect of George's coming to personal and political maturity, and reflected his growing confidence in his judgement of people and circumstances,' concludes Black. Bute's actions, however, had ensured that 'the old Whigs no longer held the Crown to ransom', as they had during the reign of his grandfather. Instead, the king was freed to make his own judgements about people and circumstances.[41]

CHAPTER 15

'So Sits Enthroned in Vegetable Pride Imperial Kew'

As the political battles of the 1760s were fought in the press and on the streets, the two most important gardens of the period, Stowe and Kew, sought to display their conflicting ideologies. The work of the Scots – Bute, Aiton and Chambers – at Kew had fuelled opposition belief that the royal gardens were paradigmatic of British government, dominated by a Scottish cabal. But, between them, this triumvirate showed horticultural and commercial foresight; they capitalised at Kew on Britain's trading links, placing the garden at the heart of a 'commonwealth of botany'.[1]

The building programme at Kew, implemented by Chambers, was devised by Augusta and Bute to display their political achievements in the face of fierce fire from Earl Temple and his supporters at Stowe. As the decade progressed, there were internal dissensions between the royal gardens at Kew and Richmond. In the 1760s, while Augusta and Bute built and developed the botanic garden at Kew, 'Capability' Brown began to work next door on the Richmond garden which George III had inherited from his grandfather; the gardens would not come under common ownership until after Augusta's death. Brown smoothed the contours of Queen Caroline's former garden, made the landscape more naturalistic and opened the view out across the river towards Syon House. He created a very different aesthetic from Augusta's across Love Lane, symbolising that these were the years when George was distancing himself not only from Bute but also from his mother, too. Richmond and Kew were finally united in 1802, but the two areas of the garden remain quite distinct even in the twenty-first century. The more cultivated areas and lawns are concentrated around the

Palm House, Temperate House and Chambers' Conservatory, near the main public gates to the gardens, while the wilder, more natural areas are on the riverside.

Chambers's work was intended to signify the role that Bute and Augusta's family played in the successful conclusion of the Seven Years War. The architect described the buildings in detail in the book of plans and elevations which was, in his words, 'undertaken by Royal Command, and nobly paid for by Royal Bounty'. The volume, already referred to, was seen as a publicity stunt, a joint promotion of the royal patron, Augusta, the visionary landscaper, Bute, and, of course, Chambers himself as the architect.[2]

The Ruined Arch (still standing) was intended to be 'triumphal' and 'to imitate a Roman antiquity', while the Temple of Victory stood, as Chambers explains, 'on a hill and was built in commemoration of the signal victory obtained, on the first of August 1759, near Minden, by the Allied Army, under Prince Ferdinand of Brunswick, over the French Army, commanded by Marshal de Contades'. The predominantly Hanoverian army was led by Brunswick, a kinsman of Augusta's, so the temple is a flattering reference to the family of the dowager princess. In 1760, the Temple of Bellona was erected, dedicated to the goddess of war, and projected by Augusta as a celebration of the victories of the Anglo-Germanic army.[3] With her British-born son on the throne, Britain's and Hanover's interests were finally aligned, rather than the latter's being seemingly privileged over the former. A Temple of Peace was also projected, which, said Chambers, would be 'richly furnished with stucco ornaments, allusive to the occasion on which it is erected'.[4] It was, however, never built; Bute and Augusta must have realised that the peace terms were too controversial to be celebrated in stone (or even in wood) adjacent to the White House.

In these turbulent years, Kew itself effectively became a conceptual battleground. Augusta, Bute and Chambers were all accused of distorting Frederick's vision, thereby causing two decades of ferocious political and aesthetic debate, as well as instability in the new reign.[5] 'Her name is Tyranny,' declared Thomas Chatterton in his epic poem, *Kew Gardens*.[6] Patrick Eyres puts the case strongly, using the vernacular of the eighteenth century. 'Bute symbolized Scottish political and sexual penetration of the English establishment, as well as the agency through which offices and privileges were appropriated by Scots perceived to be fellow travellers.'[7]

While Chambers built at Kew, Bute's enemy, John Wilkes, MP for the Buckinghamshire constituency of Aylesbury, was a frequent visitor to Stowe, where Earl Temple continued to elaborate on his own, now imperial, vision. The fruits of the Whig supremacy, he wished to demonstrate, were a world-wide empire. He erected a 100-foot stone obelisk as a memorial to General James Wolfe, killed on the Heights of Abraham in 1759 as he overcame the French at Quebec.[8] Britain's victory in the Seven Years War was commemorated by the renaming and refurbishing of the Grecian Temple, the Temple of Concord and Victory. It stood, and still stands, in an imposing position at the head of the Grecian Valley, landscaped by 'Capability' Brown. This colonnaded Ionic temple had been built some ten years before the Battle of Minden, and was based in part on the Roman *Maison Carre* in Nimes, in southern France, which Earl Temple had seen as a young man on his Grand Tour. Frederick's favourite sculptor, Peter Scheemakers, remaining in the Temples's camp rather than in Augusta's, designed a tympanum relief, *The Four Quarters of the World Bringing their various Products to Britannia*, representing Britain's new global commercial muscle. The statues of Victory and Concord respectively tower above the front and rear pediments. Inside, a frieze of stucco Victory medallions, based on a medal designed by James 'Athenian' Stuart, celebrated victories in North America and India, and contrasted with the German focus at Kew.[9]

The Seven Years War, in Temple's view, had 'raised Britain from abasement to the first position in the World'. A war that had begun disastrously, with the loss of Minorca and the execution of Admiral Byng, ended in a triumph won in part by Pitt's leadership and by wartime cabinets in which Temple and his younger brother, George Grenville, had both sat.[10] The Temple of Concord and Victory was dedicated to Pitt and promoted victory as flowing from his strategic vision, rather than the bravery of Augusta's connections.[11]

The horticultural battle continued on paper as well as on the ground, and was equally uncompromising. Visiting Stowe in 1763, the year he launched his most scathing attacks on Bute, Wilkes wrote,

I was in raptures with all the elegant beauties of Stowe. As an Englishman, I was pleased that all the patriots and heroes of my country, Alfred, King William the Third, Hampden, Sir Walter Raleigh, &c. receive there the just tribute of praise, which this nation, while it remains free, will continue to pay to superior virtue. At Stowe, ancient and modern virtue are enshrined with grateful magnificence. not only good taste, but patriotism, are conspicuous in this delightful paradise, the favourite abode of the virtues, graces and muses.[12]

The 1766 and 1768 versions of the Stowe guidebooks, published regularly since 1744, carried a poem, *To the Earl Temple: on gardening*. Written by the earl's wife, Anna Grenville, Countess Temple, the poem begins by emphasising that the new Britain, forged by a combination of commercial muscle and warfare, is now displaying that victory on a carefully designed landscape.

> By commerce, Albion, and by Arms refin'd,
> Sought for the Charms of Art and Nature join'd.

She then describes the Temple of Concord and Victory, quoting the new British national anthem, first used in 1745, and praising Pitt's war achievements which Bute's 'factious Sacrifice' had tried but failed to undermine.

> Concord and Victory with Pride proclaim
> This Mansion sacred to Britannia's Fame,
> Whose Form majestic from all Hands receives
> The various Products ev'ry Region gives,
> Pleas'd at her Feet their choicest Gifts to lay,
> And homage to her Pow'r superior pay;
> The sculptur'd Walls her Glories past declare,
> In proud Memorials of successful War.
> No factious Sacrifice to France and Spain
> These consecrated Trophies can profane;
> For public Liberty her awful Seat
> Here fixing, here protects her last Retreat.[13]

The temple, says Temple's wife, effectively embodies all that is best about Britain, and Stowe, as it had been for five decades, is a bastion of liberty. By contrast, a poem published the following year puts the case for Kew. This panegyric by Henry Jones, *Kew*

Garden: A Poem in Two Cantos (1767), sees the royal garden as embodying national values, the triumphant optimism of a new reign, and the successes of Augusta, Bute and the king himself. Jones invokes both the Tory Pope and the Whig Milton to suggest that the new monarch is, as he had intended, above party. The poem's epigraph is a quotation from Pope, describing Kew as 'At once the Monarch's, and the Muse's Seat'.[14] The poet recounts how 'At ev'ry breathing pause new wonders rise … /And manifest the works of God to man', a clear echo of Milton's aim that *Paradise Lost* will 'justify the ways of God to men'.[15]

Jones argues in the poem that 'the boast of Greece [is] by British taste improv'd'. He writes in the spirit of the Enlightenment, and echoes Wilkes by referring once again to 'taste'. What he seems to be saying is that Bute's and Augusta's garden, and by implication Britain as a whole, have advanced from the ancient world, and now provide an appropriate moral environment in which the arts, political liberties and science, can flourish. He lists places from where plants were being imported, such as the West Indies, Iberia, America and China, and by so doing, Jones hints at Bute's and Augusta's imperial vision for Kew. He also praises the building erected by Chambers to celebrate peace with France.

> The just, embellish'd, beauteous frame behold,
> That speaks the finish'd master's manly thought,
> In emblematic trophies that display
> Britannia's glory, and the vanquish'd Gaul.

He compliments Bute elaborately, stressing the earl's role as both a moral and cultural guide for the king.

> When Nature's mirror, polish'd by the hand
> Of Taste, reflects thy finest attitudes …
> Where genius, sense, and taste, and BUTE are seen,
> To chear Britannia's heart, and GEORGE'S princely soul.[16]

Yet again, taste implies moral as well as aesthetic virtues. Chambers also joined in the horticultural war of words in his *Dissertation on Oriental Gardening*, published in 1772, the year of Augusta's death. He was making a political, as much as a horticultural, point when he compared British gardening unfavourably with Chinese. 'With the

Chinese,' he wrote, 'the taste of ornamental gardening is an object of legislative attention; it being supposed to have an influence on the general culture, and consequently upon the beauty of the whole country.' Chambers was critical of the current direction of English gardening and of 'Capability' Brown, whose work he considered insufficiently polished. 'In England ... where, in opposition to the rest of the world, a new manner is universally adopted, in which no appearance of art is tolerated, our gardens differ very little from common fields, so closely is vulgar nature copied in most of them.'[17] Brown's style, which would transform the face of the British landscape, was, Chambers implied, the extreme version of the English landscape movement. There would be a further reaction, with a return to greater artifice with the Picturesque movement and the work of designers such as Humphry Repton. And, as if in riposte to Chambers, Brown would pull down many of the buildings that the Scottish architect had erected at Kew when working there subsequently for George III. Given Walpole's view that Chambers' temples were 'all of wood & very small', it seems as if the king, as he matured and found his own voice, wanted to dismantle the equally flimsy political edifice his mother and Bute had constructed.

Chambers's *Dissertation* evoked a furious poetic response from William Mason, a friend of Horace Walpole's, who satirised George III's policies, particularly towards America, and paralleled parliamentary liberty with free-flowing garden design.[18] In the preface to *An Heroic Epistle*, Mason uses heavy irony to mock Chambers's dismissal of Brown, and twists Walpole's description of Kent. 'Like thee to scorn Dame Nature's simple fence; Leap each Ha Ha of truth and common sense'. He also summons up Pope on Stowe when criticising Chambers's un-English, Oriental style.

> Replace each vista, straighten every bend;
> Shut out the Thames; shall that ignoble thing
> Approach the presence of great Ocean's King?
> No! let Barbaric glories feast his eye,
> August Pagodas round his palace rise,
> And finish'd Richmond open to his view,
> 'A work to wonder at, perhaps a' Kew.

And, of course, no attack on Kew at the time was complete without a crack at Bute. 'Here's B-te's confession and his wooden head.'[19]

But Mason's sideswipe is a mere bagatelle besides the venom which poured forth from the pen of Thomas Chatterton, who, calling up 'the Spirit of a Churchill in my Quill', wrote an epic satire on *Kew Gardens*. In April 1770, four months before his suicide, aged seventeen, 'that marvellous boy' was an ambitious poet, who patently thought that an excoriating 1,094-line attack on Bute would help him to gain patronage. It is remarkable how Bute continued to be seen as a bogey man – seven years after he had relinquished the premiership, and a long time after his estrangement from the king. He appears to have become the lightning conductor for all the government's ills, so where better to attack than Kew, which Bute continued to direct until Augusta's death? 'The Groves of Kew,' said Chatterton, were being polluted, 'To serve the purposes of Lust and Pride'. He referred in an indecent double entendre to Bute's 'Iron Rod of Favour', and claimed 'Bute barter'd Peace and wisely sold, / His King, his union'd Countrymen for Gold'.[20] Mention here of the 'union' makes it clear that Chatterton believed, or at least affected to believe, that the Scots Bute had sold the English down the river for his own financial gain, although there is no evidence whatsoever of his having done so.

The long poem, written in heroic couplets, was not really about the garden, but about politics, which would have been immediately apparent to Chatterton's contemporary readers, as Kew, Augusta and Bute continued to be the subject of rumour and innuendo.

These criticisms were rebutted by Oliver Goldsmith in a poetic tribute to Augusta after her death. *Threnodia Augustalis* connected her charitable support for orphans and war veterans with her nurturing of the gardens at Kew, and spoke of her 'blending' borrowings from abroad with the indigenous to create an artistic and conceptual whole.

> Where sculptur'd elegance and native grace
> Unite to stamp the beauties of the place,
> While sweetly blending still are seen
> The wavy lawn, the sloping green ...
> From China borrows aid to deck the scene.[21]

Oliver Goldsmith and Henry Jones were rare voices heard in favour of the landscape garden conceived by Frederick, Augusta and Bute. From Pope onwards, the more eloquent sang out for

Stowe, and Horace Walpole's comments on the lie of the land and
the buildings at Kew suggest that it was less impressive even at the
time in terms of ornamentation than the Temples' achievement at
Stowe. Certainly, the buildings constructed by Vanbrugh, Kent and
Gibbs have survived whereas all but three of Chambers' creations
were subsequently swept away by 'Capability' Brown and by the
Victorians.

Kew's increasing emphasis on its acquisition of exotic plants and
on the development of botanical science also moved it away from
the mainstream of the English landscape movement, and led critical
observers such as Walpole to decry the gardens. As a result, Kew
lost the aesthetic battle with Stowe, as simultaneously its creators
lost the publicity war of the 1760s. Yet, although based on the
more ephemeral medium of plant material rather than stone, from
the very beginning Kew had an inherent dynamism which Stowe
lacked, for all its grandeur and elegance. In the 1790s, Erasmus
Darwin, grandfather of Charles and himself a botanist and early
evolutionist, wrote an epic poem, *The Botanic Garden: A Poem in
Two Parts*, which he dedicated to Sir Joseph Banks. As the title of
its first part ('The Economy of Vegetation') suggests, the poem links
botany with economics.

> So sits enthron'd in vegetable pride
> Imperial KEW by Thames's glittering side;
> Obedient sails from realms unfurrow'd bring
> For her the unnam'd progeny of spring;
> Attendant Nymphs ...
> ... fan in glass-built fanes the stranger flowers
> With milder gales, and steep with warmer showers.
> Delighted Thames through tropic umbrage glides,
> And flowers antarctic, bending o'er his tides;
> Drinks the new tints, the sweets unknown inhales,
> And calls the sons of science to his vales ...
> The fruits and foliage of discordant skies,
> Twines the gay floret with the fragrant bough,
> And bends the wreath round GEORGE'S royal brow.[22]

Erasmus Darwin invokes the different countries from which plants
flood in to be nurtured tenderly at Kew, showing that this work,
which began with Frederick's enthusiastic plant collecting, was

continued during Augusta's lifetime, and after her death. William Aiton remained as curator at Kew until his death in 1793, when he was succeeded by his son, William Townsend Aiton. In the 1790s, a Scottish clergyman visited Kew and introduced himself 'to Mr. Aiton [probably Aiton *fils*]. He shows me the first collection of plants I ever saw, both indigenous and exotic. Mr. Aiton favours me with specimens of the following rare plants: *Lepidium alpinum*, *Erinus alpinus*, *Scrophularia aquatic* (a rare variety from Yorkshire), *Scutellaria minor*, *Asperula Cynanchica*, *Campanula pumila*, *C. Patula* ... &c.'[23]

Augusta and Bute always intended that Kew should display royal and British botanical influence both to the visiting public and to the international scientific community. A 1771 newspaper account mentions that 'Dr. Solander has presented the Princess Dowager of Wales with several curious exotic plants for her Royal Highness's gardens at Kew'. Daniel Solander was a former pupil of Linnaeus's, underlining the garden's continued links with the foremost botanist of the age. A French writer, Louis Dutens, records that Bute 'excelloit tellement dans cette science, que les plus grandes maîtres en Europe le consultoient et recherchoient sa correspondence'.[24]

After Augusta was hissed to her grave in February 1772, her estate at Kew passed to George III, and, for the first time, the two royal gardens were in the same hands.

Bute resigned on the death of the dowager princess, marking the end of the first chapter in the creation of the Royal Botanic Gardens, Kew. In the general election of 1780, Bute retired as a Scots representative peer on grounds of age and applied himself to amassing a remarkable botanical and natural history collection. He had more time for his botanical studies and in 1785 produced the twelve-volume *Botanical Tables*. George III's wife, Queen Charlotte, responded graciously to Bute's request that he might dedicate the work to her, suggesting that lines of communication were still occasionally open between the king's family and Bute. In acknowledgement, Charlotte wrote, saying, 'I can never hesitate a moment of taking under my Protection any work Lord Bute recommends; but particularly in this instance, as I know the work on British plants to be the produce of Lord Bute's studies.' She declared that she would 'endeavour not to forfeit' the earl's good opinion, but would pursue 'this study steadily'.[25] Four years later, the queen wrote again to Bute, this time to tell him about her own plans to produce a pressed plant collection.

> My Lord, I hope I shall not be accused of vanity in offering you a sight of the beginning of a herbal from impressions on black paper. The amusement being endless made me desirous of pursuing it with steadiness ... I do not dispair of coming still to greater perfection which I shall strive to do having the summer before me, & with the assistance of Aiton hope to take them quite in the botanical way.[26]

Bute's former colleague at Kew was still advising the family, and Bute himself was invited to give his imprimatur to the queen's horticultural activities.

Bute made improvements to his estates at Luton Hoo in Bedfordshire, and at Highcliffe in Hampshire. At Luton Hoo, he employed 'Capability' Brown, who took over an ancient woodland, and, as was his wont, chopped down trees to create new vistas and rolling landscape.

Some of the centuries-old trees, however, were retained, conserved like ancient buildings to be captured in pen, body colour and watercolour by Paul Sandby. Regarded by many as the father of English landscape art, Sandby had learned his craft alongside his brother, Thomas, sketching military surveys of the field of Culloden after the event. His work helped contribute to the new imagery of the nation that was evolving in the second half of the eighteenth century, and in which the gardens at Stowe and Kew also played a major part. Sandby's 1765 *View in Luton Park* shows avenues of aged beeches, with scattered clumps, screens and belts of trees. There is an allusion here to the economic role of timber on a country estate – it shows that the trees are of commercial as well as of pictorial value, and is all of a piece with the work that Bute had once done at Kew.

Bute's last tribute to Augusta was to raise a memorial to her on his estate at Luton Hoo, its pedestal engraved with a quotation from Virgil's *Aeneid*, '*Dum memor ipse mei dum spiritus hos regit artus*'.[27] The towering stone column was moved to Mount Stuart in the 1870s by the 3rd Marquess of Bute, and now stands in the Policies there, looking majestically out over the Clyde.

Bute died with his wife at his side in March 1792, at his London house in South Audley Street, largely as a result of injuries incurred while scrabbling around for specimens on the cliffs near his home at Christchurch. Most of Bute's extensive collections were auctioned off in a series of sales in the months and years after his death, and his house at Highcliffe was demolished. The English-educated and derided Scot had not returned to his native country for forty-seven years, since his departure at the time of the 1745 Jacobite rebellion.

Between them, the lives of Frederick and Bute had spanned the ninety years from the Union of the Crowns to the French Revolution, years which had seen several epoch-making wars, the establishment of the British Empire and the loss of the American colonies. This century of political upheaval had changed the nature of governance in Britain and its position in the world. It had gone from an often-disregarded offshore island, still troubled by the religious and political fallout of the seventeenth-century civil wars, to become a dominant new nation and 'master of the world'. At Bute's death, eighteen months short of the Reign of Terror, Britain was once again facing war with France, and within a decade would be engaged in a life and death struggle with Napoleon Bonaparte.

For commentators such as Walpole, Bute's botanical interests paled into insignificance beside the accomplishments of the landscaping nobility such as the Temples at Stowe. What Augusta and Bute succeeded in doing at Kew by no means vindicated them for their other shortcomings in the eyes of their outspoken and articulate contemporaries; in fact, those very achievements were decried because of their conspicuous failures in other fields. Frederick's posthumous reputation, too, was coloured by his having fallen foul of both his family and of the acerbic diarist Hervey. And his ultimate catastrophe, of course, as Prince of Wales, was not to become king. These personal disasters would destroy the standing of prince, princess and courtier, and would serve to obscure for the future their major contribution to the foundation of what remains to this day one of the world's most important botanical gardens and research institutions.

Epilogue

Stowe may have won the pitched horticultural battle of the eighteenth century, but Kew won the war, as can be seen from tracing the fortunes of both gardens over the next 200 years.

Bute's and Augusta's political antagonist at Stowe, Richard Grenville, 2nd Earl Temple, had died in 1779, having built the Corinthian Arch in 1763 as another ornament to mark Britain's triumph over the French. Crowning the main axis of the garden, it represents the gateway to a Protestant heaven, and was the final piece in the jigsaw of iconography begun half a century earlier by Lord Cobham, to contest the grand statement of Louis XIV's gardens at Versailles. In the Elysian Fields, Temple also erected a monument in 1778 to Captain Cook, the discoverer who added Australia to Britain's overseas possessions.

Over the next seventy years, the fortunes of the Temple family would wax and wane. They would make their way up the ranks of the aristocracy, with Temple's great-nephew fulfilling the family's long-standing ambitions by becoming Duke of Buckingham and Chandos in 1822. But the glory days of Cobham and Temple were over; in 1831, the horticulturalist and journalist J. C. Loudon reported that 'the number of hands being yearly lessened. In new and rare plants, trees, and shrubs, the grounds are not keeping pace with the nurseries.'[1]

The exorbitant cost of a visit from Queen Victoria and Prince Albert in 1845 undid yet another Duke of Buckingham; the second duke's assets were seized two years later and he escaped abroad. A forty-day sale by Christie's in 1848 of the contents of Stowe house raised only £75,400. The historian Thomas Babington Macaulay wrote in *The Times* of 'a spectacle of a painfully interesting and gravely historical import. One of the most splendid abodes of our almost regal aristocracy has thrown open its portals to an endless succession of visitors, who from morning to night have flowed in an uninterrupted stream from room to room ... not to enjoy the hospitality of the lord, or to congratulate him on his countless treasures of art, but to see an ancient family ruined, their place marked for destruction, and its contents scattered to the four winds of Heaven'.[2]

The house was sold and became a school in 1923. Over the next sixty years, gardens and monuments became increasingly run down until the National Trust assumed ownership in 1989, and began restoring them to their former glory. In 2012, the trust reopened the New Inn, Lord Cobham's original visitors' centre. Twenty-first-century garden pilgrims now make their way to the Bell Gate where their eighteenth-century counterparts would once have rung for admission, and follow the critical path devised by Cobham. His vision has been restored, but his garden remains a museum to eighteenth-century values, its iconography now unintelligible to most visitors without a detailed guidebook, and/or an advanced knowledge of Latin.

Kew tried but never managed to become what amounted to an upmarket eighteenth-century theme park. Instead, its reputation from the outset was soundly based on botanical excellence, and it is that which has given it continuing relevance apparent to visitors today, even without the interpretation boards which are so crucial to an understanding of Stowe. Because Bute was a disappointment as a politician, and because Augusta was an unpopular dowager, it is all too easy to overlook their initial spadework at the Royal Botanic Gardens at Kew. That work was a key contribution to the gardens' subsequent role as a showcase at home and abroad of late eighteenth and early nineteenth-century British imperial expansion. Frederick, Bute and Augusta between them laid the foundations on which Sir Joseph Banks was ultimately to build what has been called his 'patriotic project'.[3]

Banks took over what he called 'a kind of superintendence' – in fact the directorship – of the royal gardens after Bute's departure, and remained in charge until his death in 1820.[4] Banks was a wealthy botanist and naturalist who had paid for his own passage on James Cook's round the world expedition on the *Endeavour* between 1768 and 1771. He held the post of president of the Royal Society for forty-one years, and was one of the founders, in 1804, along with Josiah Wedgwood's son, John, of the Horticultural Society of London (eventually the Royal Horticultural Society). Banks, unlike Bute, was a prominent and powerful member of the British establishment, who, says John Gascoigne, identified 'the interests of the British state with his own class – the British gentry'.[5] A visionary and an entrepreneur, he had the full-hearted support of the king, and was able to develop Augusta's botanic gardens, introducing many thousands of rare and exotic plants. He understood how botany could be used in the economic and political service of the new British Empire. Kew Gardens, under Banks's aegis, became the centre of a worldwide network of botanical gardens, with Banks determined that Britain's international prestige should be bolstered by Kew's unrivalled position. He boasted that Kew 'has acquired a superiority over all similar establishments, which not one of its rivals dares to deny; in fact it is the nursing mother of all the rest, who draw from England the greater part of the exotics they cultivate in their botanic gardens'.[6]

Banks launched the great age of the plant hunting expeditions, sending out explorers across the world, including Francis Masson, William Kerr and Allen Cunningham, all of them Scots. They went to South Africa, North America, Australia, China and Brazil, where they faced great dangers and hardships. Kew Gardens' first official plant collector, Francis Masson, hid in a hut overnight from a potentially murderous party of escaped 'Hottentot' convicts in South Africa in 1773. Twenty-four years later, he was further shaken by being captured by French privateers and imprisoned for several weeks with barely enough food and water. The mutiny on HMS *Bounty* in 1789 was triggered by Banks's economic imperialism. Captain Bligh was taking breadfruit at Banks's behest from Tahiti to the West Indies to feed British slaves, and chose to water the plants rather than his crew.

Banks also commissioned another *Hortus Kewensis*, which was drawn up by William Aiton and published in 1789. This second *Hortus Kewensis* did not attract the adverse comment that had greeted Hill's volume in 1768, and reveals how many more plants had been collected in the intervening period. Nevertheless,

Bute's curator was still at the heart of the botanical garden three decades after he had been first employed by Augusta. Without their groundwork, Banks would have taken more than a few short years to establish Kew as one of the pre-eminent botanic gardens in Europe.

After Banks' death in 1820, the gardens suffered a period of neglect until Sir William Hooker became director in 1840, the year before Kew came under direct state control. Over the next fifteen years, a new arboretum was laid out, the herbarium collection was founded and the great Palm and Temperate Houses were built. Hooker's son, Joseph, was an explorer and plant collector who later took over as director from his father. In 1853, there were 4,500 herbaceous plants in cultivation. Eleven years later, there were more than 13,000 species, and over 3,000 species of trees and shrubs in the arboretum.

Scientific research expanded, fulfilling Banks's dream by supplying crops, personnel and horticultural advice to Britain's far-flung colonies. In the twentieth century, two world wars interrupted developments at Kew, but it has continued to be a centre of botanical research, and now leads on habitat and biodiversity conservation worldwide.

In 1965, Kew acquired Wakehurst Place in West Sussex, where the Millennium Seed Bank was established in 2000. In 2003 the Royal Botanic Gardens Kew were designated a UNESCO World Heritage Site, and are now visited by over one and a quarter million people a year.

Plants may seem more transient than buildings, and yet it was the emphasis on botanical science at Kew from its foundation in 1759 that has led it to become the world-respected institution it is today. It may have had its ups and downs over the intervening two and a half centuries, but it remains a living, breathing place, not an exercise in architectural history like its eighteenth-century rival, Stowe. Kew today may seem a far cry from Frederick, Prince of Wales, 'directing the plantations of Trees and exotics with the workmen' in 1750. Yet it was with that direction that this great international organisation began. There may never have been a King Frederick I of the United Kingdom of Great Britain, but he left a powerful, if often overlooked, legacy in the work that he, Augusta and Lord Bute did at Kew. I hope this book has served to shed some light on this trio's contribution to the Royal Botanic Gardens at Kew.

Acknowledgements

Although writing a book is a solitary process, many people help along the way. To name a few, thanks go to Sue Fairbairn, for alerting Amberley Publishing to my idea for this book. I also want to thank the editors at Amberley who have worked on it, namely Jonathan Jackson, Sarah Kendall and Eleri Pipien. Ellis Rea kindly took time out of her holiday to compile the index. I have been greatly helped in my research by the staff at the London Library, British Library and Kew Library, and by Agata Rutkowska at the Royal Collection, Anna McEvoy at the Stowe House Preservation Trust, Karen Horsley at the Mount Stuart Archives and Kristen McDonald at the Lewis Walpole Library at Yale. Going further back in time, I am grateful to my supervisor at Birkbeck, Laura Stewart, who encouraged me to develop my MA thesis into a book.

The greatest thanks, as ever, go my family: my elder son, Nicholas, a fellow historian, who has always been a perceptive guide, and my younger son, Matthew, for his good humour and encouragement. Lastly, I would have written nothing without the support of my husband, Chris Evans, who has read every word more than once and been unfailingly reassuring over more than thirty-five years.

Notes

Introduction

1. Flora Fraser, *Princesses: The Six Daughters of George III* (London: John Murray, 2004), p. 30.
2. Horace Walpole, *The Yale Edition of Horace Walpole's Correspondence*, 48 Vols (ed.) W. S. Lewis (Oxford: Oxford University Press, 1937–65), Vol. 23, p. 379.
3. *Middlesex Journal or Chronicle of Liberty* (London), Thursday 13 February, 1772; Issue 449, *Seventeenth & Eighteenth Century Burney Collection Newspapers*.
4. Fraser, *Princesses*, p. 30.
5. Mrs Henrietta Hill, calling herself Lady Hill, *An Address to the Public by the Honourable Lady Hill; setting forth the consequences of the late Sir John Hill's Acquaintance with the Earl of Bute* (London: 1788), p. 7.
6. Edward Salisbury, 'The Royal Botanic Gardens, Kew', *Proceedings of the Royal Society of London. Series A, Mathematical and Physical Sciences*, 195:1043 (3 February 1949), p. 423.
7. *Letters from George III to Lord Bute 1756–1766* (ed.) Romney Sedgwick (London: Macmillan, 1939); J. A. Lovat-Fraser, *John Stuart Earl of Bute* (Cambridge: Cambridge University Press, 1912), pp. 8–9.
8. George Rude, *Wilkes and Liberty: A Social Study* (Oxford: Clarendon Press, 1962; 2nd edition, with new preface, London: Lawrence & Wishart, 1983), pp. 19–21.
9. Horace Walpole, *Memoirs of the Reign of King George III*, Vol. I (ed.) Derek Jarrett (New Haven & London: Yale University Press, 2000), p. 7.
10. *London Evening Post*, Thursday, 31 May, 1770; Issue 6642, *Burney Collection*.

Part I

1. A Chilly Summons

1. Tobias Smollett, *Peregrine Pickle* (1751), quoted, Morris Marples, *Poor Fred and the Butcher: Sons of George III* (London: Michael Joseph, 1970), p. 14.

2. *The Flying Post or Weekly Medley*, Saturday 7 December 1728. *Burney Collection.*
3. Quoted, Frances Vivian, *A Life of Frederick, Prince of Wales, 1707–1751: A Connoisseur of the Arts* (ed.) R. White (Lewiston, Lampeter: The Edwin Mellen Press, 2006), pp. 63–64.
4. Charles Maitland, quoted, Matthew Kilburn, 'Frederick Lewis, prince of Wales (1707–1751)', *Oxford Dictionary of National Biography* (Oxford, 2004; online edn, May 2009).
5. Friedrich Ernst Von Fabrice, *The Genuine Letters of Baron Fabricus* (London: 1761), pp. iv, vi.
6. Vivian, *A Life of Frederick*, p.95.
7. Vivian, ibid, p. 87.
8. R. L. Arkell, *Caroline of Ansbach: George II's Queen* (London: Oxford University Press, 1939), p. 152.
9. Andrew C. Thompson, *George II: King and Elector* (New Haven & London: Yale University Press, 2011), pp. 51–52
10. Arkell, *Caroline of Ansbach*, pp. 100–101.
11. Arkell, ibid, pp. 102,108.
12. Quoted, Edward Pearce, *The Great Man: Sir Robert Walpole: Scoundrel, Genius and Britain's First Prime Minister* (London: Jonathan Cape, 2007; Pimlico Paperback, 2008), p. 219.
13. John, Lord Hervey, *Some Materials towards Memoirs of the Reign of King George II*, 3 Vols (ed.) Romney Sedgwick (London: King's Printers, 1931), Vol.I, pp. 24, 25, 23.
14. Pearce, *The Great Man*, p. 221.
15. Hervey, *Memoirs*, Vol. III, p. 904.
16. Edmund Curll, *The Rarities of Richmond: Being Exact Descriptions of the Royal Hermitage and Merlin's Cave. With his Life and Prophecies* (2nd edition, London: 1736), Part I, pull-outs, facing pp. 7, 11.
17. Hervey, *Memoirs*, Vol. I, p. 35.
18. Arkell, *Caroline of Ansbach*, p. 163.
19. Hervey, *Memoirs*, Vol. I, p. 95.
20. Michael De-La-Noy, *The King Who Never Was: The Story of Frederick, Prince of Wales* (London: Peter Owen, 1996), p. 87.
   Hervey, *Memoirs*, Vol. I, p. 95.

2. A Boy in a Man's World

1. Arkell, *Caroline of Ansbach*, p. 151.
2. Vivian, *A Life of Frederick*, p. 14.
3. Horace Walpole, *Memoirs of King George II*, Vol.1, January 1751–1754 (ed.) John Brooke (New Haven and London: Yale University Press, 1985), p. 51.
4. Quoted, Hannah Smith, in *Georgian Monarchy: Politics and Culture, 1714–1760* (Cambridge: Cambridge University Press, 2006), p. 34.
5. Vivian, *A Life of Frederick*, p. 14.
6. Quoted, Stephen Taylor, 'Caroline (1683–1737)', *Oxford Dictionary of National Biography* (Oxford, 2004). [http://www.oxforddnb.com.ezproxy.londonlibrary.co.uk/view/article/4720, accessed 10 Nov 2011]

7. J. H. Plumb, *The First Four Georges* (London: Batsford, 1956; Fontana paperback, 1972), p. 71.
8. Quoted, Henry Curties, *A Forgotten Prince of Wales* (London: Everett & Co, 1912), pp. 2–3.
9. Marples, *Poor Fred*, p. 4.
10. Quoted, George Young, in *Poor Fred, The People's Prince* (London: Oxford University Press, 1937), p. 10.
11. Vivian, *A Life of Frederick*, p. 5.
12. Vivian, ibid., p. 17.
13. Kilburn, 'Frederick Lewis, Prince of Wales (1707–1751)'.
14. Hervey, *Memoirs*, Vol.III, p. 861.
15. Vivian, *A Life of Frederick*, p. 18.
16. Quoted, Young, *Poor Fred*, p. 19.
17. Quoted, Curties, *A Forgotten Prince of Wales*, pp. 12–13.
18. John Walters, *The Royal Griffin: Frederick Princes of Wales, 1707–51* (London: Jarrolds, 1972), p. 37.
19. *The Flying Post or Weekly Medley*, Saturday 7 December 1728. *Burney Collection.*
20. Quoted, Marples, *Poor Fred*, p. 6.
21. Vivian, *A Life of Frederick*, pp. 20–21.
22. Walters, *The Royal Griffin*, p. 28.
23. Quoted, Vivian, *A Life of Frederick*, p. 21.
24. Walters, *The Royal Griffin*, p. 32.
25. Hervey, *Memoirs*, Vol.III, p. 858.
26. Walters, *The Royal Griffin*, p. 27.
27. Quoted, De-La-Noy, *The King Who Never Was*, pp. 89–90.
28. John Perceval, First Earl of Egmont, *Manuscripts of the Earl of Egmont: Diary of Viscount Perceval, Afterwards First Earl of Egmont*, 3 vols (ed.) R. A. Roberts (London: Historical Manuscripts Commission, 1920–1923), Vol. III, p. 327.

3. 'The Opulence of a Free Country'

1. Celia Fiennes, *The Journeys of Celia Fiennes* (ed.) Christopher Morris (London: Cresset Press, 1947), pp. 29–30 [Note: When quoting contemporary authors, I have kept their spelling and punctuation but not their insistent use of capitals, which is sometimes confusing. I have also substituted the modern 's' for their archaic use of a sloping 'f' for 's'.]
2. John Martin Robinson, *Temples of Delight: Stowe Landscape Gardens* (London: National Trust, 1990; 2nd edition, 1994), pp. 82, 12, 28.
3. Jenny Uglow, 'A pastoral painter', *RA Magazine*, 106 (Spring 2010), p. 52.
4. Basil Williams, *The Whig Supremacy: 1714–1760*, 2nd edition, revised by C. H. Stuart (Oxford: Clarendon Press, 1960), p. 13.
5. Desmond Shawe-Taylor, 'Ruling a Free Nation', in (ed.) Desmond Shawe-Taylor, *The First Georgians: Art & Monarchy 1714–1760* (London: *Royal Collection, 2014*), *p. 14.*
6. Williams, *The Whig Supremacy*, p. 1
7. Williams, ibid., pp. 157, 156.

8. Cesar de Saussure, *A Foreign View of England in the Reigns of George I and George II: The Letters of Monsieur Cesar de Saussure to his family*: translated and edited by Madame Van Muyden (London: John Murray, 1902), pp. 336, 337.

9. Horace Walpole, *The History of the Modern Taste in Gardening* (ed.) John Dixon Hunt (New York: Ursus Press, 1995), pp. 29–30.

10. Edmund Burke, *A Philosophical Enquiry into the Origin of our Ideas of the Sublime and the Beautiful* (London, 1757), (ed.) Adam Phillips (Oxford: Oxford World's Classics paperback, 2008), p. 22.

11. Quoted, H. F. Clark, *The English Landscape Garden* (London: Pleiades Books, 1948), p. 10.

12. Quoted, Timothy Mowl, *William Kent: Architect, Designer, Opportunist* (London: Jonathan Cape, 2006; Pimlico paperback, 2007), p. 37.

13. Joseph Addison, 'Primary pleasures: the effects of nature and art compared and contrasted', Wednesday, 25 June 1712, in *Selections from The Tatler and The Spectator* (1709–1712), (ed.) Angus Ross (London: Penguin, 1982), p. 378.

14. Walpole, *Modern Taste*, p. 43.

15. Jeremy Black, *Culture in Eighteenth-Century England: A Subject for Taste* (London: Hambledon Continuum, 2005; paperback, 2007), p. 48.

16. Quoted, Charles Quest-Ritson, *The English Garden: A Social History* (London: Viking, 2001), p. 117.

17. Humphry Repton to Uvedale Price, 1794; quoted, Dana Arnold, *Rural Urbanism: London Landscapes in the early nineteenth century* (Manchester: Manchester University Press, 2005), p. 156.

18. Martin Robinson, *Temples of Delight*, pp. 60, 28.

19. H. T. Dickinson, *Liberty and Property: Political Ideology in Eighteenth-Century Britain* (London: Weidenfeld & Nicolson, 1977), p. 57.

20. Horace Walpole, *Last Journals*, Vol. 2, quoted, John Cannon, *Aristocratic Century: The peerage of eighteenth-century England* (Cambridge: Cambridge University Press, 1984), p. 3.

21. Roger White, *Chiswick House and Gardens* (London: English Heritage, 2001), p. 24.

22. Martin Robinson, *Temples of Delight*, p. 20.

23. Quoted, Christopher Hussey, *English Gardens and Landscapes 1700–1750* (London: Country Life, 1967), p. 95.

24. Dana Arnold, *Rural Urbanism*, p. 24.

25. Walpole, *Modern Taste*, p. 58.

26. Daniel Defoe, *A Tour through the Whole Island of Great Britain* (eds) G. D. H. Cole and D. C. Browning (London, 1928; reprinted in one volume, London: J. M. Dent, 1974), p. 2.

27. John Ogilby, *Britannia* (London, 1675). [http://www.fulltable.com/vts/m/map/ogilby/b/SH950.jpg, accessed 20 September 2010]

28. George Bickham, *The Beauties of Stowe or a Description of the Most Noble House, Gardens & Magnificent Buildings therein of the Right Honourable Earl Temple, Viscount & Baron Cobham* (London, 1753), p. 38.

29. Carole Fabricant, 'The Literature of Domestic Tourism and the Public

Consumption of Private Property', in (eds) Felicity Nussbaum and Laura Brown, *The New Eighteenth Century: Theory, Politics, English Literature* (London: Methuen, 1987), pp. 261, 256, 257.

30. Bickham, *The Beauties of Stowe*, p. 39.
31. *The Gentleman's Magazine*, 5 (December 1735), p. 715.
32. Bickham, *The Beauties of Stowe*, p. 38.
33. John Byng, Viscount Torrington, *The Torrington Diaries: Containing the Tours through England and Wales of the Hon. John Byng*, Vol. II (ed.) C. Bruyn Andrews, London: Eyre & Spottiswoode, 1935), p. 121.
34. Adam Smith, *The Wealth of Nations*, 2 vols (eds) R. H. Campbell and A. S. Skinner (Oxford: Clarendon Press, 1976), Vol. 1, p. 190.
35. Lewis M. Wiggin, *The Faction of Cousins: A Political Account of the Grenvilles, 1733–1763* (New Haven: Yale University Press, 1958), p. 1.
36. Adrian Tinniswood, *The Polite Tourist: A History of Country House Visiting* (2nd edition, London: National Trust, 1998), p. 74.
37. Wilfrid Blunt, *In For a Penny: A Prospect of Kew Gardens, Their Flora, Fauna and Falballas* (London: Hamish Hamilton, 1978), p. 1.
38. Williams, *The Whig Supremacy*, p. 157.
39. W. Thistleton-Dyer, 'Historical Account of Kew to 1841', *Kew Bulletin*, 60 (1891), p. 283.
40. Jonathan Marsden, in (ed.) Desmond Shawe-Taylor, *The First Georgians*, p. 279.
41. Edmund Curll, *The Rarities of Richmond* Part I, pull-outs, facing pp. 7, 11.
42. Judith Colton, 'Merlin's Cave and Queen Caroline: Garden Art as Political Propaganda', *Eighteenth-Century Studies*, 10:1 (Autumn 1976), pp. 6, 16, 19.
43. *The Gentleman's Magazine*, 5 (December 1735), p. 715.

4. *'This Is Not a Son I Need Be Much Afraid Of'*

1. *Daily Post*, 8 December 1728, *Burney Collection*.
2. Egmont, *Manuscripts*, Vol. III, p. 327.
3. Young, *Poor Fred*, p. 14.
4. Averyl Edwards, *Frederick Louis Princes of Wales 1707–1751* (London: Staples Press, 1947), p. 16.
5. *Brice's Weekly Journal*, No. 129, 13 December 1728, *Burney Collection*.
6. *Daily Post*, 13 December 1728, *Burney Collection*.
7. Kimerly Rorschach, *Frederick, Prince of Wales (1707–1751) as a Patron of the Visual Arts: Princely Patriotism and Political Propaganda* (unpublished PhD dissertation, Yale University, 1985), p. 18.
8. *British Gazeteer*, No. 193, 1 February 1729, *Burney Collection*.
9. Vivian, *A Life of Frederick*, pp. 113–116.
10. *Applebee's Original Weekly Journal*, 8 March 1729, *Burney Collection*.
11. Quoted, Walters, *The Royal Griffin*, p. 52.
12. Hervey, *Memoirs*, Vol. I, p. 95.
13. Hervey, ibid, Vol. I, p. 96.
14. Egmont, *Manuscripts*, Vol. I, p. xv.
15. Egmont, ibid, Vol. I, p. 92.

16. De-la-Noy, *The King who Never Was*, p. 105.
17. Hervey, *Memoirs*, Vol. I, pp. 308–309.
18. Quoted, De-La-Noy, *The King who Never Was*, p. 151.
19. Robert Sackville-West, *Inheritance: The Story of Knole and the Sackvilles* (London: Bloomsbury, 2010), p. 107.
20. Egmont, *Manuscripts*, Vol. I, p. 10.
21. Quoted, Edwards, *Frederick Louis Prince of Wales*, p. 21.
22. Quoted, Edwards, ibid, p. 22.
23. Alexander Pope, *Epistle to Dr. Arbuthnot*, ll. 305–310, from *The Poems of Alexander Pope* (ed.) John Butt (London: Methuen, 1963), pp. 607–608.
24. John van der Kiste, *King George II and Queen Caroline* (Stroud: Alan Sutton, 1997), p. 114.
25. De-la-Noy, *The King who Never Was*, p. 117.
26. Hannah Smith and Stephen Taylor, 'Hephaestion and Alexander: Lord Hervey, Frederick, Prince of Wales, and the Royal Favourite in England in the 1730s', *English Historical Review*, 124:507 (April 2009), pp. 283–284.
27. Quoted, Edwards, *Frederick Louis Prince of Wales*, p. 31.
28. Edwards, *Frederick Louis Prince of Wales*, p. 31.
29. *The Humours of the Court: Or, Modern Gallantry: A New Ballad Opera* (London: 1732), pp. iii, 10,16, 17, 25.
30. *The Fair Concubine: Or, the Secret History of the Beautiful Vanella* (London: 1732), pp. 20, 37.
31. Hervey, *Memoirs*, Vol. II, p. 388.
32. Hervey, ibid., pp. 483.

5. 'Fretz's Popularity Makes Me Vomit'

1. Quoted, Walters, *The Royal Griffin*, p. 9.
2. Desmond Shawe-Taylor, *The King's Ransom* (Video, 2014: A Royal Collection Trust and BBC partnership).
3. Hervey, *Memoirs of the Reign of King George II*, Vol. I, pp. 309, 310.
4. Hervey, ibid., Vol. I, pp. 274, 273.
5. Quoted, John Martin Robinson, *Buckingham Palace: The Official Illustrated History* (London: Royal Collection, 2000; reprint, 2007), pp. 27–29.
6. Veronica Baker-Smith, *Royal Discord: The Family of George II* (London: Athena Press, 2010), p. 52.
7. Hervey, *Memoirs*, Vol. II, p. 628.
8. Hervey, ibid., Vol. I, p. 97.
9. Archibald S. Foord, *His Majesty's Opposition 1714–1830* (Oxford: Clarendon Press, 1964), p. 128n.
10. Quoted, De-La-Noy, *The King who Never Was*, p. 151.
11. Hervey, *Memoirs*, Vol. II, p. 645.
12. Mavis Batey, *Oxford Gardens: The university's influence on garden history* (Amersham: Scolar Press, 1982), p. 100.
13. Tim Richardson, *The Arcadian Friends: Inventing the English Landscape Garden* (London: Bantam Press, 2007; paperback, 2008), pp. 216–220.
14. Isaac Kramnick, *Bolingbroke & His Circle: The Politics of Nostalgia in the Age of Walpole* (London: Oxford University Press, 1968; paperback

edition, Ithaca and London: Cornell University Press, 1992), pp. viii, 12, 13–14.

15. Wiggin, *The Faction of Cousins*, pp. 1–2.
16. H. T. Dickinson, *Walpole and the Whig Supremacy* (London: English Universities Press, 1973), pp. 178–179.
17. Vivian, *A Life of Frederick*, p. 224.
18. Quoted, Shawe-Taylor Desmond, *The Conversation Piece: Scenes of fashionable life* (London: Royal Collection, 2009), p. 69.

6. 'There Is a New Taste in Gardening'

1. Thomas Whately, *Observations on Modern Gardening and Laying-Out Pleasure Grounds, Parks, Farms, Ridings, &c. Illustrated by Descriptions. To Which is Added, An Essay on the Different Natural Situations of Gardens* (A new edition with notes by Horace (late) Earl of Orford, London, 1801), p. 1.
2. Hervey, *Memoirs*, Vol. II, p. 501.
3. Egmont, *Manuscripts*, Vol. II, p. 355.
4. John Evelyn, *The Diary of John Evelyn* (selected from 1959 Oxford University Press edition, ed. E. S. de Beer; London: Everyman's Library, 2006), pp. 583, 781.
5. Jenny Uglow, *A Little History of British Gardening* (London: Chatto & Windus, 2004), p. 130.
6. Lucy Worsley, *Courtiers: The Secret History of Kensington Palace* (London: Faber & Faber, 2010), p. 75.
7. Hervey, *Memoirs*, Vol.II, p. 581.
8. Walpole, *Modern Taste*, pp. 43–44.
9. Colton, 'Merlin's Cave and Queen Caroline', pp. 6, 16, 19.
10. Hervey, *Memoirs*, Vol. III, p. 844.
11. Timothy Mowl, *William Kent*, p. 204–206.
12. William Chambers, *Plans, Elevations, Sections, and Perspective Views of the Gardens and Buildings at Kew in Surry, the seat of Her Royal Highness the Princess Dowager of Wales* (London: 1763), pp. 1, 2.
13. Horace Walpole, *Memoirs of King George II*, p. 54.
14. Quoted, Young, *Poor Fred*, p. 143.
15. E. P. Thompson, 'Eighteenth-century English society class struggle without class?', *Social History*, 3:2 (May 1978), p. 140.
16. Pope, *Epistle to Cobham* (1734), p. 559.
17. Pope, *Epistle IV. To Richard Boyle, Earl of Burlington* (1731), pp. 590, 592.
18. Anne Jennings, *Georgian Gardens* (London: English Heritage and the Museum of Garden History, 2005), pp. 17–18.
19. Shawe-Taylor (ed.), *The First Georgians*, p. 38.
20. Edwards, *Frederick Louis, Prince of Wales*, pp. 128, 118.
21. Arthur Young, *The Farmer's Tour through the East of England* (London: W. Strahan, 1771), pp. 32–33, 39–40.
22. Bickham, *The Beauties of Stowe*, pp. 17, 20.
23. Benton Seeley, *Stowe: The Gardens of the Right Honourable the Lord Viscount Cobham* (London: 1751); Bickham, *The Beauties of Stowe*.
24. Bickham, *The Beauties of Stow*, frontispiece; Benton Seeley, *Stow: A*

Description of the Magnificent Gardens of the Right Honourable Richard, Earl Temple, Viscount and Baron Cobham (London, 1756); Benton Seeley, *Stowe: A Description of the Magnificent House and Gardens of the Right Honourable Richard, Earl Temple, Viscount and Baron Cobham* (London, 1759); frontispieces. [Please note that the spelling of the word 'Stow/Stowe' is not consistent in these guides; I have followed the spelling as used in each individual guide].

25. [William Gilpin], *A Dialogue upon the Gardens of the Right Honourable the Lord Viscount Cobham at Stowe in Buckinghamshire* (London, 1748).

26. [Gilpin], *A Dialogue*, p. 1.

27. Seeley, *Stowe* (1751), pp. 2, 18; [Gilpin], *A Dialogue*, p. 35.

28. Seeley, *Stowe* (1751), pp. 12, 20–21, 12.

29. David Coombs, 'The Garden at Carlton House of Frederick Prince of Wales and Augusta Dowager Duchess of Wales: Bills in their Household Accounts 1728–1772', *Garden History*, 25:2 (Winter 1997), pp. 153–177.

30. Letter from Sir Thomas Robinson, Historic Manuscripts Commission, *Carlisle*, pp. 143–144, quoted by Tom Williamson, *Polite Landscapes: Gardens & Society in Eighteenth-Century England* (Stroud: Allan Sutton, 1995), p. 59.

Part II

7. 'As Anxious as a Good Child to Please'

1. Sarah, Duchess of Marlborough, *Memoirs of Sarah, Duchess of Marlborough together with her Characters of her Contemporaries and her Opinions* (ed.) William King (London: Routledge, 1930), pp. 316–317.

2. Ophelia Field, *The Favourite: Sarah, Duchess of Marlborough* (London: Hodder & Stoughton, 2002; Sceptre paperback, 2003), p. 408.

3. Marples, *Poor Fred*, p. 31.

4. Hervey, *Memoirs*, Vol. I, p. 231.

5. Charles Chevenix Trench, *George II* (London: Allen Lane, 1973), p. 184.

6. Baker-Smith, *Royal Discord*, p. 65; Arkell, *Caroline of Ansbach*, p. 214.

7. Hervey, *Memoirs*, Vol. I, pp. 230–231.

8. Hervey, ibid, pp. 232–233.

9. Baker-Smith, *Royal Discord*, p. 70.

10. Quoted, Arkell, *Caroline of Ansbach*, p. 212.

11. Egmont, *Manuscripts*, Vol. II, pp. 121, 197.

12. Hervey, *Memoirs*, Vol. II, p. 548.

13. Hervey, ibid., p. 550.

14. Quoted, Michael De-La-Noy, *The King who Never Was*, p. 143.

15. Hervey, *Memoirs*, Vol. II, p. 548.

16. Quoted, Vivian, *A Life of Frederick, Prince of Wales*, p. 203.

17. Edwards, *Frederick Louis Prince of Wales*, p. 54.

18. Quoted, Vivian, *A Life of Frederick, Prince of Wales*, p. 204.

19. John L. Bullion, '"To play what game she pleased without observation:" Princess Augusta and the political drama of succession, 1736–1756', in (ed.) Clarissa Campbell Orr, *Queenship in Britain 1660–1837: Royal patronage,*

court culture and dynastic politics (Manchester: Manchester University Press, 2002), p. 214.

20. *The Gentleman's Magazine*, 6 (April 1736), p. 230.
21. Egmont, *Manuscripts*, Vol. II, p. 265.
22. Hervey, *Memoirs*, Vol. II, p. 550.
23. Hervey, ibid, pp. 551–552.
24. Egmont, *Manuscripts*, Vol. II, p. 263
25. *The Gentleman's Magazine*, 6 (April 1736), pp. 230–231.
26. Quoted, De-La-Noy, *The King who Never Was*, pp. 142–143.
27. Edward Pearce, *Pitt the Elder: Man of War* (London: The Bodley Head, 2010; Pimlico Paperback, 2011), p. 40.
28. *The Gentleman's Magazine*, 6 (May 1736), p. 289.
29. Quoted, Edwards, *Frederick Louis Prince of Wales*, p. 60.
30. Hervey, *Memoirs*, Vol.II, p. 560–561.
31. Vivian, *A Life of Frederick, Prince of Wales*, p. 203.
32. Hervey, *Memoirs*, Vol.II, pp. 554, 563.
33. Hervey, ibid., p. 553.
34. Edwards, *Frederick Louis Prince of Wales*, p. 61.
35. Baker-Smith, *Royal Discord*, p. 89.
36. Hervey, *Memoirs*, Vol. II, p. 556.
37. Hervey, ibid., p. 564.
38. Hervey, ibid., p. 566.
39. Egmont, *Manuscripts*, Vol. II, pp. 321–322.
40. Hervey, *Memoirs*, Vol. II, p. 635.
41. Hervey, ibid., pp. 647–648.
42. Hervey, ibid., p. 626.

8. 'Under a Fool's Direction'

1. Richard Savage, *The Poetical Works of Richard Savage, with the Life of the Author by Samuel Johnson* (New York: William A. Davis, 1805), pp. 88–90.
2. Hervey, *Memoirs*, Vol. III, p. 797.
3. Quoted, Edwards, *Frederick Louis Prince of Wales*, pp. 83–84.
4. Foord, *His Majesty's Opposition*, p. 127.
5. Hervey, *Memoirs*, Vol. II, p. 564.
6. Hervey, ibid, Vol. II, p. 553.
7. *The Gentleman's Magazine*, 7 (October 1737), p. 639.
8. Hervey, *Memoirs*, Vol. III, pp. 749–750.
9. Hervey, ibid, Vol. III, p.757.
10. Sarah, Duchess of Marlborough, *Memoirs*, p. 318.
11. Hervey, *Memoirs*, Vol. III, pp. 757–759.
12. Lord Fitzmaurice, *Life of William Earl of Shelburne Afterwards First Marquess of Lansdowne, with Extracts from his Papers and Correspondence* (Second and revised edition, in two volumes, London: Macmillan, 1912), p. 50.
13. Hervey, *Memoirs*, Vol. III, p. 793.
14. BL. Add Ms. 32795, f. 352, Mr Courand to Sir Benjamin Keene, Madrid, 12 September 1737.

15. *The Gentleman's Magazine*, 7 (October 1737), p. 677.
16. BL. Add Ms. 32795, f. 354.
17. *The Gentleman's Magazine*, 7 (October 1737), pp. 678–679, 680, 681, 682.
18. BL. ADD Ms. 32795, ff. 356–357.
19. Egmont, *Manuscripts*, Vol. II, p. 432.
20. Young, *Poor Fred*, p. 127; Egmont, *Manuscripts of the Earl of Egmont*, Vol. II, p. 425.
21. Quoted, Young, *Poor Fred*, p. 131.
22. Egmont, *Manuscripts*, Vol. II, p. 436.
23. Shawe-Taylor (ed.), *The First Georgians*, pp. 375–377.
24. Egmont, *Manuscripts*, Vol. II, p. 432.
25. Hervey, *Memoirs*, Vol. III, pp. 886–887.
26. Egmont, *Manuscripts*, Vol. II, p. 445.
27. van der Kiste, *King George II*, pp. 124, 164.
28. Quoted, Arkell, *Caroline of Ansbach*, pp. 225, 229.
29. Thompson, *George II*, p. 126.
30. Egmont, *Manuscripts*, Vol. II, p. 459.

9. 'A Declared Head to Range Themselves Under'

1. Egmont, *Manuscripts*, Vol. II, pp. 263–264.
2. Fitzmaurice, *Life of William Earl of Shelburne*, pp. 49, 47, 49.
3. Smith, *Georgian Monarchy*, p. 222.
4. Fitzmaurice, *Life of William Earl of Shelburne*, p. 49.
5. Hervey, *Memoirs of the Reign of King George II*, Vol. II, p. 564.
6. Quoted, Gervase Jackson-Stops, 'Cliveden, Buckinghamshire – II', *Country Life*, 161i (3 March 1977), p. 500.
7. Jeremiah Miles, Ms *A Journey from London to Holyhead in 1742*. BL. Add Ms. 15776, ff. 118–119.
8. Sarah, Duchess of Marlborough, *Memoirs*, p. 322.
9. Jackson-Stops, 'Cliveden – II', p. 501.
10. Thompson, *George II*, pp. 126–127.
11. Quoted, Edwards, *Frederick Louis, Prince of Wales*, p. 130.
12. Walpole, *Memoirs of King George II*, p. 52.
13. Thompson, *George II*, p. 129.
14. van der Kiste, *King George II*, p. 173.
15. Egmont, *Manuscripts*, Vol.III, p. 240.
16. Rorschach, *Frederick, Prince of Wales*, pp. 189–190.
17. Quoted, Edwards, *Frederick Louis, Prince of Wales*, p. 134.
18. Thompson, *George II*, p. 142.
19. Pearce, *The Great Man*, p. 414.
20. van der Kiste, *King George II*, p. 176.
21. Thompson, *George II*, p. 143.
22. Baker-Smith, *Royal Discord*, pp. 114, 117, 118.
23. Walpole, *The Yale Edition*, Vol. 18. pp. 340–341.
24. Baker-Smith, *Royal Discord*, pp. 119, 122.
25. Shawe-Taylor (ed.), *The First Georgians*, pp. 38–39.
26. Quoted, Edwards, *Frederick Louis, Prince of Wales*, p. 142.

27. Vivian, *A Life of Frederick, Prince of Wales*, p. 357.
28. Martin Robinson, *Temples of Delight*, p. 125.
29. Quoted, Edwards, *Frederick Louis, Prince of Wales*, p. 143.
30. Vivian, *A Life of Frederick, Prince of Wales*, p. 367.
31. Edwards, *Frederick Louis, Prince of Wales*, p. 149.
32. *Letters of Horace Walpole*, selected by W. S. Lewis, with an introduction by R. W. Ketton-Cremer (London: The Folio Society, 1951), pp. 51, 52.

Part III

10. *'An Odd Accident'*

1. *Horace Walpole's Miscellany 1786–1795* (ed. Lars E. Troide, New Haven and London: Yale University Press, 1978), pp. 80, 81.
2. Francis Russell, *John, 3rd Earl of Bute: Patron & Collector* (London: Merrion Press, 2004), p. xv.
3. Roger L. Emerson, 'Lord Bute and the Scottish Universities 1760–1792', in (ed.) Karl W. Schweizer, *Lord Bute: Essays in Re-interpretation* (Leicester: Leicester University Press, 1988), p. 170.
4. Fitzmaurice, *Life of William Earl of Shelburne*, pp. 110, 111.
5. Russell, *John, 3rd Earl of Bute*, p. 55.
6. Richard B. Sher, '"The favourite of the favourite": John Home, Bute and the politics of patriotic poetry', in (ed.) Schweizer, *Lord Bute*, p. 188.
7. Quoted, Romney Sedgwick, 'William Pitt and Lord Bute: An Intrigue of 1755-1758', *History Today*, 6:10 (October 1956), p. 649.
8. Quoted, David P. Miller, '"My favourite studdys": Lord Bute as naturalist', in (ed.) Karl W. Schweizer, *Lord Bute*, p. 217.
9. Russell, *John, 3rd Earl of Bute*, p. 2.
10. Isobel Grundy, *Lady Mary Wortley Montagu* (Oxford: Oxford University Press, 1999), p. 307.
11. Grundy, ibid, p.317.
12. Walpole, *Memoirs of the Reign of King George III*, p. 25.
13. Walpole, *Memoirs of the Reign of King George II*, p. 187.
14. Pearce, *The Great Man*, pp. 371, 372.
15. Walpole, *Memoirs of the Reign of King George II*, p. 187.
16. James Alexander Sinclair, 'The Gardens and Policies', *Mount Stuart: Isle of Bute* (Isle of Bute: The Mount Stuart Trust, 2001), p. 40.
17. Lady Mary Wortley Montagu, *The Complete Letters of Lady Mary Wortley Montagu*, 3 Vols (ed.) Robert Halsband (Oxford: Clarendon Press, 1966), Vol.II, pp. 438–439.
18. Quoted, Russell, *John, 3rd Earl of Bute*, p. 18.
19. Walpole, quoted in Wortley Montagu, *The Complete Letters*, Vol. II, p. 401 (note).
20. Edwards, *Frederick Louis, Prince of Wales*, pp. 116–117, 161–162.
21. Wortley Montagu, *The Complete Letters*, Vol. II, pp. 408, 416, 421.
22. Wortley Montagu, ibid., p. 427.
23. Tom Williamson, *Polite Landscapes*, p. 64.
24. Quoted, Edwards, *Frederick Louis, Prince of Wales*, pp. 142–143.

25. George Bubb Dodington, *The Political Journal of George Bubb Dodington* (eds) John Carswell and Lewis Arnold Dralle (Oxford: Clarendon Press, 1965), p. 6.

11. 'Gardening and Planting Have Lost Their Best Friend'

1. Dodington, *Political Journal*, pp. 59, 67.
2. William Chambers, *The Gardens and Buildings at Kew*, p. 2.
3. Ray Desmond, *Kew: The History of the Royal Botanic Gardens* (London: 1995, Harvill Press; paperback version, 1998), pp. 26–27.
4. George Vertue, 'Notebooks', *The Walpole Society*, Vol. 26 (1937–8), Vol. 30 (1951–1952), pp. 148, 149, 153.
5. Martin Robinson, *Temples of Delight*, p. 125.
6. Desmond, *Kew*, p. 28.
7. Kimerly Rorschach, 'Frederick, Prince of Wales: Taste, politics and power', *Apollo*, 134:156, New Series (October 1991), p. 243.
8. William Chambers, *A Dissertation on Oriental Gardening*, 2nd edition, with additions, London: 1773), p. 13.
9. Richardson, *The Arcadian Friends*, pp. 319–320; Desmond, *Kew*, p. 27.
10. Timothy Mowl, *Gentlemen & Players: Gardeners of the English Landscape* (Stroud: Alan Sutton, 2000), p. 63.
11. Richard Quaintance, 'Kew Gardens 1731–1778: Can We Look At Both Sides Now?', *New Arcadian Journal*, 51/52 (2001), p. 20.
12. Aubrey N. Newman, 'The Political Patronage of Frederick Lewis, Prince of Wales', *Historical Journal*, 1:1 (1958), pp. 70–71.
13. Quoted, Aubrey N. Newman, 'Leicester House Politics, 1750–1760, from the Papers of John, Second Earl of Egmont', *Camden Miscellany* (London: Royal Historical Society, 1969), Vol. 23, p. 90.
14. Robert Filmer, *Patriarcha* (London: 1680), pp. i, iv.
15. Newman, 'The Political Patronage of Frederick', p. 73.
16. Plantagent Somerset Fry, *The Kings & Queens of England & Scotland* (London: Dorling Kindersley, 1990), p. 163.
17. Quoted, Marples, *Poor Fred*, p. 107.
18. Dodington, *Political Journal*, p. 106.
19. Newman (ed.), 'Leicester House Politics', pp. 87–88, 174–175, 117, 93, 190–191.
20. Walpole, *Memoirs of King George II*, p. 55.
21. Newman, 'Leicester House Politics', p. 195.
22. Dodington, *Political Journal*, p. 104.
23. Walpole, *Memoirs of King George II*, Vol. I p. 50
24. Dodington, *Political Journal*, pp. 105–106.
25. Hervey, *Memoirs of the Reign of King George II*, Vol. III, p. 844.
26. Walpole, *Memoirs of King George II*, pp. 54–55.
27. Walpole, ibid., p. 63.
28. Robin Eagles, '"No more to be said?" Reactions to the death of Frederick Lewis, prince of Wales', *Historical Research*, 80:209 (August 2007), pp. 354, 355, 350, 355.
29. Dodington, *Political Journal*, p. 112.

30. Eagles. '"No more to be said?"', p. 356.
31. Dodington, *Diary*, pp. 112–113.
32. Walpole, *Memoirs of King George II*, p. 152.
33. Quoted, Eagles, 'No more to be said?', p. 350.
34. Quoted, Marples, *Poor Fred*, pp. 115, 117, 118.
35. Quoted, Christine Gerrard, *The Patriot Opposition to Walpole: Politics, Poetry, and National Myth, 1725-1742* (Oxford: Clarendon Press, 1994), p. 66.
36. Quoted, Desmond, *Kew*, p. 29.
37. Wortley Montagu, *The Complete Letters*, Vol. II, p. 513.

12. *'To Play What Game She Pleased Without Observation'*
 1. Dodington, *Political Journal*, p. 106; Walpole, *Memoirs of King George II*, p. 54.
 2. Newman, 'Leicester House Politics', pp. 198, 199.
 3. John L. Bullion, 'The Prince's Mentor: A New Perspective on the Friendship between George III and Lord Bute during the 1750s', *Albion*, 21:1 (Spring 1989), p. 39.
 4. Walpole, *Memoirs of King George II*, p. 60.
 5. Newman, 'Leicester House Politics', p. 205.
 6. Dodington, *Political Journal*, p. 177.
 7. Young, *Poor Fred*, pp. 172–175.
 8. Foord, *His Majesty's Opposition*, pp. 278–279; Newman, 'Leicester House Politics', p. 93.
 9. Fitzmaurice, *Life of William Earl of Shelburne*, pp. 52, 54, 49, 46.
10. James, 2nd Earl of Waldegrave, *The Memoirs and Speeches of James, 2nd Earl of Waldegrave, 1742–1763* (ed.) J. C. D. Clark (Cambridge: Cambridge University Press, 1988), p. 54.
11. Quoted, Desmond, *Kew*, p. 30.
12. Letter from Sir William Chambers to Robert Wood, quoted, John Harris, 'George III's parents: Frederick and Augusta', in *The Wisdom of George the Third: Papers from a Symposium at The Queen's Gallery, Buckingham Palace, June 2004*, (ed.) Jonathan Marsden (London: Royal Collection, 2005), p. 24.
13. Chambers, *The Gardens and Buildings at Kew*, p. 7.
14. Allen Paterson, *The Gardens at Kew* (London: Frances Lincoln, 2008), p. 27.
15. Chambers, *The Gardens and Buildings at Kew*, pp. 5, 6.
16. Quoted, Blunt, *In for a Penny*, p. 19.
17. Quoted, Madeline Bingham, *The Making of Kew* (London: Michael Joseph, 1975), p. 4.
18. *Middlesex Journal or Chronicle of Liberty* (London), Thursday, 13 February, 1772; Issue 449; Burney Collection.
19. Chambers, *The Gardens and Buildings at Kew*, p. 2.
20. Dodington, *Political Journal*, p. 178.
21. Walpole, *Memoirs of King George II*, p. 60.
22. Walpole, ibid., p. 194.
23. Waldegrave, *Memoirs and Speeches*, p. 55.

24. Walpole, *Memoirs of King George II*, pp. 199–200.
25. Waldegrave, *Memoirs and Speeches*, p. 145.
26. Waldegrave, ibid., pp. 176, 177.
27. Dodington, *Political Journals*, p. 178.
28. Russell, *John, 3rd Earl of Bute*, p. 20.
29. Waldegrave, *Memoirs and Speeches*, pp. 163–164.
30. Quoted, Blunt, *In for a Penny*, p. 24.
31. J. A. Lovat-Fraser, *John Stuart, Earl of Bute* (Cambridge: Cambridge University Press, 1912), p. 10.
32. Quoted, Edward Pearce, *Pitt the Elder*, p. 257.
33. Copies of the Letters of the Earl of Bute, 1756–1765, BL. Add. Ms. 36797, ff. 65, 64, 65.
34. Quoted, Jeremy Black, *George III: America's Last King* (New Haven and London: Yale University Press, 2006; paperback, 2008), p. 15.
35. Romney Sedgwick (ed.), 'Letters from William Pitt to Lord Bute: 1755–1758' in (ed.) Richard Pares and A. J. P. Taylor, *Essays Presented to Sir Lewis Namier* (London: Macmillan, 1956), pp. 156, 152, 166.
36. Walpole, *Memoirs of the Reign of King George III*, p. 11.

13. 'The Paradise of Our World, Where All Plants Are Found'

1. Andrea Wulf, *The Founding Gardeners: How the Revolutionary Generation Created an American Eden* (London: William Heinemann, 2011), pp. 22, 25, 26, 123, 201n.
2. Frank McLynn, *1759: The Year Britain Became Master of the World* (London: Jonathan Cape, 2004).
3. Desmond, *Kew*, pp. 34, 35.
4. Quoted, Miller, 'My favourite studdys,' p. 217.
5. The Earl of Bute to Peter Collinson from Mount Stuart, 7 March 1745, and from Twickenham, 4 March 1746. The Duke of Richmond to Peter Collinson from Goodwood, 27 June 1746. *Letters to Peter Collinson 1725–1790*, Vol. 1. BL. Add. Ms. 28726, ff. 154–155, 159, 157.
6. Quoted, Miller, 'My favourite studdys', p. 217–218.
7. Quoted, Desmond, *Kew*, p. 42.
8. Quoted, Norman G. Brett-James, *The Life of Peter Collinson FRS, FSA* (London: Edgar G. Dunstan & Co, 1925), pp. 87, 133.
9. Desmond, *Kew*, pp. 42, 40, 41, 42.
10. *St James's Chronicle*, Tuesday, 6 November, 1763; Issue 419, Burney Collection.
11. Quoted, Miller, 'My favourite studdys', p. 215.
12. Desmond, *Kew*, p. 41.
13. Walpole, *Memoirs of King George III*, Vol. 1, p. 16.
14. John Stuart, 3rd Earl of Bute, *Botanical Tables, Containing the Different Familys of British Plants, distinguished by a few obvious parts of fructification rang'd in a synoptical method* (London: 1785), pp. 3, 6, 12, 14.
15. The Duke of Richmond to Peter Collinson from Goodwood, 22 November 1741 and 5 December 1742. *Letters to Peter Collinson*, Vol. 1. BL. Add. Ms. 28726, ff. 108, 123.

16. Dr. J. Hill, *An Idea of a Botanical Garden, In England: with Lectures on the Science. Without Expence to the Public, or to the Students* (London, 1758), pp. 4–5.
17. Hill, *An Address to the Public*, pp. 7, 8–9, 10.
18. Desmond, *Kew*, p. 43.
19. Quoted, Miller, 'My favourite studdys', p. 220.
20. Hill, *An Address to the Public*, pp. 9, 26.
21. Horace Walpole, 'Horace Walpole's Journals of Visits to Country Seats, &c', (ed.) Paget Toynbee, *The Walpole Society*, Vol. 16 (1927–1928), pp. 26, 23.
22. Horace Walpole, *Memoirs of King George the Third*, 4 Vols, published from the original MSS (ed.) Sir Denis Le Marchant (London, 1845), Vol. I, p. 11, note 1.
23. Linda Levy Peck, *Consuming Splendor: Society and Culture in Seventeenth-Century England* (Cambridge: Cambridge University Press, 2005), p. 228.
24. Quoted, W. Thistleton-Dyer, 'Historical Account of Kew', p. 283.
25. Chambers, *The Gardens and Buildings at Kew*, p. 2.
26. *Gazetteer and New Daily Advertiser* (London), Wednesday, 14 August, 1765; Issue 11364. *Burney Collection*.
27. Arthur Young, *A Six Weeks Tour through the Southern Counties of England and Wales* (London: 1768), pp. 96–97.
28. *Middlesex Journal* (London), Tuesday, 16 June, 1772; Issue 502, *Burney Collection*.
29. *Morning Chronicle and London Advertiser* (London), Thursday, 16 July, 1772: Issue 982. *Burney Collection*.
30. *St James's Chronicle or the British Evening Post* (London), Saturday, 25 September, 1773; Issue 1969. *Burney Collection*.
31. *General Evening Post* (London), Tuesday, 26 July, 1774; Issue 6371. *Burney Collection*.
32. *Daily Advertiser* (London), Tuesday, 16 June, 1772; Issue 12942. *Burney Collection*.

14. 'A Passionate Domineering Woman and a Favourite Without Talents'

* Admiral Byng's naval actions were responsible for the loss of Menorca. He was tried, sentenced and executed for treason, or, as Voltaire has it, '*pour encourager les autres*'.
1. Walpole, *Memoirs of the Reign of King George III*, Vol. I, p. 7.
2. Walpole, ibid., pp. 6–7.
3. Walpole, ibid., p. 15.
4. Thomas Nuthall to Lady Chatham, and Thomas Birch to Lord Royston, quoted, Waldegrave, *Memoirs and Speeches*, p. 240, note 13.
5. The Earl of Bute to Mr. Worsley, 28 November, 1762. Copies of Letters of the Earl of Bute 1756–1765. BL. Add. Ms. 36797, f. 24.
6. The Earl of Bute to Lord Holdernesse, 13 March, 1761. BL. Add. Ms. 36797, f. 46.
7. The Earl of Bute to the King, 24 March, 1761. BL. Add. Ms. 36797, ff. 47, 48.
8. Walpole, *Memoirs of the Reign of King George III*, Vol. I, p. 14.
9. Walpole, ibid., p. 11, note 5.

10. Miller, 'My favourite studdy', p. 220.
11. Walpole, *Memoirs of the Reign of King George III*, Vol. I, p. 15.
12. Richard Pares, *King George III and the Politicians* (Oxford: Clarendon Press, 1953), p. 100.
13. John Adolphus, *History of England* (1802), quoted by Karl W. Schweizer, 'Introduction: Lord Bute: interpreted in history', in (ed.) Schweizer, *Lord Bute*, p. 3.
14. John Brewer, 'The Misfortunes of Lord Bute: A Case-Study in Eighteenth-Century Political Argument and Public Opinion', *The Historical Journal*, 16:1 (March 1973), p. 19.
15. Paul Langford, *Eighteenth-Century Britain: A Very Short Introduction* (Oxford: Oxford University Press, 2000), p. 80.
16. Linda Colley, *Britons: Forging the Nation 1707–1837* (London: Yale University Press, 1992; Vintage paperback, 1996), pp. 115–116.
17. Quoted, Lovat-Fraser, *Earl of Bute*, p. 25.
18. Quoted, Marie Peters, *Pitt and Popularity: The Patriot Minister and London Opinion during the Seven Years War* (Oxford: Clarendon Press, 1980), p. 242.
19. The Earl of Bute to the Marquis of Granby, 5 November, 1762. Liverpool Papers, Vol. XI. BL. Add. Ms. 38200, f. 93.
20. Liverpool Papers, Vol. CXLVII. BL. Add. Ms, 38336, ff. 154, 265, 267.
21. The Earl of Bute to the Duke of Bedford, 28 September, 1762. BL. Add. Ms. 36797, f. 11.
22. John L. Bullion, 'Securing the peace: Lord Bute, the plan for the army, and the origins of the American Revolution', in (ed.) Schweizer, *Lord Bute*, pp. 19, 18.
23. The Earl of Bute to the Marquis of Granby, 5 November, 1762. Liverpool Papers, Vol. XI. BL. Add. Ms. 38200, f. 94.
24. William Strahan to Benjamin Franklin, 18 August 1763, ALS: Historical Society of Pennsylvania (www.franklinpapers.org. Accessed 6 October 2014).
25. Paul Langford, *The Excise Crisis: Society and Politics in the Age of Walpole* (Oxford, 1975), p.2. *Note: It is ironic that another unpopular Scottish prime minister, Gordon Brown, also fell foul of a projected tax on cider as recently as 2010.
26. The Earl of Bute to Dr Campbell, 30 January 1763, quoted, Sedgwick, *Letters from George III to Lord Bute*, p. lxi.
27. The Earl of Bute to Major-General George Townshend, 2 November, 1762. Liverpool Papers, Liverpool Papers, Vol. XI. BL. Add. Ms. 38200, f. 89.
28. The Earl of Bute to the Duke of Bedford, 2 April, 1763. BL. Add. Ms. 36797, ff. 38, 37.
29. Blunt, *In for a Penny*, p. 28.
30. Quoted, Rude, *Wilkes and Liberty*, p. 22.
31. Rude, ibid., pp. 24, 27, 26; Patrick Eyres, 'Kew and Stowe, 1757–1779: the Polarised Agendas of Royal and Whig iconographies', *New Arcadian Journal*, 51/52 (2001), p. 82.
32. The Earl of Bute after 1756 to George, Prince of Wales, and to Augusta, Dowager Princess of Wales. BL. Add. Ms. 36797, ff. 67, 69.

33. Diana Donald, *The Age of Caricature: Satirical Prints in the Reign of George III* (London and New Haven: Yale University Press, 1996), p. 5

34. Brewer, 'The Misfortunes of Lord Bute', pp. 7, 5–6, 18.

35. Philip Dormer Stanhope, 4th Earl of Chesterfield, *Lord Chesterfield's Letters* (ed.) David Roberts (Oxford: Oxford World's Classics, 1992; reissued, 2008), pp. 354–355, 359.

36. *Letters from George III to Lord Bute 1756–1766*, pp. 255, 256, 255.

37. John Brooke, *King George III* (London: Constable, 1972), p. 136.

38. Letter from William Strahan to Benjamin Franklin.

39. Quoted, Russell, *John Stuart*, p. 75.

40. Quoted, Brooke, *King George III*, p. 136.

41. Black, *George III*, p.88; Peter D. Brown, 'Bute in Retirement', in (ed.) Schweizer, *Lord Bute*, p. 271.

15. 'So Sits Enthroned in Vegetable Pride Imperial Kew'

1. Thistleton-Dyer, 'Historical Account of Kew', p. 289–290.

2. Chambers, *The Gardens and Buildings at Kew*, p. 8; Patrick Eyres, 'Kew and Stowe', p. 56.

3. Eyres, 'Kew and Stowe', p. 56.

4. Chambers, *The Gardens and Buildings at Kew*, pp. 5, 7.

5. Patrick Eyres, 'Editorial', *New Arcadian Journal*, 51/52 (2001), p. 6.

6. Thomas Chatterton, *Kew Gardens* (1770), *The Complete Works of Thomas Chatterton: A Bicentenary Edition*, 2 vols (ed.) Donald S. Taylor (Oxford: Clarendon Press, 1971), p. 517.

7. Eyres, 'Kew and Stowe', p. 64.

8. Martin Robinson, *Temples of Delight*, p. 113.

9. Eyres, 'Kew and Stowe', p. 70.

10. Martin Robinson, *Temples of Delight*, pp. 140–142.

11. Quaintance, 'Kew Gardens', pp. 58, 63.

12. Quoted, Eyres, 'Kew and Stowe', p. 78.

13. [Stowe. A description of the House and Gardens of ... Richard East Temple ... embellished with a general plan of the Gardens, and also a separate plan of each Building ... A new edition, etc.] (Buckingham: B. Seeley, 1768).

14. Henry Jones, *Kew Garden: A Poem in Two Cantos* (London: 1767), p. 41.

15. John Milton, *Paradise Lost* (1667), (ed.) Christopher Ricks (New York: New American Library, 1968; London: Penguin, 1989), Book I, p. 5.

16. Jones, *Kew Garden*, pp. 10, 44.

17. William Chambers, *A Dissertation on Oriental Gardening*, pp. 14, v.

18. Samuel Kliger, 'Whig Aesthetics: A Phase of Eighteenth-Century Taste', *ELH*, 16:2 (June 1949), p. 139.

19. William Mason, *An Heroic Epistle to Sir William Chambers, Knight, Comptroller General of His Majesty's Work, and Author of a Late Dissertation on Oriental Gardening* (3rd edition, London: 1773), pp. 3, 6, 10, 12.

20. Chatterton, *Kew Gardens*, p. 523, 517, 531.

21. Oliver Goldsmith, *Threnodia Augustalis* (1772), *The Complete Works of Oliver Goldsmith* (ed.) Austin Dobson (London: Oxford University Press), p. 74.

22. Erasmus Darwin, *The Botanic Garden: A Poem in Two Parts* (London: J. Johnson, 1791), p. 207.
23. Rev. William MacRitchie, *Diary of a Tour through Great Britain in 1795*, with introduction and notes by David MacRitchie (London: Elliot Stock, 1897), pp. 94–5.
24. Blanche Henrey, *British Botanical and Horticultural Literature before 1800, Vol. II, The Eighteenth Century History* (London: Oxford University Press, 1975), p. 243. Bute 'so excelled in this science the great European masters consulted him and sought to correspond with him.'
25. Letter from Queen Charlotte to Lord Bute, 18 July 1784. Kew Papers, PrP87-0002/3.
26. Letter from Queen Charlotte to Lord Bute, 19 March 1788. Kew Papers, PrP87-0002/4/2.
27. Alexander Sinclair, 'The Gardens and Policies', p. 41. [You will remain in my memory] 'So long as I am conscious and my spirit controls my limbs'.

Epilogue

1. Quoted by Michael Bevington, 'The First Marquess and the first Duke', in Michael Bevington with George Clarke, Jonathan Marsden and Tim Knox, *Stowe: The People and the Place* (London: National Trust, 2011), p. 60.
2. Bevington, 'Decline and Fall' in *Stowe*, pp. 62–65.
3. Jenny Uglow, *The Lunar Men: The Friends who made the Future 1730–1810* (London: Faber and Faber, 2002; paperback, 2003), p. 268.
4. Paul Cloutman, *Royal Botanic Gardens Kew: Souvenir Guide* (London: The Royal Botanic Gardens Kew, 2001; revised edition, 2004), p. 82.
5. John Gascoigne, *Science in the Service of Empire: Joseph Banks, the British State and the uses of Science in the Age of Revolution* (Cambridge: Cambridge University Press, 1998), p. 5.
6. Gascoigne, ibid., p. 134.

Bibliography

MANUSCRIPT SOURCES
London, British Library
Additional Ms. 15776
Additional Ms. 28726
Additional Ms. 32871
Additional Ms. 32795
Additional Ms. 35155
Additional Ms. 36595
Additional Ms. 36796
Additional Ms. 36797
Additional Ms. 38200
Additional Ms. 38336
Sloane Ms. 4076

London, Library, Royal Botanic Gardens, Kew
PrP87-0002/3
PrP87-0002/4/1

PRIMARY PRINTED SOURCES
Addison, Joseph, *Selections from The Tatler and The Spectator* (1709–1712), (ed.) Angus Ross (London: Penguin, 1982)
Anonymous, *The Fair Concubine: Or, the Secret History of the Beautiful Vanella* (London, 1732)
Anonymous, *The Humours of the Court: Or, Modern Gallantry: A New Ballad Opera* (London, 1732)
Ashley Cooper, Anthony, 3rd Earl of Shaftesbury, *Characteristics of Men, Manners, Opinions, Times* (1711), (ed.) Lawrence E Klein (Cambridge: Cambridge University Press, 1999)
Bickham, George, *The Beauties of Stow or a Description of the Most Noble House, Gardens & Magnificent Buildings therein of the Right Honourable Earl Temple, Viscount & Baron Cobham* (London, 1753)
Burke, Edmund, *A Philosophical Enquiry into the Origin of our Ideas of the*

Sublime and the Beautiful (London, 1757) (ed.) Adam Phillips (Oxford: Oxford World's Classics paperback, 2008)

Burke, Edmund, *Select Works of Edmund Burke, Vol. I: Thoughts on the Cause of the Present Discontents; Two Speeches on America* (ed.) E. J. Payne (Originally published Oxford, 1874–1878; new edition, with introduction by Francis Canavan, Indianapolis: Liberty Fund, 1999)

Bute, John Stuart, 3rd Earl of, *Botanical Tables, Containing the Different Familys of British Plants, distinguished by a few obvious parts of fructification rang'd in a synoptical method* (London: 1785)

Byng, John, Viscount Torrington, *The Torrington Diaries: Containing the Tours through England and Wales of the Hon. John Byng*, Vol. II (ed.) C. Bruyn Andrews, London: Eyre & Spottiswoode, 1935)

Chambers, William, *Plans, Elevations, Sections, and Perspective Views of the Gardens and Buildings at Kew in Surry, the seat of Her Royal Highness the Princess Dowager of Wales* (London: 1763)

Chambers, William, *A Dissertation on Oriental Gardening* (2nd edition, with additions, London: 1773)

Chatterton, Thomas, *The Complete Works of Thomas Chatterton: A Bicentenary Edition*, 2 vols (ed.) Donald S. Taylor (Oxford: Clarendon Press, 1971)

Chesterfield, Philip Dormer Stanhope, 4th Earl of, *Lord Chesterfield's Letters* (ed.) David Roberts (Oxford: Oxford World's Classics, 1992; reissued, 2008)

Coombs, David, 'The Garden at Carlton House of Frederick Prince of Wales and Augusta Dowager Duchess of Wales: Bills in their Household Accounts 1728–1772', *Garden History*, 25:2 (Winter 1997), pp. 153–177

Curll, Edmund, *The Rarities of Richmond: Being Exact Descriptions of the Royal Hermitage and Merlin's Cave. With his Life and Prophecies* (2nd edition, London: 1736)

Darwin, Erasmus, *The Botanic Garden: A Poem in Two Parts* (London: J. Johnson, 1791)

de Saussure, Cesar, *A Foreign View of England in the Reigns of George I and George II: The Letters of Monsieur Cesar de Saussure to his Family*: translated and edited by Madame van Muyden (London: John Murray, 1902)

Defoe, Daniel, *A Tour through the Whole Island of Great Britain* (eds) G. D. H. Cole and D. C. Browning (London: 1928; reprinted in one volume, London: J. M. Dent, 1974)

Dodington, George Bubb, *The Political Journal of George Bubb Dodington* (eds) John Carswell and Lewis Arnold Dralle (Oxford: Clarendon Press, 1965)

Evelyn, John, *The Diary of John Evelyn* (selected from 1959 Oxford University Press edition, ed. E. S. de Beer; London: Everyman's Library, 2006)

Fabrice, Freidrich Ernst von, *The Genuine Letters of Baron Fabricius* (London: 1761)

Fiennes, Celia, *The Journeys of Celia Fiennes* (ed.) Christopher Morris (London: Cresset Press, 1947)

Filmer, Robert, *Patriarcha* (London: 1680)

Fitzmaurice, Lord, *Life of William, Earl of Shelburne, Afterwards First Marquess of Lansdowne, with Extracts from His Papers and Correspondence* (second and revised edition in two volumes, London: Macmillan, 1912)

The Gentleman's Magazine, 6 (1736); 5 (1735); 7 (1737)

George III, *Letters from George III to Lord Bute 1756–1766* (ed.) Romney Sedgwick (London: Macmillan, 1939)

Gilpin, William, *A Dialogue upon the Gardens of the Right Honourable the Lord Viscount Cobham at Stow in Buckinghamshire* (London, 1748)

Goldsmith Oliver, *Threnodia Augustalis* (1772), *The Complete Works of Oliver Goldsmith* (ed.) Austin Dobson (London: Oxford University Press)

Hervey, John, Lord, *Some Materials towards Memoirs of the Reign of King George II*, 3 Vols (ed.) Romney Sedgwick (London: King's Printers, 1931)

Hill, Henrietta, Mrs, calling herself Lady Hill, *An address to the Public by Lady Hill, setting forth the consequences of the late Sir John Hill's acquaintance with the Earl of Bute* (London: 1788)

Hill, Dr J., *An Idea of a Botanical Garden in England: with Lectures on the Science, without Expence to the Public, or to the Students* (London: 1758)

Jones, Henry, *Kew Garden: A Poem in Two Cantos* (London: 1767)

MacRitchie, Revd William, *Diary of a Tour through Great Britain in 1795*, with introduction and notes by David MacRitchie (London: Elliot Stock, 1897)

Marlborough, Sarah, Duchess of, *Memoirs of Sarah, Duchess of Marlborough together with her Characters of her Contemporaries and her Opinions* (ed.) William King (London: Routledge, 1930)

Milton, John, *Paradise Lost* (1667), (ed.) Christopher Ricks (New York: New American Library, 1968; London: Penguin, 1989)

Perceval, John, First Earl of Egmont, *Manuscripts of the Earl of Egmont: Diary of Viscount Perceval, Afterwards First Earl of Egmont*, 3 vols (ed.) R. A. Roberts (London: Historical Manuscripts Commission, 1920–1923)

Pitt, William, 'Letters from William Pitt to Lord Bute: 1755–1758', edited by Romney Sedgwick in (ed.) Richard Pares and A. J. P. Taylor, *Essays Presented to Sir Lewis Namier* (London: Macmillan, 1956), pp. 108–166

Pope, Alexander, *The Poems of Alexander Pope* (ed.) John Butt (London: Methuen, 1963)

Savage, Richard, *The Poetical Works of Richard Savage, with the Life of the Author by Samuel Johnson* (New York: William A. Davis, 1805)

Seeley, Benton, *Stowe: The Gardens of the Right Honourable the Lord Viscount Cobham* (3rd edition, London: 1751)

Seeley, Benton, *Stow: A Description of the Magnificent Gardens of the Right Honourable Richard, Earl Temple, Viscount and Baron Cobham* (London, 1756)

Seeley, Benton, *Stowe: A Description of the Magnificent House and Gardens of the Right Honourable Richard, Earl Temple, Viscount and Baron Cobham* (London, 1759)

Smith, Adam, *The Wealth of Nations*, 2 Vols (Oxford: Clarendon Press, 1976) (eds) R. H. Campbell and A. S. Skinner

'Stowe. A description of the House and Gardens of … Richard East Temple … embellished with a general plan of the Gardens, and also a separate plan of each Building … A new edition, etc.' (Buckingham: B. Seeley, 1768)

Vertue, George, 'Notebooks', *The Walpole Society*, Vol. 26 (1937–1938), Vol. 30 (1951–1952)

Waldegrave, James, 2nd Earl of, *The Memoirs and Speeches of James, 2nd Earl of Waldegrave, 1742–1763* (ed.) J. C. D. Clark (Cambridge: Cambridge University Press, 1988)

Walpole, Horace, *The History of the Modern Taste in Gardening* (ed.) John Dixon Hunt (New York: Ursus Press, 1995)

Walpole, Horace, 'Horace Walpole's Journals of Visits to Country Seats, &c', (ed.) Paget Toynbee, *The Walpole Society*, Vol. 16 (1927–1928), pp. 9–80

Walpole, Horace, *Letters of Horace Walpole*, selected by W. S. Lewis, with an introduction by R. W. Ketton-Cremer (London: The Folio Society, 1951)

Walpole, Horace, *Memoirs of King George II*, Vol. I, January 1751–March 1754 (ed.) John Brooke (New Haven and London: Yale University Press, 1985)

Walpole, Horace, *Memoirs of the Reign of King George the Third*, 4 Vols, published from the original MSS (ed.) Sir Denis Le Marchant (London: 1845)

Walpole, Horace, *Memoirs of the Reign of King George III*, Vol. I (ed.) Derek Jarrett (New Haven and London: Yale University Press, 2000)

Walpole, Horace, *The Yale Edition of Horace Walpole's Correspondence*, 48 Vols (ed.) W. S. Lewis (Oxford: Oxford University Press, 1937–1965)

Walpole, Horace, *Horace Walpole's Miscellany 1786–1795* (ed.) Lars E Troide (New Haven and London: Yale University Press, 1978)

Whately, Thomas, *Observations on Modern Gardening and Laying-Out Pleasure Grounds, Parks, Farms, Ridings, &c. Illustrated by Descriptions. To Which is Added, An Essay on the Different Natural Situations of Gardens* (A new edition with notes by Horace (late) Earl of Orford, London, 1801)

Wortley Montagu, Lady Mary, *The Complete Letters of Lady Mary Wortley Montagu*, 3 vols (ed.) Robert Halsband (Oxford: Clarendon Press, 1966)

Young, Arthur, *A Six Weeks Tour through the Southern Counties of England and Wales* (London: 1768)

Young, Arthur, *The Farmer's Tour through the East of England* (London: W. Strahan, 1771)

SECONDARY SOURCES

Alcorn, Ellenor M., 'A Chandelier for the King', William Kent, George II, and Hanover', *The Burlington Magazine*, 139:1126 (January 1997), pp. 40–43

Alexander Sinclair, James, 'The Gardens and Policies', *Mount Stuart: Isle of Bute* (Isle of Bute: The Mount Stuart Trust, 2001), pp. 39–47.

Arkell, R. L., *Caroline of Ansbach: George II's Queen* (London: Oxford University Press, 1939)

Arnold, Dana, *Rural Urbanism: London Landscapes in the early nineteenth century* (Manchester: Manchester University Press, 2005)

Baker-Smith, Veronica, *Royal Discord: The Family of George II* (London: Athena Press, 2008)

Batey, Mavis, *Oxford Gardens: The university's influence on garden history* (Amersham: Scolar Press, 1982)

Bevington, Michael, with Clarke, George, Marsden, Jonathan and Knox, Tim, *Stowe: The People and the Place* (London: National Trust, 2011)

Bingham, Madeleine, *The Making of Kew* (Michael Joseph: London, 1975)

Black, Jeremy, *The Hanoverians: The History of a Dynasty* (London: Hambledon Continuum, 2004)

Black, Jeremy, *Culture in Eighteenth-Century England: A Subject for Taste* (London: Hambledon Continuum, 2005; paperback, 2007)

Black, Jeremy, *George III: America's Last King* (New Haven and London: Yale University Press, 2006)

Black, Jeremy, *Eighteenth-Century Britain: 1688–1783* (Basingstoke: Palgrave Macmillan, 2001; 2nd edition, 2008)

Blunt, Wilfrid, *In for a Penny, A Prospect of Kew Gardens: Their Flora, Fauna and Falballas* (London: Hamish Hamilton, 1978)

Borman, Tracy, *King's Mistress, Queen's Servant: The Life and Times of Henrietta Howard* (London: Vintage Books, 2007)

Brett-James, Norman G., *The Life of Peter Collinson FRS FSA* (London: Edgar G. Dunstan & Co, 1925)

Brewer, John, 'The Misfortunes of Lord Bute: A Case-Study in Eighteenth-Century Political Argument and Opinion', *Historical Jourrnal*, 16:1 (March 1973), pp. 3–43

Brewer, John, *The Pleasures of the Imagination in the Eighteenth Century* (London: HarperCollins, 1997)

Brooke, John, *King George III* (London: Constable, 1972)

Brown, Jane, *The Omnipotent Magician: Lancelot 'Capability' Brown 1716–1783* (London: Chatto & Windus, 2011)

Bullion, J. L., 'The Prince's Mentor: A New Perspective on the Friendship between George III and Lord Bute during the 1750s', *Albion*, 21:1 (Spring 1989), pp. 34–55

Bullion, J. L., 'The Origins and Significance of Gossip about Princess Augusta and Lord Bute, 1755-1756', *Studies in Eighteenth-Century Culture*, 21 (1992), pp. 245–265

Bullion, J. L., '"George, Be a King!": The Relationship between Princess Augusta and George III', in (eds) Stephen Taylor, Richard Connors and Clyve Jones, *Hanoverian Britain and Empire: Essays in Memory of Philip Lawson* (Woodbridge: Boydell Press, 1998), pp. 177–197

Bullion, J. L., '"To play what game she pleased without observation": Princess Augusta and the political drama of succession, 1736–56', in (ed.) Clarissa Campbell Orr, *Queenship in Britain 1660–1837: Royal patronage, court culture and dynastic politics* (Manchester: Manchester University Press, 2002), pp. 207–235

Campbell-Culver, *The Origin of Plants: The people and plants that have shaped Britain's garden history since the year 1000* (London: Eden Project Books, 2004)

Cannon, John, *Aristocratic Century: The peerage of eighteenth-century England* (Cambridge: Cambridge University Press, 1984)

Chessum, Sophie, Rogers, Kevin and Rowell, Christopher, *Claremont* (London: National Trust, 2000)

Chevenix Trench, Charles, *George II* (London: Allen Lane, 1973)

Coats, Alice M., *Lord Bute: An illustrated life of John Stuart, third Earl of Bute 1713–1792* (Aylesbury: Shire Publications, 1975)

Clark, H. F., *The English Landscape Garden* (London: Pleiades Books, 1948)

Cloutman, Paul, *Royal Botanic Gardens Kew: Souvenir Guide* (London: The Royal Botanic Gardens Kew, 2001; revised edition, 2004)

Colley, Linda, 'The Apotheosis of George III: Loyalty, Royalty and the British Nation, 1760–1820', *Past and Present*, 102 (1984), pp. 94–129

Colley, Linda, *Britons: Forging the Nation 1707–1837* (London: Yale University Press, 1992; Vintage paperback, 1996)

Colton, Judith, 'Merlin's Cave and Queen Caroline: Garden Art as Political Propaganda', *Eighteenth-Century Studies*, 10:1 (Autumn 1976), pp. 1–20

Coombs, David, 'The Garden at Carlton House of Frederick Prince of Wales and Augusta Princess Dowager of Wales: Bills in their Household Accounts 1728 to 1772', *Garden History*, 25:2 (Winter 1997), pp. 169–173

Curties, Henry, *A Forgotten Prince of Wales* (London: Everett & Co., 1912)

De-la-Noy, Michael, *The King who Never Was: The Story of Frederick, Prince of Wales* (London: Peter Owen, 1996)

Desmond, Ray, *Kew: The History of the Royal Botanic Gardens* (London: The Harvill Press with the Royal Botanic Gardens, Kew, 1995)

Dickinson, H. T., *Walpole and the Whig Supremacy* (London: English Universities Press, 1973)

Dickinson, H. T., *Liberty and Property: Political Ideology in Eighteenth-Century Britain* (London: Weidenfeld & Nicolson, 1977)

Donald, Diana, *The Age of Caricature. Satirical Prints in the Reign of George III* (London and New Haven: Yale University Press, 1996)

Eagles, Robin, '"No more to be said"? Reactions to the death of Frederick Lewis, prince of Wales', *Historical Research*, 80:209 (August 2007), pp. 346–367

Edwards, Averyl, *Frederick Louis Prince of Wales 1707–1751* (London: Staples Press, 1947)

Eyres, Patrick (ed), 'Kew Gardens: A Controversial Georgian Landscape', *New Arcadian Journal*, 51/52 (2001)

Fabricant, Carole, 'The Literature of Domestic Tourism and the Public Consumption of Private Property', in (eds) Felicity Nussbaum and Laura Brown, *The New Eighteenth Century: Theory, Politics, English Literature* (London: Methuen, 1987), pp. 254–275

Fearnley-Whittingstall, Jane, *The Garden: An English Love Affair: One Thousand Years of Gardening* (London: Weidenfeld & Nicolson, 2002)

Ferguson, Niall, *Empire: How Britain Made the Modern World* (London: Allen Lane, 2003)

Field, Ophelia, *The Favourite: Sarah, Duchess of Marlborough* (London: Hodder & Stoughton, 2002; Sceptre paperback, 2003)

Field, Ophelia, *The Kit-Cat Club: Friends Who Imagined a Nation* (London: Harper Press, 2008)

Foord, Archibald S., *His Majesty's Opposition 1714–1830* (Oxford: Clarendon Press, 1964)

Fraser, Flora, *Princesses: The Six Daughters of George III* (London: John Murray, 2004)

Fry, Carolyn, *The World of Kew* (London: BBC Books, 2006)

Gascoigne, John, *Science in the Service of Empire: Joseph Banks, the British*

State and the uses of Science in the Age of Revolution (Cambridge: Cambridge University Press, 1998)

Gerrard, Christine, *The Patriot Opposition to Walpole: Politics, Poetry, and National Myth, 1725–1742* (Oxford: Clarendon Press, 1994)

Gerrard, Christine, 'Queens-in-Waiting: Caroline of Anspach and Augusta of Saxe-Gotha as Princesses of Wales' in (ed.) Clarissa Campbell Orr, *Queenship in Britain 1660–1837: Royal patronage, court culture and dynastic politics* (Manchester & New York: Manchester University Press, 2002), pp. 143–161

Grundy, Isobel, *Lady Mary Wortley Montagu* (Oxford: Oxford University Press, 1999)

Hanham, Andrew, 'Caroline of Brandenburg-Ansbach and the "Anglicisation" of the House of Hanover' in (ed.) Clarissa Campbell Orr, *Queenship in Europe 1660–1815: The Role of the Consort* (Cambridge: Cambridge University Press, 2004), pp. 276–299

Harding Nick, *Hanover and the British Empire, 1700–1837* (Woodbridge: Boydell Press, 2007)

Harris, John, 'George III's parents: Frederick and Augusta', in *The Wisdom of George the Third: Papers from a Symposium at The Queen's Gallery, Buckingham Palace, June 2004*, (ed.) Jonathan Marsden (London: Royal Collection, 2005), pp. 15–27

Henrey, Blanche, *British Botanical and Horticultural Literature before 1800, Vol. II, The Eighteenth Century History* (London: Oxford University Press, 1975)

Hussey, Christopher, *English Gardens and Landscapes 1700–1750* (London: Country Life, 1967)

Jackson-Stops, Gervase, 'The Cliveden Album: drawings by Archer, Leoni and Gibbs for the 1st Earl of Orkney', *Architectural History*, 19 (1976–1977), pp. 5–16

Jackson-Stops, Gervase, 'Cliveden, Buckinhamshire I and II', *Country Life*, 161i (24 February 1977 and 3 March 1977), pp. 438–441 and pp. 498–501

Jennings, Anne, *Georgian Gardens* (London: English Heritage and the Museum of Garden History, 2005)

Jones, Stephen, *Frederick, Prince of Wales and his Circle* (Sudbury, Suffolk: Gainsborough House, exhibition catalogue, 1981)

Kenny, Ruth, 2013. 'Defaced Coins' in (eds) Tabitha Barber and Stacy Boldrick, *Art Under Attack. Histories of British Iconoclasm* (London: Tate Publishing, 2013)

King, Ronald, *Royal Kew* (London: Constable, 1985)

Kliger, Samuel, 'Whig Aesthetics: A Phase of Eighteenth-Century Taste', *ELH*, 16:2 (June 1949), pp. 135–150

Kramnick, Isaac, *Bolingbroke & His Circle: The Politics of Nostalgia in the Age of Walpole* (London: Oxford University Press, 1968; paperback edition, Ithaca and London: Cornell University Press, 1992)

Langford, Paul, *The Excise Crisis: Society and Politics in the Age of Walpole* (Oxford, 1975)

Langford, Paul, *Eighteenth-Century Britain: A Very Short Introduction* (Oxford: Oxford University Press, 2000)

Lees-Milne, *Earls of Creation: Five Great Patrons of Eighteenth-Century Art* (London: Classic Penguin, 2001)

Levy Peck, Linda, *Consuming Splendor: Society and Culture in Seventeenth-Century England* (Cambridge: Cambridge University Press, 2005)

Lovat-Fraser, J. A., *John Stuart Earl of Bute* (Cambridge: Cambridge University Press, 1912)

Marples, Morris, *Poor Fred and the Butcher: Sons of George III* (London: Michael Joseph, 1970)

Marsden, Jonathan (ed.), *The Wisdom of George the Third: Papers from a Symposium at The Queen's Gallery, Buckingham Palace, June 2004* (London: Royall Collection, 2005)

Martin Robinson, John, *Temples of Delight: Stowe Landscape Gardens* (London: National Trust, 1990; 2nd edition, 1994, 2002)

Martin Robinson, John, *Buckingham Palace: The Official Illustrated History* (London: Royal Collection, 2000; reprinted, 2007)

Mason William, *An Heroic Epistle to Sir William Chambers, Knight, Comptroller General of His Majesty's Work, and Author of a Late Dissertation on Oriental Gardening* (3rd edition, London: 1773)

McLynn, Frank, *1759: The Year Britain Became Master of the World* (London: Jonathan Cape, 2004)

Moore, Lucy, *Amphibious Thing: The Life of Lord Hervey* (London: Viking, 2000)

Mount, Harry, *How England made the English: From Hedgerows to Heathrow* (London: Viking, 2012)

Mowl, Timothy, *Gentlemen & Players: Gardeners of the English Landscape* (Stroud: Alan Sutton, 2000)

Mowl, Timothy, *William Kent: Architect, Designer, Opportunist* (London: Jonathan Cape, 2006; Pimlico paperback, 2007)

Newman, Aubrey N., 'The Political Patronage of Frederick Lewis, Prince of Wales', *Historical Journal*, 1:1 (1958), pp. 68–75

Newman, Aubrey N., 'Leicester House Politics, 1749–71', *English Historical Review*, 76:301 (October 1961), pp. 577–589

Newman, Aubrey N. (ed.), 'Leicester House Politics, 1750–1760, from the Papers of John, Second Earl of Egmont', *Camden Miscellany* (London: Royal Historical Society, 1969), Vol. 23, pp. 85–228

Pares, Richard, *King George III and the Politicians* (Oxford: Clarendon Press, 1953)

Paterson, Allen, *The Gardens at Kew* (London: Frances Lincoln, 2008)

Pavord, Anna, *The Naming of Names: The Search for Order in the World of Plants* (London: Bloomsbury, 2005)

Pearce, Edward, *The Great Man: Sir Robert Walpole: Scoundrel, Genius and Britain's First Prime Minister* (London: Jonathan Cape, 2007; Pimlico Paperback, 2008)

Pearce, Edward, *Pitt the Elder: Man of War* (London: The Bodley Head, 2010; Pimlico Paperback, 2011)

Peters, Marie, *Pitt and Popularity: The Patriot Minister and London Opinion during the Seven Years War* (Oxford: Clarendon Press, 1980)

Plumb, J. H., *The First Four Georges* (London: Batsford, 1956)

Quaintance, Richard, 'Kew Gardens 1731–1778: Can We Look At Both Sides Now?', *New Arcadian Journal*, 51/52 (2001), pp. 14–51

Quennell, Peter, *Caroline of England: An Augustan Portrait* (London: Collins, 1939)

Quest-Ritson, Charles, *The English Garden: A Social History* (London: Viking, 2001)

Richardson, Tim, *The Arcadian Friends: Inventing the English Landscape Garden* (London: Bantam Press, 2007; paperback, 2008)

Rorschach, Kimerly, *Frederick, Prince of Wales (1707–1751) as a Patron of the Visual Arts: Princely Patriotism and Political Propaganda* (unpublished PhD dissertation, Yale University, 1985)

Rorschach, Kimerly, 'Frederick, Prince of Wales (1707–1751), as collector and patron', *The Walpole Society*, Vol. 55 (1989–1990), pp. 1–76

Rorschach, Kimerly, 'Frederick, Prince of Wales: Taste, politics and power', *Apollo*, 134:156, New Series (October 1991), pp. 239–245

Rude, George, *Wilkes and Liberty: A Social Study* (Oxford: Clarendon Press, 1962; 2nd edition, with new preface, London: Lawrence & Wishart, 1983)

Russell, Francis, *John, 3rd Earl of Bute, Patron & Collector* (London: Merrion Press, 2004)

Sackville-West, Robert, *Inheritance: The Story of Knole and the Sackvilles* (London: Bloomsbury, 2010)

Salisbury, Edward, 'The Royal Botanic Gardens, Kew', *Proceedings of the Royal Society of London*, Series A, Mathematical and Physical Sciences, 195:1043 (3 February 1949), pp. 423–433

Schweizer, Karl W. (ed.), *Lord Bute: Essays in Re-interpretation* (Leicester: Leicester University Press, 1988)

Schweizer, Karl W., *Frederick the Great, William Pitt, and Lord Bute: The Anglo-Prussian Alliance, 1756–1763* (London: Garland Publishing, 1991)

Sedgwick, Romney, 'William Pitt and Lord Bute: An Intrigue of 1755–1758', *History Today*, 6:10 (October 1956), pp. 647–654

Shawe-Taylor, Desmond, *The Conversation Piece: Scenes of Fashionable Life* (London: Royal Collection, 2009)

Shawe-Taylor, Desmond (ed.), *The First Georgians: Art & Monarchy 1714–1760* (London: Royal Collection, 2014)

Smith, Hannah, *Georgian Monarchy: Politics and Culture, 1714–1760* (Cambridge: Cambridge University Press, 2006)

Smith, Hannah and Taylor, Stephen, 'Hephaestion and Alexander: Lord Hervey, Frederick, Prince of Wales, and the Royal Favourite in England in the 1730s', *English Historical Review*, 124:507 (April 2009), pp. 283–312

Somerset, Anne, *Queen Anne: The Politics of Passion* (London: Harper Press, 2012)

Somerset Fry, Plantagenet, *The Kings & Queens of England & Scotland* (London: Dorling Kindersley, 1990)

Symes, Michael, 'William Pitt the Elder: The Gran Mago of Landscape Gardening', *Garden History*, 24:1 (Summer 1996), pp. 126–136

Thistleton-Dyer, W., 'Historical Account of Kew to 1841', *Kew Bulletin*, 60 (1891), pp. 279–327

Thompson, Andrew C, *George II: King and Elector* (New Haven and London: Yale University Press, 2011)

Thompson, E. P., 'Eighteenth-century English society class struggle without class?', *Social History*, 3:2 (May 1978), pp. 133–165

Tillyard, Stella, *Aristocrats: Caroline, Emily, Louisa and Sarah Lennox 1740–1832* (London: Chatto & Windus, 1994)

Tinniswood, Adrian, *The Polite Tourist: A History of Country House Visiting* (2nd edition, London: National Trust, 1998)

Trevelyan, George Macaulay, (ed.) T. F. Henderson, *History of England* (London: Routledge, 1907)

Uglow, Jenny, *The Lunar Men: The Friends who made the Future 1730–1810* (London: Faber & Faber, 2002; paperback, 2003)

Uglow, Jenny, *A Little History of British Gardening* (London: Chatto & Windus, 2004)

Uglow, Jenny, 'A pastoral painter', *RA Magazine*, 106 (Spring 2010), pp. 52–53

van der Kiste, John, *King George II and Queen Caroline* (Stroud: Alan Sutton, 1997)

Vivian, Frances, *A Life of Frederick, Prince of Wales, 1707–1751: A Connoisseur of the Arts* (ed.) R. White (Lewiston, Lampeter: The Edward Mellen Press, 2006)

Walters, John, *The Royal Griffin: Frederick Prince of Wales 1707–51* (London: Jarrolds, 1972)

Wheeler, Richard, 'Prince Frederick and Liberty: The Gardens of Hartwell House, Buckinghamshire, in the Mid-Eighteenth Century, *Garden History*, 34:1 (Summer 2006), pp. 80–91

White, Jerry, *London in the Eighteenth Century: A Great and Monstrous Thing* (London: The Bodley Head, 2012)

White, Roger, *Chiswick House and Gardens* (London: English Heritage, 2001)

Wiggin, Lewis M., *The Faction of Cousins: A Political Account of the Grenvilles, 1733–63* (New Haven: Yale University Press, 1958)

Williams, Basil, *The Whig Supremacy: 1714–1760* (2nd edition, revised by C. H. Stuart, Oxford: Clarendon Press, 1960)

Williamson, Tom, *Polite Landscapes: Gardens & Society in Eighteenth-Century England* (Stroud: Allan Sutton, 1995)

Worden, Blair, 'Favourites on the English Stage', in (eds) J. H. Elliott and L. W. B Brockliss, *The World of the Favourite* (New Haven and London: Yale University Press, 1999), pp. 159–183

Worsley, Lucy, *Courtiers: The Secret History of Kensington Palace* (London: Faber & Faber, 2010)

Wulf, Andrea, *The Brother Gardeners: Botany, Empire and the Birth of an Obsession* (London: William Heinemann, 2008)

Wulf, Andrea, *The Founding Gardeners: How the Revolutionary Generation Created an American Eden* (London: William Heinemann, 2011)

Young, George, *Poor Fred: The People's Prince* (London: Oxford University Press, 1937)

NEWSPAPERS/ONLINE SOURCES

Clark, Robert, 'Stowe Landscape Gardens', *The Literary Encyclopedia*, 15 January, 2010 [www.litencyc.com/php/stopics.php?rec=true&UID=7210, accessed 6 August 2010]

Kilburn, Matthew, 'Frederick Lewis, prince of Wales (1707–1751)', *Oxford Dictionary of National Biography*, (Oxford: 2004; online edn, May 2009) [www.oxforddnb.com.ezproxy.londonlibrary.co.uk/view/article/10140, accessed 10 Nov 2011]

Ogilby, John, *Britannia* (London, 1675) [www.fulltable.com/vts/m/map/ogilby/b/ SH950.jpg, accessed 20 September 2010]

Seventeenth & Eighteenth Century Burney Collection Newspapers [find.galegroup.com/bncn/retrieve.do, accessed through Birkbeck, University of London, e-library, using Basic Search: Kew Gardens, 1728-1774. 144 items retrieved, 20 September 2010]

Shawe-Taylor, Desmond, *The King's Ransom* (Video, 2014: A Royal Collection Trust and BBC partnership)

Letter from William Strahan to Benjamin Franklin, 18 August 1763, ALS: Historical Society of Pennsylvania [www.franklinpapers.org. Accessed 6 October 2014]

Taylor, Stephen, 'Caroline (1683–1737)', *Oxford Dictionary of National Biography* (Oxford: 2004; online edn, May 2009) [www.oxforddnb.com.ezproxy.londonlibrary.co.uk/view/article/4720, accessed 10 Nov 2011]

About the Author

Vanessa Berridge was educated at the universities of Bristol, East Anglia and London, taking an MA with distinction in British History at Birkbeck College. She edited *Country Homes & Interiors* magazine, and then conceived, launched and edited *The English Garden* magazine. She is now a widely published freelance writer on gardening, garden history and heritage issues. Her first book, *The Joy of Gardening*, was published in 2014. As both an editor and a writer, she has appeared on gardening television programmes, broadcast for BBC local radio across the country, and set up and chaired events at the Cheltenham Festival of Literature. Married with two grown-up sons, she lives and gardens in Gloucestershire.

Timeline

Act of Union (between England and Scotland)	1707	Birth of Frederick
Treaty of Utrecht (ends War of Spanish Succession)	1713	Birth of John Stuart, 3rd Earl of Bute Lord Cobham begins work at Stowe
Death of Queen Anne Accession of George I	1714	
First Jacobite Rebellion	1715	
Breakdown of relations between George I and Prince & Princess of Wales First Whig split	1717	Opening of the New Inn at Stowe
	1719	Birth of Augusta
South Sea Bubble bursts	1720	
	1721	Birth of William, Duke of Cumberland George Augustus & Caroline lease Richmond Lodge & garden
Accession of George II	1727	
	1728	Charles Bridgeman appointed Royal Gardener Arrival of Frederick in London
George II returns to Hanover for the first of many visits	1729	Frederick made Prince of Wales
	1730	Frederick buys lease on Kew
	1731	Frederick commissions Royal Barge from William Kent
	1732	Hermitage at Richmond designed by Kent for Queen Caroline Kent appointed architect to Frederick

Excise Crisis divides the Whigs Cobham is sacked from his regiment by George II for his opposition to Walpole	1733	Frederick buys lease on Carlton House and begins work on the garden Kent starts to create the Elysian fields at Stowe (completed 1739)
Marriage of Princess Anne to William of Orange	1734	
	1736	Marriage of Frederick to Augusta of Saxe-Gotha-Altenburg (April)
Death of Queen Caroline (November)	1737	Birth of Princess Augusta (July) leads to estrangement between Frederick and his parents
Birth of the future George III (June)	1738	
Start of the War of Jenkins' Ear	1739	
War of Austrian Succession (until 1748)	1740	
	1741	'Capability' Brown appointed head gardener at Stowe
Fall of Walpole	1742	Building of Temple of Friendship at Stowe
Battle of Dettingen Henry Pelham ministry begins	1743	
Second Jacobite Rebellion	1745	
Battle of Culloden	1746	
	1747	Frederick meets Bute and begins work on the gardens at Kew
Treaty of Aix-la-Chapelle ends War of Austrian Succession	1748	
	1749	Death of Lord Cobham Dodington rejoins Frederick's household and works with him and Egmont on his succession
	1751	Death of Frederick, Prince of Wales (March)

Newcastle ministry begins	**1754**	
Seven Years' War begins	**1756**	Bute becomes head of the Prince of Wales's household
Capture of Quebec from the French; battles of Quiberon and of Minden	**1759**	Appointment of William Aiton as curator marks the foundation of the Royal Botanic Gardens Kew. William Chambers at work on the buildings including the Temple of Victory
Death of George II (October)	**1760**	
	1761	Remodelling of Temple of Concord and Victory at Stowe (completed 1764). Ideological clash with Kew
	1762	Bute becomes prime minister (May)
Treaty of Paris ends Seven Years' War	**1763**	Bute leaves office (April) Ferocious Wilkesite attacks on Bute and Augusta
Pitt becomes prime minister and Earl of Chatham	**1766**	
	1772	Death of Augusta, Dowager Princess of Wales (February) Sir Joseph Banks takes over from Bute at Kew
Boston Tea Party	**1773**	
American Declaration of Independence	**1776**	
	1779	Death of Earl Temple
Gordon Riots	**1780**	Bute's London home attacked
French Revolution begins	**1789**	
	1792	Death of John Stuart, 3rd Earl of Bute

Index